# Regulating the City

# Regulating the City

## Competition, Scandal and Reform

**Michael Clarke**

*Department of Sociology,*
*University of Birmingham*

OPEN UNIVERSITY PRESS

*Milton Keynes : Philadelphia*

Open University Press
Open University Educational Enterprises Limited
12 Cofferidge Close
Stony Stratford
Milton Keynes MK11 1BY, England

*and*

242 Cherry Street
Philadelphia, PA 19106, USA

First published 1986

**British Library Cataloguing in Publication Data**
Clarke, Michael, *1945–*
    Regulating the city: competition, scandal and
    reform.
    1. Financial institutions—England—
    London
    I. Title
    332.1'09421'2        HG186.G7

    ISBN 0-335-15381-X
    ISBN 0-335-15382-8 PBK            1497378

**Library of Congress Cataloging in Publication Data**
Clarke, Michael, *1945–*
    Regulating the city.
    1. Financial institutions–England–London–Corrupt
    practices.    2. Financial institutions–government
    policy–England–London        I. Title
    HG186.G7C53 1985        332.1'09421'2        85-29715

    ISBN 0-335-15381-X
    ISBN 0-335-15382-8 (Pbk)

Text design by Clarke Williams

Typeset by Gilbert Composing Services, Leighton Buzzard, Bedfordshire

Printed in Great Britain by J.W. Arrowsmith Ltd, Bristol BS3 2NT

# Contents

# Preface

The original impetus to write this book came from a combination of two circumstances. In 1984 I was due to run a course on white-collar crime as part of the graduate socio-legal studies programme, and I was aware of the paucity of adequate social scientific literature on the regulation of the City of London, an essential topic for inclusion in such a course. I was also asked to provide a paper for a panel on corruption at the 1984 Political Studies Association conference by the panel convenor, Alan Doig. I undertook an initial investigation and produced what turned out to be a long paper, as a result of which I became convinced that fairly substantial changes were afoot, accompanied by, but not simply the product of, a series of scandals in various sectors of the City. I should like to thank Alan Doig for his encouragement and support, both then and later. It is not likely, however, that the project would have resulted in this book, but for the interest in it displayed by Stephen Barr of the Open University Press, who encouraged me to develop it, which I was able to do during study leave granted to me by the University of Birmingham in Spring 1985. Happily, this proved to be a point by which the pattern of reforms, though far from finally settled, had at least become reasonably clear. Whether I am correct in my assessments I leave the reader to judge and time to show.

Finally, the manuscript would not have reached the printers but for the diligence of June Brough and Chris Marlow in producing a typescript: my thanks to them also.

*Michael Clarke*
*Birmingham*

# Acknowledgements

Grateful acknowledgement is made to the following sources of material used in this book.

*Text* pp 67–9 from Godfrey Hodgson, *Lloyds of London: A Reputation at Risk,* Allen Lane, 1984, © Godfrey Hodgson, pp 258–9, 261–2, 269, by permission of Penguin Books Ltd; pp 167–8 from 'In the City', *Private Eye*, 10 August 1984, p. 25, by permission of *Private Eye* & Michael Gillard.

*Tables*   Chapter 2, tables 1–3, from A. Sampson, *The Changing Anatomy of Britain*, Hodder & Stoughton, 1982, by permission of Hodder & Stoughton Ltd; table 10 from M. Reid, *The Secondary Banking Crisis*, Macmillan, 1982, by permission of Macmillan, London and Basingstoke. Chapter 5, table 1 by permission of Noel Alexander Associates, Marketing and Executive Recruitment Consultants to banks and stockbrokers; table 2 from M. Lisle-Williams, 'Beyond the Market: The Survival of Family Capitalism in the English Merchant Bank', *British Journal of Sociology*, June 1984, by permission of Routledge and Kegan Paul; table 4 from J. Farrar and M. Russell, 'The Impact of Institutional Investment on Company Law', *Company Lawyer* vol. 5, no. 3, p. 115, by permission of Longman Professional.

# 1

# Introduction

It can scarcely have escaped the attention of even the casual reader of the business pages of a British newspaper in the last five years that the City of London seems embroiled in feverish reform and regulation. In the latter 1970s it was the banks, in the early 1980s Lloyds, and in the mid-1980s the Stock Exchange which predominated, with such matters as investor/depositor protection, self-regulation, state intervention and public access constituting repeated topics, and bodies such as the Bank of England, the Department of Trade and the Office of Fair Trading making frequent appearances. It is the object of this book to analyse why there is such current zeal for reform and regulation and to assess its significance. As to whether widespread reforms really are taking place, the following chapters will consider a number of major City institutions in turn which will provide ample evidence that this is indeed the case.

The more interesting questions are not whether attempts at regulation and reform are being made, still less how much public pontification takes place about them, but whether they amount to substantial changes or not, and if so, for what reasons. For it is a familiar feature of many social institutions that when things go wrong with them and they fail to function efficiently or are abused by individual members of them for private gain, there are calls for reform, vociferous public debates, committees of inquiry and, frequently, scapegoats. And it is intrinsic to the City that it is prone to scandals: its business is money, very large sums of it, much of it other people's, and some of it the state's money; and although some of its institutions perform financial functions that are simple and stable, the work of most is to perform complex and ever-evolving manipulations with money so as to make it available to others on attractive terms with a view to a profit or fee. Such

1

business inevitably gives rise both to fraudsters, whose object is to manipulate money for private ends regardless of purported public service, and to innovators who invent new manipulations, which may on the one hand constitute a more efficient or otherwise desirable service, or no more than sleight of hand and a quick profit. Effective sanctions must be available to deal with fraud, and effective decision-making procedures are required to discriminate those innovations which are legitimate and beneficial from those which are not.

Regulation is hence an intrinsic part of City life. It is essential for regulation to be effective that it be constantly brought up to date to deal with innovations, and that it be capable of discriminating between the market operator who plays it fast and loose for personal gain, and the imaginative innovator who provides a new or better service. It follows that formal, lawlike regulation, while desirable on the grounds of clarity and public accessibility, carries the danger of irrelevance, either because of innovation in a specific area for which there is no regulation, or because of the broader change in the nature of financial business which makes what used to be an undesirable practice legitimate or vice versa. The alternative recourse is to general principles of conduct which can be referred to as a guide in situations of novelty or doubt. The difficulty here lies in obtaining a sure interpretation of principles in a given case. It is easy to lay down, for example, that one should always act to protect one's clients' interests, but less easy to define in all relevant respects what those interests are, and less easy still to prescribe in all cases what the essential action is, given that the environment for action is a market whose behaviour is always to some degree unpredictable. It is the more difficult to determine the acceptability of conduct in a particular instance, given the fact that at the core of the City are a series of markets for money in various forms, and for financial services. While these markets are not entirely unregulated they are, to a substantial extent, free, and are the basis therefore of very substantial gains and losses by those who enter them on a significant scale. While most of the transactions in these markets are by agents on behalf of principals who provide the funds, many of the agents also act for themselves, and in any case derive their standing as agents from their success in acting to achieve gains. Now just as military men will claim that the essence of their way of life consists in comradeship, physical activity and fitness, discipline, or indeed anything else but a refined capacity for death and destruction, so the men of the City will insist that their life revolves around professional expertise, the satisfaction of a job well done, cooperation with others, service to clients and anything but a refined capacity to make a great deal of money. Just as the military claims only its fully professional members can properly understand what military life is all about, so also in the City.

The outcome of this has been a strong emphasis upon membership of the City and its institutions as distinctive and as conferring a moral identity, that of the City gentleman whose word is his bond, that is, who can be trusted for what he is. This has in the past been sustained, for the upper echelons of the City, by a common socio-economic background, education and experience. Aristocratic connections, or at any rate upper-middle or upper class status, some inherited wealth, major public school education followed by Oxbridge, and perhaps an early career in one of the Guards regiments has been the ideal, an ideal now often honoured in the breach, no doubt, but honoured none the less, and reflected quite powerfully in the sustained domination of City institutions by men (never, of course, women) of such background at a time when industry and the Conservative party have become much more diverse in their membership; not that a career in the City is not still a quite common preliminary to a career in Conservative politics, it still being held quite widely necessary to secure one's fortune before embarking upon the pursuit of public office. This pattern has had a critical significance for the problem of regulation in the City. Common background implies common outlook, based not only on common circumstances but common experiences. This in turn involves common contacts and knowledge of others, and thereby the prospect of evaluating others with whom one has to deal professionally not only by reference to their presenting characteristics, but to what is known of their careers, family and friends. Commonality of background and outlook provides the ground upon which discussion of the application of principles to particular situations can take place, with reduced chances of mutual incomprehension, or of talking past each other. Not only is the practical meaning of principles more likely to be held in common, but it can be clarified and debated by reference to common experiences, and the dangers of an individual's weaknesses, understood by reference to the same common experiences: thus it might be said that the qualities that make a future Governor of the Bank of England are first displayed on the playing fields of Eton, and the qualities of those who become City innovators of the undesirable sort may also be visible, if not on the playing fields, at least in the common rooms and studies.

The outcome which is most publicly visible is, of course, the old boy network by which new members are recruited to the City, and outsiders excluded, or at any rate deflected. It is easy to denigrate such a practice as that of a self-interested elite, and there is little doubt that there is some truth in such a claim: social and cultural closure conduces to complacency and excludes able and energetic outsiders. The point for present purposes, however, is that such a system effectively resolves the problem of regulation which, as I have suggested, is intrinsically an acute one for the City, because there are evident tensions between the large fiduciary role of its members in their management of other's money, and their interests in making money for themselves. The greater the mutual knowledge of members of City institutions, the more extensive their shared backgrounds, and more importantly the greater store they set by membership of an exclusive institution, both because of its social rewards and because of its financial and career opportunities, the greater the possibility of effective internal self-regulation and the maintenance of mutual internal trust. Trust, and its connotations – faith, confidence, respect and so on – have played a salient part in the ideology of City institutions. Much emphasis has been placed upon the binding handshake, the verbal bonds to make bargains among members of the Stock Exchange, the sanctity of the initialled slip and the 'utmost good faith' of the Lloyds underwriter, and there has been much in the past to be said for this. Mutual trust facilitates business transactions and avoids reliance on cumbersome legal formalities; externally, it projects an image of absolute integrity, while at the same time supporting informal methods of internal regulation and sanction. Social and cultural exclusiveness thus comes to be reinforced by the emphasis upon trust.

Informal exclusiveness is also reinforced by the similarity of the organizations which structure the experience of the ideal typical City figure. Throughout his life, a relatively small male peer group is central not only to work but to recreation. At public school it is not the school as a whole but the much smaller house in which the boy lives and shares his life with others: at Oxbridge the very similar College; in the Guards the relatively restricted regimental officers' mess; in the City his peers in the institution of which he is a member (as it expressed, rather than that he works there); and the exclusive gentlemen's clubs of the West End where he may spend some of his leisure time. All of these organizations are socially exclusive, numerically small, relatively intimate, male, and largely restricted in age range. Even if steady progress through them does not constitute the career of all or even most of the majority of senior figures in the City any more – and statistical proof would be a lengthy undertaking indeed – it does none the less remain as a model, and the values and style of these organizations have remained until the present exceptionally potent as a basis for managing City affairs, and a model of how critical issues should be coped with. Thus, for example, the Governor of the Bank of England used to be able to manage important banking issues by summoning the leading bankers to his office for discussion within half an hour.[1]*

It will be one of the main arguments of this book that the changes now in progress amount to the almost complete abandonment of the exclusive, informal gentleman's club model of self-regulation and the establishment of formal, public and bureaucratic regulation with a large measure of external supervision. To return to one of the questions posed earlier, it will therefore be maintained that the current concern with regulation is not simply a matter of debate and self-justification but also of substance, in that the regulatory machinery now being introduced in institution after institution is of a completely different character to that which has governed them up to now, and indeed in many respects is opposite in character and has been bitterly opposed by members of these institutions in the past. In the chapters which follow, I shall attempt to demonstrate the extent and significance of these changes in regulation in banks, in the Stock Exchange and in Lloyds before going on to discuss related changes in other areas. Granted for the moment that I am correct in this generalization, the immediate questions which arise are why the change has come about now and whether the new regulatory arrangements will be effective in maintaining high standards and in eliminating wrong doing, bearing in mind the difficulties in achieving this that I have outlined above.

The Achilles' heel of the informal and exclusive method of social control is the perception of wrongdoing by the public. If members of important organizations with significant public and client responsibilities are presented as socially distinctive, socially cohesive and socially exclusive, the danger is that the public will see any wrongdoing by an individual as contaminating the group and hence the organization as a whole. For it can be argued that the very features of common background and circumstances that give rise to adherence to a common code of conduct, the enforcement of which is facilitated by informal social contacts, surely implies that either individuals will not deviate from the code or that, if they do, this

*Superscript numerals refer to numbered footnotes at the end of each chapter.

will be picked up and corrected at a very early stage. The difficulty here in practice is that the notion at the centre of the code is trust, which entails the presumption that others within the organization are behaving correctly. Thus, the key quality of the code makes the kind of normal caution and probing characteristic of business relations less likely: a chap is assumed to be a good chap until it is clear that he is a rotter; by which time it may be too late for his clients. The problem then is that when deviance becomes exposed it creates a scandal, and the informality of self-regulation and social exclusiveness of City organizations provide a basis for public conclusions that if things were not as they seemed in this case, why should it be assumed that others are the models of probity that they present themselves as. Since there is no formal and public mode of accountability and verification, there is no means of demonstrating the rectitude of the majority: that has to be taken on trust by the public. Scandal, therefore, always threatens the autonomy of City institutions based on informal and exclusive and private methods of control. Over the past five years or so there has been no shortage of scandals, and their public significance has been increasingly to throw into question the effectiveness of traditional methods of self-regulation and to raise doubts as to whether the public interest is really secured by them. Ultimately, scandals have been instrumental in generating and, more particularly, in sustaining, effective pressure to alter, in some instances by legislation, the method of regulation in the direction of a formal, bureaucratic and public model of accountability – the Banking Act 1979, the Lloyds Act 1982, and the legislation on the Stock Exchange planned for 1986 are obvious examples.

Additional problems arise with the informal methods of control when wrongdoing is detected at a relatively early stage, because of the instinctive reaction of organizations to deal with the matter privately and informally, so as to preserve public confidence. In so far as rumours that there is a problem do not leak out, this may work very well, but where the public and the press have become more inquisitive and suspicious, as there is reason to suggest they have in recent years, and hints of scandal begin to circulate, private and informal methods tend to look like a cover-up. Further, when questions arise about losses to clients because of unethical behaviour, public interest may turn sceptical if clients are expected to bear such losses as part of the normal risks of market involvement – and, in truth, it is very often difficult to disentangle what part unethical behaviour plays in such cases. Doubt then comes to be expressed about the adequacy of the account presented to clients and the public, and questions begin to be raised about compensation of clients by the institution as a whole. Now the more informal the institution, and the greater the emphasis on trust in it, the less likely it is to have made formal provision by way of a subscription fund or insurance by members to meet such a contingency. In practice such matters have been dealt with *ad hoc* as a result of public and client pressure in a politically and professionally messy way, the case of Lloyds (see Chapter 3) being perhaps the most prominent recent example, though by no means the only one. The general term for this issue is of course investor/depositor protection, and it has been the subject of major debate and change in most, if not all, City institutions recently.

Yet the existence of scandals and the protection of investors is scarcely a new issue in the City – it has been a problem ever since the City developed: every schoolchild learns of the South Sea Bubble, and any historian of the City uncovers a stream of substantial scandals throughout the nineteenth and twentieth centuries. Why then should scandals recently have apparently led to the implementation of reforms substantial enough to involve the elimination of the traditional informal method of self-regulation? Are contemporary scandals greater, or more persistent, than those of the past? I do not believe they are. Their significance derives from the altered circumstances in which they have taken place, which have given them added weight as levers of change. There are several aspects to this, which, although distinct, are quite closely interrelated in practice. They may be identified as the change in the structure of the City, in particular the rise of the so-called institutions – pension funds, unit trusts, life assurance and building societies; the increase in international competition, associated with technological changes which promise to obliterate the traditional boundaries of the City as a secluded enclave in world financial markets and to integrate it into the world markets, with enormous consequences for the survival of existing organizations; and finally, the political interests of the Thatcher government, keen to extend as far as possible unfettered free market principles, to sustain the City's international competitiveness on that basis, and to promote much wider public participation in the City – the flotation of British Telecom in 1984 being perhaps the most publicly obvious, but not the most significant step in this direction.

The importance of the rise of the Institutions is more of a background factor than a source of direct pressure towards reform of other City organizations. In each case the growth of the Institutions has been the product, albeit not a consciously intended one, of the tax concessions made during the long period of post-war economic growth in Britain to the financially secure property-owning majority of the population. Home ownership has increased to around 60% with the assistance of the building societies, which have also expanded very rapidly as high street competitors to the banks for small savers, who are offered longer opening hours and privileged rates of interest. Similarly, the proportion of the population with occupational pension schemes has increased vastly in post-war years and, given the preference in Britain for funded schemes, in which members' savings are invested rather than recycled directly to existing pensioners, this has created very large pension funds. Life assurance, the premiums of which were until recently allowable against tax, has also grown substantially, in part because of endowment-linked mortgages, and in part because of endowment policies as a form of saving taking advantage of the tax privileges on the premiums. This also has produced very large sums for investment on behalf of policy holders. Finally, unit trusts were a post-war innovation deliberately aimed at making the stock market accessible to the small saver by allowing him to buy units in a fund which was invested in a portfolio sufficiently diverse to ensure security, but sufficiently astutely compiled to give the hope of capital growth. The increase in the diversity and specialization of unit trusts in the last 20 years has led to competition between them, and to increased specialization of some funds in different areas, e.g. Japanese investments, electronics.

The introduction of large numbers of small savers to the City in this way has of course been by proxy. Their savings have been managed by fund managers, merchant banks and stockbrokers (either directly or as advisors), but the institutions have none the less created a very large and direct public interest in the efficient workings of the City, and raised in an unavoidable fashion the issue of securing the value of their savings. Prudent and ethically proper investment conduct on the part of those managing the funds of small savers has thus become at least a latent issue. It has remained largely latent because the rise of the institutions has been largely a success story, and while there have been instances of wrongdoing by individuals, the cashflow has been so enormous that public disasters have been avoided. I shall say more in detail on fund management in a later chapter. More immediately significant has been the very size of the funds managed, which have had implications for banking; for government borrowing, since the institutions buy a large amount of government stock (gilt edged securities); for the stock market, where they have become major buyers of equities, and capable through their buying and selling power of greatly increasing or reducing the value of the stock – the success of the BT launch was almost entirely due to the desire of the institutions to buy up, even at a substantial premium, what they regarded as a new blue chip stock; and for individual quoted companies, where the institutions may, even in the case of some large plcs (public limited companies), come to own enough of the stock to be able to influence company policy and obtain representation on the board of directors. Their position in the market is thus different from even that of the wealthy private investor, in that they manage such large funds, and that they do so for the purpose of investment only (they have not, so far, engaged in entrepreneurial activities such as takeovers to any great extent, though they may be important actors in such situations) on behalf, not of themselves, but of an anonymous army of small clients. They are, hence, extremely influential in the City, but relative newcomers and not part of the traditional pattern. Their size, and their responsibility to the small savers who fund them, put them in a position to exercise a critical view of some City practices. Of the three factors mentioned above as enhancing the significance of scandal in promoting substantial concern for reform and regulation, the institutions are least directly important, but they have raised for the first time as a sustained public issue the viability of existing City institutions for the small saver.

Very much more important is international competition. This has a number of different aspects. First, developments in telecommunications and data processing have led to the emergence of the capacity for worldwide round the clock trading in equities, hard currencies and commodities. Rather than existing, as in the past, as an enclave structured substantially around the needs and interests of the British economy, the City stands to become one of perhaps half a dozen major financial centres in the world, a role it has prepared for itself by establishing itself in the nineteenth century as the financial centre of the empire, and in the last decade or two as a major centre for currency trading outside the US (the so-called Eurodollar market). In order to compete, however, firms will need to be vastly better capitalized than at present in most cases, and will need to invest heavily in skilled manpower and sophisticated equipment, and to establish a substantial presence in other trading centres: Britain presently ranks way below the USA, Japan and West Germany in the volume of business it transacts. The price of failure to compete will be, at best, to become marginalized in the international financial trading system and, more likely, to be preyed upon by the successful multinationals. Unless they can compete, City firms hence face the options of being squeezed out of existence by foreign competition or putting up barriers to keep them out at the price of opting out of the lucrative international system.

One effect of the emerging competition is that it will make worldwide continuous trading possible. The second is the need for increased capitalization and investment to stay in the large markets. The third is the emergence of huge financial conglomerates which are in part made necessary by the requirements of increased capitalization and in part constitute an attempt to create new opportunities and market strength. In brief, what this involves is that organizations previously limited in function, say to retail banking or stockbroking, come to offer a range of financial services. In theory, it should be more cost-effective to have services available in-house rather than go out and buy them as needed. It should attract more customers, who can be offered additional services, which they might not even have considered seeking before, and it will enable the capital strength of one part of the conglomerate to be used to support the expansion of others. The fourth and final aspect of international competition is the attempt by the emergent conglomerates to create new institutions attracting new customers who have not up to now participated in the financial markets, the so-called 'financial supermarket' idea. In a number of cases, large organizations with established retail outlets, such as department stores and retail banks, have taken over or merged with stockbroking and insurance broking firms to provide a range of financial services to their customers. The proposed diversification of the building societies to allow them to offer conveyancing, estate agency, insurance and banking facilities is a similar though distinctive development. The importance of this fourth aspect is that it is the one most associated with the object of expanding the total financial market by drawing in new customers.

The implications of these sort of changes for City regulation are not far to seek. It may have been that the City gentleman established himself internationally as a figure of trust and repute in the late nineteenth and early twentieth centuries, when British banking and insurance dominated large areas of the world, but in the late twentieth century, when other nations have developed their own and often larger financial centres, trust in the integrity of the gentleman and the regulatory effectiveness of the gentlemen's clubs of the City is not likely. Foreign professionals and investors want to be able to see that control is present and that it works. The USA, dominant in this as in so many other fields, has had a completely different history of regulation, by no means lacking in crimes, scandals and disasters. Access to financial institutions and markets, though restricted in the twentieth century by the enormous power of the bankers and 'robber barons' of the late nineteenth century, and the establishment in the Ivy League universities and the East Coast 'aristocracy' of something akin to British social exclusiveness, has never been subject to the same degree of restriction of access and social exclusiveness. Participation in financial markets has been on a larger scale, without social inhibitions, and organizations have flourished and died subject to the control not only of the law but, following the great crash of 1929, of the Securities and

Exchange Commission (SEC) with its wide powers of investigation, denunciation and prosecution: in brief, control has been formal, public and bureaucratic, and there has been considerable suspicion of organizations that are unduly secretive, and an unwillingness to rely on the good faith of honest men; the penchant has been to see that they are honest, competent and prudent.

International competition hence produces pressure for the City of London to conform to the regulatory style which dominates the rest of the world and to abandon its distinctive system. Further, the expansion in size and in particular the unheard-of diversification of new organizations begins to make formal regulation imperative. Increased size, particularly when it involves going international in a big way, clearly makes nonsense of the informal methods of control, based as they are on frequent social contact. Diversification creates new regulatory problems, for what are now required are not just bodies capable of policing functionally specialized organizations, which may be credibly attempted through a professional body, but bodies to police large organizations with a range of professionals working in sub-units within them, where the issue which arises is not just that of conventional probity and competence, but endemic conflict of interest. If an organization provides banking services, for example, and wishes its client who takes out a large loan to insure his life in that amount by way of security, and the organization also provides life assurance on behalf of a certain company which is part of the same conglomerate, is the client likely to get the best possible terms for his assurance, or indeed disinterested advice? As we shall see later, this area of difficulty is one that is only beginning to be seriously contemplated, and is very far from resolution. It is certain, however, that the traditional institutions of City self-regulation are not the instrument appropriate to achieve it.

The final element in the pressure for regulatory reform of the City is the existence in the Thatcher government since 1979 of a strong political will to shift politics in Britain firmly to the right and incontestably in support of the free enterprise economy. It has not been lost on the government that in the USA, which fits this model of politics, levels of home ownership are high and participation in the financial markets is widespread, both of these giving the individual citizen direct ownership of property with a good chance of a capital gain, and direct participation in the markets whereby such gains may be achieved. The Thatcher government inherited a system which supported home ownership through the subsidy of mortgages, and had permitted it to rise above 50%. It achieved a further rise to around 60% today by maintaining the subsidy, and by promoting the sale of council houses to sitting tenants at a substantial discount. It is clear that this aspect of the extension of property ownership is now past the peak of its expansion, and that with unemployment at its present levels many families will remain unable to aspire to own their homes. Inducing increased participation in the financial markets is an attractive second avenue to pursue, and the changes in the shape of financial institutions referred to above are, in this connection, entirely opportune. In addition, the ground has been prepared by the growth of the 'Institutions' referred to earlier, which have had the effect of making a large section of the population aware of the existence and importance of financial markets and, through pensions and life assurance, of providing an underpinning of financial security. The time is hence ripe for the provision of facilities to tempt those with some cash to spare to start thinking beyond the confines of the bank, the building society or unit trusts, and to contemplate the stock market in particular. An associated development which has been an entirely welcome product of the recession to the government, has been the buy-out by employees of a number of industrial and commercial firms threatened with bankruptcy, perhaps most notably the formerly nationalized freight company, the National Freight Consortium, which after a management buy-out in 1982 had done so well by 1985 as to raise the value of its £1 shares to £8.60. The argument is, that once workers have a direct stake in the profitability of their firms, restrictive practices and timeserving will end, and ingenuity and effort will pay off. In the case of shareholdings in companies through the stock market the interest is less sharp, but the chance to back winners and make money, active participation in the stock markets central to the capitalist economy, and a lively interest in the fate of companies invested in, may reasonably be expected to induce greater faith in the system as long as it works.

In order to ensure that it does, and to end the diffidence, to say the least, of most of the population about approaching a stockbroker, the traditional socially exclusive image of the City clearly has to be altered, access improved by developing local outlets, and potential investors' confidence assured by reforming regulatory machinery and ensuring that it is more public, and by taking measures to secure investor protection by legislation and by establishing funds to cover unacceptable losses. The interests of the government, in other words, are doubly behind regulatory reform – first, to support the international image and competitiveness of the City and secondly, to encourage participation in its markets and in the retail outlets of the new conglomerates by a much wider public. One test of initial success here will be whether the success of the BT share issue will result in small shareholders keeping their shares rather than selling them for a quick profit, and whether the British Airways flotation due in 1985 will be as successful in obtaining a wide public response.

All of these factors conducing to regulatory reform spell the end of the traditional system of the gentlemen's club, but the practitioners have not been willing to abandon established habits and practices easily and have clung persistently to their tradition and its privileges. As a result, scandals which have emerged have acquired an enhanced significance in pointing up the weaknesses of the traditional system. It is also the case, though this has so far been given much less attention, that scandals have in some instances suggested some of the problems that may lie ahead with the new order of larger, diversified international institutions catering for a mass public that is emerging. The central argument of this book is that the importance of scandal in achieving an effective reforming response, as opposed to either an apathetic one or pious sentiment but no effective action, lies in their contextual significance at the time they occur. There is no doubt that the scandals which have occurred, some of which will be referred to in later chapters, have provided powerful publicity and contributed to pressure for real change, but it would be a mistake to believe that they could have achieved anything nearly so radical as the end of informal self-regulation without the influence of the other factors outlined above. This book is hence an attempt to contribute to the understanding of the importance of crime and scandal in financial institutions, and to understand the reasons for initiatives for regulatory reform. These matters need to be considered in detail in respect of the major sectors of the City and the following chapters will undertake this. It will be seen that there are strong lines of similarity in different sectors, but that the balance of importance of different factors varies from sector to sector, and the detailed history is unique to each.

Chapter 2 will deal with banking, where reform was supposed to have been achieved by the 1979 Act, but where recent events have cast doubt upon its effectiveness. Chapter 3 will be concerned with Lloyds, where radical reforms were achieved by the Lloyds Act 1982, but which is still in the process of implementation, while major scandals have rumbled on and proved difficult for the new machinery to resolve. Chapter 4 deals with the Stock Exchange, where, although progress has been made, the final shape of the new reformed institutions and its method of regulation is only beginning to take shape in 1985. Chapter 5 deals with the issue of reform in a number of other areas in which, although central City institutions are not directly the focus of regulation, the raising of standards in the control of sharp practice, and in general the search for capitalism's acceptance face are at issue. The areas involved are tax avoidance, insolvency, the role of the Office of Fair Trading and that of the 'Institutions'. As will be seen, what is at issue here is, as in the central City institutions, the creation of secure, publicly accountable conditions for capitalism to function, which are publicly defensible, and form a basis for the encouragement of wider public participation. The role of the government is substantial. In Chapter 6 attention shifts to begin to consider some of the problems raised by reform: first, the persistent difficulties experienced in mounting successful fraud prosecutions and, secondly, some of the problems raised by the new, larger, diversified financial institutions that are emerging. Finally, Chapter 7 will go on to consider the implications of closer government involvement in the promotion of greater public participation in capitalist institutions. It will project the issues onto a larger canvas to ask what implications the changes that have been discussed have for the development of capitalism in Britain. In particular, the potential rise of very large and multinational financial institutions will be a focus of attention, and the problems these may pose for government and the state, if they are associated with increased public participation in such institutions, with government support.

## Notes

1. I have not attempted to document the quite general points I make in the Introduction, since to do so would require footnotes of inordinate length and many of the points are made in more detail in later chapters, where references are given.

# 2

# Banks: Regulation by the Bank of England?

## Introduction

British Banks in the mid–1980s are supposed to have undergone substantial regulatory reform as a result of changes in their market in the 1960s and 1970s and of the financial crisis of 1974, which centred upon the so-called secondary banks. The Banking Act of 1979 was proclaimed as an instrument to regularize the position of these new banks, to establish a formal basis for depositor protection, and to formalize the supervision of banking. In particular, the traditionally highly informal relationship between the Bank of England and the other banks was supposed to have been modified in the light of the proliferation of the new secondary banks and of the influx of foreign banks establishing themselves in the City. In fact, the Bank of England, jealous of its independence from the Government and Whitehall and keen to preserve the speed and flexibility involved in its informal style of control, took steps to limit severely the formalization of control and accountability implied by the 1979 Act, and the consequences of this became evermore embarrassingly plain in the wake of the failure of a bank in 1984. Banking thus provides an example of changing economic circumstances acting with well-publicized scandals to achieve apparently substantial regulatory reform; just how thorough-going and effective this reform has been has only recently become apparent. In having purportedly completed its process of reform, banking contrasts with the Stock Exchange which is in the midst of regulatory reform due to be completed in 1986, and with Lloyds insurance market which was reformed by the Lloyds Act 1982, and is hence at an early stage of working under the new regime. The history of regulation in the banking sector may provide some pointers in evaluating progress in the other sectors.

## The History of Banking Regulation

In order to understand that history, it is necessary to consider the nature of regulation in British banking up to the 1979 Act, and in particular the role of the Bank of England. Central banks may have more or less limited functions, but perhaps the most familiar is a monopoly of issuing notes and coins. In the past these were redeemable in many countries (in Britiain up to 1931) against gold, a commitment which was long held to be an essential discipline against printing an excessive number of notes. The strength of a currency, however, as the British people are now daily reminded by politicians and the media, is ultimately dependent upon the productive and market strengths of the economy as a whole, though it may be manipulated over the short term by such tactics as raising of lowering interest rates to depositors. The major purpose of the gold standard was to provide an internationally accepted reference standard for currencies which would sustain confidence in what, after all, are at best fancy pieces of paper, and these days more often an electronic record and the print-outs ensuing from it. In a world in which the gold standard has been abandoned the role of central banks in sustaining confidence in the currency is less critical.

In a modern economy a linked function of the bank is to provide means whereby governments can borrow, which in turn gives them a much greater degree of flexibility in economic policy than if they could not. It has long been a major part of the Bank of England's job to manage the sale of government stock (so-called gilt-edged securities), as well as to arrange short-term borrowing. In order to discharge these and other functions the Bank has to ensure that confidence is sustained in the other banking institutions with which it deals, and which go to make up the British banking system as a whole. These are arranged in what may be thought of as concentric circles around the bank, with trust and intimacy declining from centre to periphery. The other factor which interacts with centrality to the system is the size of the institutions and the proportion of the whole banking market which they constitute.

Closest to the Bank are the 11 Discount Houses,[1] quite small but highly-privileged organizations, who make their money by currency transactions and by taking on surplus funds from the banks and investing it in mainly short-term deposits. In December 1982 their total sterling borrowings were £5 124 000 000, of which £4 701 000 000 was overnight or at call. Since they deal only in wholesale funds and not directly with the public, and since these funds effectively represent the credit-worthiness of other banks, or the central government, they are allowed to borrow a much higher multiple of their capital and reserves than retail banks and may take much greater risks in interest rate mis-matching. In virtue of an agreement reached between the Bank, the clearers and the Discount Houses, a comprehensive set of restrictive practices was agreed by the 1930s, whereby the clearers did not compete with the Discount Houses in tendering for Treasury Bills; the Houses agreed to a common tender price, allocating bills between each other by an agreed formula, and the clearers were protected by a minimum interest rate for their funds from the Discount Houses. Most important of all, the Bank of England was assured of a stable and reliable outlet for government funds by which it could, through increasing or reducing the flow onto the market through the Discount Houses, influence interest rates and market government debt. The importance of this for the regulatory function and style of the Bank is elucidated by Moran.[2]

In the 1930s there began

> a practice which still persists: the Governor (of the Bank) or his deputy met representatives of the houses weekly . . . The representatives heard the Bank's view of the immediate economic prospects and fixed their offer price (for Treasury bills) accordingly. The Bank in return was able to keep close contact with institutions which were virtually its agents to communicate views via the discount houses and to gather from them information about the financial community . . . Thus were created the connections between debt management, credit control and restrictive practices which were an inseparable part of the socially cohesive banking community . . . Informality and trust could be relied upon in regulating financial life because entry into markets was tightly controlled and competition between existing members severely curtailed. The penalties of exclusion and the rewards for inclusion were powerful incentives to acceptable behaviour.

The extent of the social cohesion and closure still prevalent in 1980 is evident from recent research,[3] which showed that a third of the directors of Discount Houses came from families with large shareholdings in a House, two thirds were from families with entries in Burke's Peerage, every owner-director had been to a Clarendon School and three quarters of these were old Etonians; and here it should be borne in mind that 47% of the Etonians had fathers at the same school, by far the largest proportion for any public school.[4]

The significance of Eton in particular was emphasized by Lord Poole, a former Conservative party Chairman and director of Lazard's Merchant Bank, who replied to Lord Cowdray's enquiry as to how he had managed to avoid lending to failed financiers in the secondary banking boom: 'Quite simple: I only lent money to people who had been at Eton'.[5] The point about the coincidence of social closure and exclusiveness, restrictive practices and informal regulation is that they are interdependent and form a stable system of financial management: eliminate any one of them and you threaten the other. Thus, threaten exclusiveness and you get outside competition and rate-cutting, if not corner-cutting; end restrictive practices and internal competition, with the same dangers, arises; and substitute formal for informal control and you slow down information flow, limit flexibility and allow lawyers to act by the letter of regulation and not its spirit. Conversely, social exclusiveness contributes to security, lack of fear of competition, easier communication and a shared set of standards; restrictive practices enshrine the most dangerous areas of competition in a code; and informal regulation ensures that information flows are rapid, intervention prompt, respect sustained and people treated as friends as well as businessmen, whose interest it is much harder to compromise by self-interested action.

This system of knowledge, trust and mutual support could only exist in a society where the banking institutions had a degree of social continuity, established in the case of Britain in the eighteenth and especially the nineteenth centuries, when the banking system thrived with the Industrial Revolution and extension of the Empire and provided a basis for trading and investing in sterling world wide and for providing large loans to foreign governments. As Sampson puts it:[5]

> For a century after the Napoleonic Wars in 1815 London was the world's financial centre enriched by growing private fortunes and international trade which increased with each stage of the Industrial Revolution. As the trade extended so it transformed the nature of banking. London was not only the richest city it was also the city which made the most effective use of its money. Its banks were able to attract the savings of the whole country, lending them wherever the profit was greatest, first within Britain then across the world, carefully attuning interest rates to the risks. As they became more confident, the bankers felt able to lend greater sums compared to their own capital and foreigners began to deposit their funds in London banks and to borrow money from them.

By 1873 these amounted to £120 000 000 compared to £40 000 000 in New York, £13 000 000 in Paris and £8 000 000 in Germany.

In the latter part of the nineteenth century, and increasingly in the twentieth, the private banks also engaged in these ventures were joined by the new joint stock banks, who took large quantities of small depositors' money and lent both to them and, on a large scale, to corporations and governments. Once the British banking system had emerged from the crisis of the great crash of 1929, which it did more successfully than the USA, where the crash began and where 325 banks failed in one month in 1929, and 7000 between 1929 and 1933, a stable, not to say complacent, pattern emerged in Britain, dominated by the big four clearing banks, with the established merchant banks, the Accepting Houses, forming a second tier, and the discount houses a small role. They were all, however, clearly established in the social as well as the institutional sense, as Tables 1–3 indicate. Hence, regulation was conducted neither through pressure groups nor by bureaucratic procedure. The Governor of the Bank of England, himself traditionally a scion of the established banking families, said to the Radcliffe Committee in 1957: 'If I want to talk to the representatives of the British financial community, we can usually get together in one room in half an hour.'[8]

Smallness of numbers, fairly intimate knowledge, frequent and easy contact and shared social expectations meant that what was said in that one room was privileged, both in the sense that a degree of straightforwardness was possible and that any revelations could be reckoned to go no further than the four walls, but that appropriate and collective action would be taken to secure the soundness of the British banking system as a whole on the basis of this information. The importance of mutual support and of the role of the Bank of England as lender of last resort in a financial crisis had finally been established in 1890, when Barings, over-exposed to the extent of £21 000 000 as a result of loans to Argentina, which was as politically unstable and ravaged by inflation then as it is now, was on the brink of collapse. The Bank of England's reserves were only £10 000 000 (it remained a private corporation until 1946).

As alarm mounted at the prospect of a collapse, with its inevitable consequences and dangers for other banks with whom Barings was involved, for international banking, and for the reputation of London, the Government promised to underwrite half of Barings losses, and a special Argentine committee was set up under Lord Rothschild which persuaded merchant and joint stock banks to raise

**Table 1.   Accepting Houses**

| Founded | Bank | Assets 1981 (£ million) | Chairman | Education |
|---|---|---|---|---|
| 1763 | Baring Brothers | 489 | John Baring | Eton; Oxford |
| 1804 | Rothschild's | 603 | Evelyn de Rothschild | Harrow; Cambridge |
| 1804 | Schroder Wagg | 1845 | Lord Airlie | Eton; Guards |
| 1810 | Brown Shipley | 252 | Lord Farnham | Eton; Harvard |
| 1830 | Kleinwort, Benson | 2713 | Robert Henderson | Eton; Cambridge |
| 1831 | Hill Samuel | 1443 | Sir Robert Clark | Highgate; Cambridge |
| 1833 | Arbuthnot Latham | 206 | Andrew Arbuthnot | Eton; Guards |
| 1836 | Guinness Mahon | 332 | Graham Hill | Winchester; Oxford |
| 1838 | Morgan Grenfell | 1578 | Lord Catto | Eton; Cambridge |
| 1839 | Hambros | 1389 | Jocelyn Hambro | Eton; Cambridge |
| 1853 | Samuel Montagu (Midland) | 1580 | Malcolm Wilcox | Wallasey GS |
| 1870 | Lazard Brothers | 735 | Ian Fraser | Ampleforth; Oxford |
| 1880 | Charterhouse Japhet | 485 | Malcolm Wells | Eton |
| 1907 | Singer & Friedlander | 283 | Keith Wickenden | East Grinstead GS |
| 1919 | Rea Brothers | 109 | Walter Salomon | Hamburg |
| 1932 | Robert Fleming | 194 | W. R. Merton | |
| | | | Lord Roll | Abroad; Birmingham |
| 1946 | S. G. Warburg | 981 | D. G. Scholey | Wellington; Oxford |

Source: A. Sampson, *The Changing Anatomy of Britain*, Hodder & Stoughton, 1982, p. 281.

Table 2.   **Major Clearing Banks**

| Bank | Gross deposits (£ million) | Chairman | Education |
|------|------|------|------|
| 1 Barclays | 42 834 | Timothy Bevan | Eton; Guards |
| 2 National Westminster | 39 709 | Robin Leigh-Pemberton | Eton; Oxford; Guards |
| 3 Midland | 38 000 | Sir David Barran | Winchester; Cambridge |
| 4 Lloyds | 25 309 | Sir Jeremy Morse | Winchester; Oxford |
| 5 Royal Bank of Scotland | 6698.8 | Sir Michael Herries | Eton; Cambridge |
| 6 Bank of Scotland | 2524.6 | T. N. Risk (Governor) | Kelvinside; Glasgow |

*Source: A. Sampson, The Changing Anatomy of Britain, Hodder & Stoughton, 1982, p. 274.*

£17 000 000 to avert the crisis. Barings was re-constructed and paid off the debts in four years. Since this time, the role of the Bank of England as the lender of the last resort and co-ordinator of financial rescues has been established, and likewise the principle of mutual obligation among British banks, with cash contributions. The horrors of 1929 on Wall Street where, despite the efforts of leading banks, enough money and collective will was not mobilized, remain as a warning.

For this system of collective security to operate, access to banking markets must be controlled, ethical and prudential norms established and observed, and early warning given of trouble, so that it can be localized. Informal control by a limited number of organizations with common standards and of long financial standing is one way to manage this. The difficulty is that it tends to become conservative and inward-looking. For the British banking system in the post-war period it looked for some time as though this mattered little: 'The traditional banks', said Jack Hambro in 1960, 'are like the British Empire. There's nothing more to gain and quite a lot to lose.'[9] Or as Lord Franks, chairman of Lloyds put it: 'it was like driving a powerful motor car at 20 miles an hour. The banks were anaesthetised – it was a kind of dream life.'[10]

Another aspect of the inward-looking nature of the banks was their concern with banking and financial matters to the exclusion of everything else. The concern to manage the currency in particular was held to be the prerogative of the Bank of England, which resented interference by the Treasury or by government. Equally, banks came ever-increasingly to think that their own stability and profitability were to be pursued in isolation from the rest of the economy, but that they should be free to impose whatever terms they wanted upon borrowers, regardless of the economic

**Table 3.   Directors of the Bank of England, 1982**

| Name | Jobs | School and University |
|------|------|----------------------|
| Sir Gordon Richardson[a] | Governor | Nottingham High School; Cambridge |
| Kit McMahon | Deputy Governor | Melbourne Grammar School; Oxford |
| George Blunden | Bank of England | City of London School; Oxford |
| Sir Adrian Cadbury | Cadbury Schweppes | Eton; Cambridge |
| Sir Robert Clark | Hill Samuel Bank | Highgate; Cambridge |
| John Clay | Hambros Bank | Eton; Oxford |
| Leopold de Rothschild | Rothschild's Bank | Harrow; Cambridge |
| Geoffrey Drain | General Secretary, NALGO | Preston Grammar School; London |
| John Standish Fforde | Bank of England | Rossall; Oxford |
| Sir Jasper Hollom | Chairman, Panel on Takeovers | King's School, Brunton |
| Sir Hector Laing | United Biscuits | Loretto; Cambridge |
| Anthony Loehnis | Bank of England | Eton; Oxford |
| Lord Nelson of Stafford | General Electric | Oundle; Cambridge |
| John Brangwyn Page | Bank of England | Highgate; Cambridge |
| Sir Alastair Pilkington | Pilkington | Sherborne; Cambridge |
| David Scholey | Warburg's Bank | Wellington; Oxford |
| Sir David Steel | British Petroleum | Rugby; Oxford |
| Lord Weir | Chairman, Weir Group | Eton; Cambridge |

[a]Sir Gordon Richardson was succeeded as Governor by Robin Leigh-Pemberton, formerly Chairman of National Westminster (see Table 2).

Source: A. Sampson, *The Changing Anatomy of Britain*, Hodder & Stoughton, 1982, p. 266.

and industrial consequences. The independence of the financial sector is an issue remarked on long ago by Lenin, and much commented on since down to the establishment of the Wilson committee on the functioning of financial institutions in the 1970s, in part to investigate whether terms for industrial borrowers had become unnecessarily oppressive, and were indirectly a cause of industrial decline and unemployment.[11] Whether prudent or not in its more negative aspects, the independence of the financial sector as a whole, of banking in particular, and of the Bank of England, most notably, is not in dispute. The process of bringing the latter under Treasury control has been a long and contested one.

Under the gold standard the management of monetary policy was presented by the Bank as a purely technical banking matter. With the end of the gold standard in 1931 monetary policy clearly needed more widely co-ordinated economic management, and yet it was not until the 1950s that it was conceded that bank rate could not be altered without Treasury consent. Even nationalization in 1946 and the deep suspicion by labour radicals of the Bank failed to curb its power, for paradoxically the complex regulations, on, for example, exchange control and the management of nationalizations, only re-emphasized the Bank's monopoly of the relevant expertise with effective and constant contact with the major banks, and the power to persuade them, by what was technically only advice, to vary their interest rates and to restrict or expand credit. When these advantages were coupled with the determined control of what it considered its own affairs it is not surprising that its independence was sustained. The select committee on nationalized industries learned in 1969 that the Bank published no conventional accounts, was not restricted by the usual limits on bodies managing public money, and did not reveal even to the Treasury what its Senior officials were paid.[12] Although the Charter enacted when it was nationalized formally enabled the Bank to issue directions to a banker if so authorized by the Treasury, the Bank continued to exercise its own direct and informal influence to achieve its ends rather than rely on the Treasury.

This long-established position of the Bank is important for enduring reasons. First, the commitment of the Bank to independence and informal control was powerfully instrumental in sustaining the same system throughout the city in circumstances where it was plainly inappropriate. Secondly, the persistence on the part of the Bank in maintaining itself as an itermediary between the Treasury and the Government and the City, helped to sustain the autonomy of the City as a financial sector with its own rules and objectives incommensurable with those of the rest of society and the economy. Finally, the sustained independent power of the Bank is of vital importance in the process of regulatory reform, since, as we shall see, the Bank has emerged with enhanced formal regulatory and supervisory power from this process, with powers of representation and intervention under the new systems of control which it did not have before. If the institution which is to be responsible for overseeing the effectiveness of new regulatory regimes elsewhere in the City is itself still wedded to its traditional autonomy, social exclusiveness and informal methods, it bodes ill for its capacity to understand the nature of the changes in resources, methods and style called for, and hence for its effectiveness.

Two developments took place in the 1960s and continued apace thereafter that were jointly to tranform British banking and especially its regulations. Both of them reflected the continuing substantial rise of the City of London as a world financial centre, albeit one now somewhat circumscribed by a preoccupation with the sterling area, the legacy of a fading Empire that was fast gaining independence. More importantly, the informality of control of financial institutions in London was coupled with the presumption that, since the main opportunities for Banking and the provision of financial services in the City were already distributed to established operators who dominated the markets, anything in the way of new business would be bound to come to and through them. But loosely exercised control made it easy for new institutions to set up in London. Lack of competitive urgency among the established institutions encouraged the emergence of the new and home-grown secondary banks developing out of finance houses, share dealing and property speculation. Before they became substantial, however, the development of the Euro-currency market brought in a flood of branch establishments of foreign banks.

## The Euro-currency market

The Euro-dollar market began quietly in 1949[13] when the Chinese, following the Revolution, placed their dollars in a Soviet-owned bank in Paris, fearful that the US authorities might retaliate against the Revolution by seizing them. With the cold war at its height, the Russians also began to keep their dollars in Paris and at the Moscow Narodny Bank in London. Dollars were then, as now, of central importance to international trade in the West, and in the ensuing decade many companies and banks came to see the advantages of keeping their dollars in Europe, away from the control of the US authorities who, in particular during this period, restricted interest rates.

Why was it that London should have become the centre of the Euro-dollar market? One advantage often cited is its advantageous geographical location for worldwide trade, which enables currency dealers in a normal working day to talk to Tokyo in the morning, New York in the afternoon, California in the evening and Europe all day. But the period from the late 1950s onwards was one in which the Bretton Woods agreement of 1945, which had pegged the European currencies within a 2% range of variation to the dollar, and the dollar to gold, in an attempt to secure the international stability of currencies, was gradually breaking down, because the US began to run a trade deficit from 1958 and its overwhelming predominance in world markets gradually receded with the recovery of Europe, most notably Germany, and Japan. By 1973, when the stresses of the South East Asia war had vastly increased the US trade deficit, fixed parities were abandoned, and the dollar, followed by other currencies, was allowed to float. Currency speculation, with other currencies following the dollar into less-regulated havens, saw increased interest rate advantages. As multinational corporations began to expand rapidly in Europe and elsewhere, they too saw the advantages of having unrestricted access to dollars which could be used for deals and developments or transferred easily to where they were needed. The Euro-dollar market tripled in 1959 and doubled again in 1960, when it was first mentioned by the *Times*. Up to this point 'the Euro-dollar market was . . . hidden from economists and other readers of the financial press by a remarkable conspiracy of silence . . . Several bankers emphatically asked me not to write about the new practice.'[14] The market was further boosted by President Kennedy's move in 1963 to make foreign borrowing in America more expensive, which was designed to strengthen the dollar and preserve the Bretton Woods agreement, but which generated greater interest in the uncontrolled Euro-dollar market.

With the rise in size of the Eurodollar market, its funds began to be organized into blocks for large loans, initially as bonds bearing a fixed rate of interest, the breakthrough being a $15 million bond to finance the Italian autostrada arranged by Warburgs in 1963. These bonds were then sold by the banks for quick profits. As the loans became larger, however, and as more institutions and countries of less than absolute credit-worthiness were drawn into the market, Euro-credits with variable rates of interest drawn on banks rather than individuals, came to be favoured. Increased demand also resulted in these being syndicated, the first major loan being that of $200 million by 22 banks to the Bank of Italy in 1969 to tide it over a currency crisis. The interest rate for such loans is based on the London Inter-Bank Offer Rate, LIBOR, that is the rate at which banks in London will lend to each other with a margin according to the risk of the loan on top of this. It seems hard to estimate at any given time how great a share of the total market is held by British- or London-based institutions, but the predominance of London is demonstrated by the acceptance of LIBOR as the basis for calculating loan rates. When, in 1981, New York attempted to challenge London by substituting its prime rate for Euro-dollar loans on the grounds of profit advantages, the experiment failed and LIBOR was restored.

The growth of the Euro-currency market since 1970 is shown in Table 4. An important part of its growth since the quadrupling of oil prices in 1973 and their further rapid increase in 1978–9 has been the recycling of oil money. The members of the Organization of Petroleum Exporting Countries (OPEC), already used to a substantial dollar income from oil, were by all accounts somewhat taken aback by the success of the cartel in 1973 and did not make decisions in advance as to what to do with the increased revenue, which they left on deposit with major banks in London and New York. Since the banks had to pay interest on the deposits, they had to lend the money out to pay for the interest, and it went increasingly in the form of loans to the Third World, to tide countries over the oil shock and finance development.

The nature of the Euro-currency market and the consequences of increased lending to sovereign states in the Third World and Communist Bloc, and of consequent impending defaults in the 1980s need not concern us here. What is important in its impact on banking regulation in Britain is that the Euro-currency market became centred upon London, and that it attracted a very large number of foreign institutions to participate in it. In 1959 there were 45 overseas banks with a recognized presence in London. By 1983 the figure had risen to 351, of which 65 were American and 25 were Japanese. The extent of their presence varies from a few people in a small office engaging only in limited transactions under the direction of the parent bank, to the vast new towers of the European headquarters of major US banks with a complete spread of activities. It was certainly no longer

**Table 4.   Eurocurrency Market Size, 1970–1980 ($ billion)**

|  | 1970 | 1971 | 9172 | 1973 | 1974 | 1975 | 1976 | 1977 | 1978 | 1979 | 1980 | 1981 | 1982 |
|---|---|---|---|---|---|---|---|---|---|---|---|---|---|
| Gross size | 110 | 145 | 200 | 315 | 395 | 485 | 595 | 740 | 950 | 1235 | 1525 | 1860 | 2015 |
| Net size | 60 | 85 | 110 | 160 | 220 | 225 | 320 | 390 | 495 | 590 | 730 | 890 | 940 |
| Eurodollars % of all eurocurrencies | 81 | 76 | 78 | 74 | 76 | 78 | 80 | 76 | 74 | 72 | 75 | 78 | 81 |

Source: *World Financial Markets*, New York, Morgan Guaranty, cited in J. Coakley and L. Harris, *The City of Capital*, Basil Blackwell, 1983, p. 52.

possible for the Governor of the Bank of England to gather all the heads of even the major institutions in one room within half an hour. On the other hand, he had to reckon with the fact that the business in which they were involved, together with British banks, brought enormous profits to the City and went a long way in sustaining claims by the Bank on behalf of the City that it was a major foreign exchange earner, vital to the economy as a whole, and should be left to manage its own affairs; in sustaining, in other words, the traditional City claim to autonomy.

By the mid-1970s the vulnerability of the new market to crisis was plain enough. The vast new revenues of OPEC were flowing into it, and with such a large amount of money seeking outlets it was all but inevitable that the quality of the risks would decline and mistakes would be made. The dangers of the market were amply displayed in 1974 when the German *Bankhaus Herstadt* collapsed after disastrous foreign exchange dealings, and significant losses were reported from other banks for the same reason. With increasing amounts of money being deposited as surplus funds with other banks for short periods – one estimate gives $1000 billion in 1982[15], and large numbers of foreign-based banks trading in London, the responsiblities and capacities of banks and banking systems to ensure prudence and mount rescues had to be established. Some of Herstadt's liabilities were to London banks, and the Governor of the Bank of England, Sir Gordon Richardson, responded by persuading his fellow central bankers at the meeting of the Bank for International Settlements in July 1974 to accept the doctrine of parental responsiblity; that is, that subsidiaries of foreign banks would be the parents' responsiblity rather than that of the central bank in the host country. This was followed up by requiring letters of comfort from the parents of banks operating in London, undertaking to assume responsibility in case of difficulties.[16]

This in turn was followed by an initiative by the Group of Ten major industrialized nations, plus Switzerland and Luxembourg, through a standing committee, to reach agreement on the international supervision of banks. It resulted in a concordat in 1975 whereby, in the words of one authority in the Bank of England:[17]

'supervision was deemed to be the joint responsibility of parent and host authorities, with both having a duty to ensure that surveillance of banks' foreign establishments was adequate. The supervision of liquidity was seen as the responsibility of host authorities in the first instance (on the grounds that foreign establishments generally have to conform to local rules on liquidity management). The solvency of branches which are an integral part of the parent bank was seen as primarily a matter for parent authorities, whilst that of subsidiaries fell rather to the host; though it was recognised that parent supervisors in their supervision of the parent bank needed to take account of its foreign subsidiaries and joint ventures in view of its moral commitment in their regard.'

A later recommendation of the committee which developed out of the concordat was that supervision of banks' international business should be carried out on the basis of consolidated data in order to provide a global picture of the bank's activities. This tended to reinforce the perception of an overall supervisory duty of the parent authority to monitor the totality of a bank's international operations, including both branches and subsidiaries.

By 1982 the same authority claimed that 'the essential structure is in place within which international banking can operate soundly and confidently . . . There are no rogue herds of unregulated banks tramping through international markets.' It was in 1982 that the Banco Ambrosiano failed, necessitating a $325 million rescue by seven leading Italian banks and involving the loss of $400 million as a result of complicated and at least partially fraudulent transactions through a network of overseas companies, notably in Luxembourg, Nassau, Nicaragua and Peru. The Bank of Italy did not feel obliged to mount a rescue of the Luxembourg subsidiary. 69% owned by Ambrosiano, which was the conduit for a good deal of the irrecoverable funds, and the subsidiary was left to default on its loans. The response of Mr Cooke of the Bank of England to this apparent deviation from the terms of the concordat, was to stress that it referred to supervision, not lender of last resort responsibilities. Although, in the view of the one well-placed commentator,[18] such a débâcle is exceedingly unlikely in Britain, because supervision of the Ambrosiano[19] was inadequate and underpinned by inadequate information, and supervision in Luxembourg was inadequate in part because of banking secrecy, the affair gives pertinence to Sir Gordon Richardson's letters of comfort. It makes sense to clarify and publicize the arrangements for supervising foreign banks, and such a system no doubt goes a long way to ensure that in most cases recklessness and fraud do not go undetected as a result of various potential supervisors thinking that their intervention is the responsibility of others; however, there will always be devious operators and inadequate supervisors, and hence there will always be problems.

However, the question remains as to who mounts the rescue and pays for it, and here the British banking system appears still to be dependent on the letters of comfort, which may sound reassuring, but which are not clear, unequivocal, legal undertakings. When a revised concordat was published in 1983, it did something to clear up this issue, emphasizing that the central banks had agreed on supervision, not as lenders of last resort, and pointed to the improved flow of relevant information that had been achieved since 1975. What will happen when a major foreign-based subsidiary slips through the net, gets into bad trouble and threatens both other banks in the host country and its parent remains to be seen. Who pays in the last analysis will, as circumstances stand at present, depend upon the exercise of political-economic power.

It was not, then, the Euro-currency market and the influx of foreign banks which gave rise directly to formal changes in banking regulation in Britain, though they did give rise to defensive moves. Most of the incoming banks were branches or subsidiaries of well-established parents, quite acceptable to the Bank of England for recognition as financial institutions of long-established good standing and therefore as banks in Britain. Furthermore, the possibility of entering the British markets by degrees, without having to pass through cumbersome legal and bureaucratic red tape, made the establishment of foreign banks in London easier. The challenge to banking conventions and to the very definition of what a bank is, came substantially from home-grown fringe institutions.

# The secondary banks

*Finance Houses*

Besides banks, there had long been other retail lending institutions in Britain. The expansion of the British car industry in the 1950s and 1960s was significantly helped by the invention of hire puchase, which enabled many customers who did not have bank accounts to obtain new cars and pay for them by instalments. The retail banks were forced to compete by introducing personal loans. Credit through the finance houses was controlled by the Government, specifying a minimum percentage deposit and a maximum repayment period. These controls were, however, exercised through the Bank of England as part of its wider obligations in managing credit and the money supply. It was bad enough that the Bank should have to request an increasing number of foreign banks to comply with its restrictions, but at least in this sector it was dealing mainly with established banks for whom it could make life exceedingly difficult if they would not comply. Finance houses were less easy to deal with. There were far more of them, and they ranged from the large and respectable to the small and fly-by-night. The Radcliffe Committee in 1959 estimated that approximately 1200 organizations, accounting for 10% of the instalment credit market, were 'sufficiently insecure to resent well-meaning interference and requests for moderation in an environment of fierce competition'.[20] As long as they remained financially insignificant, however, they did not impinge on the overall problems of credit control, and the Bank concentrated on trying to strengthen the Finance Houses' Association, through whom it channelled its 'requests' from 1961, and whose members controlled 90% of instalment credit by 1969.

In 1966 the banking status of finance houses came to a head, in a case involving one of the largest, United Dominions Trust (UDT). UDT had fallen foul of the provisions of the legislation governing money-lenders, which constrained them in recovering their debts in certain circumstances. Lord Denning, hearing the case in the Court of Appeal,[21] recommended that: 'If any other concern should wish to be regarded by the courts as a banker, it ought to ask the Board of Trade for a certificate that it should be treated as a banker.' Accordingly, in the Companies Act 1967 the distinction was made between Section 127, which provided for a list of full banks agreed by the Treasury, the Bank of England and the Board of Trade (later the Department of Trade and Industry), and other deposit-taking institutions which were covered by Section 123 of the Act and permitted exemption from the Money-lenders Act, but were not allowed to refer to themselves as banks in their advertising.

Whereas under Section 127 banks were subject to liquidity constraints, disclosures and the constant scrutiny of the Bank of England, the only requirement of fringe or secondary banks under Section 123 was that they should be bona fide in banking business. This reflected the fact that, in the words of a Bank of England review of subsequent events,[22] 'It was always (and still is) open to any company or partnership to take deposits and to on-lend them. If such a deposit-taking institution prospered and its reputation and standing in the market-place equally grew, it could eventually come to be accepted as a full member of the banking community.' In other words, the gradual and informal system of recognition by the banking community and the Bank in particular remained in place after the Act, thus begging the really important aspect of the question thrown up by the UDT case: it was all very well to create a special legal category for secondary banks, but how were they to be regulated and, especially, what measures were to be taken to protect retail customers? How were they to be prevented from engaging in reckless ventures, and how was any failure by such an institution to be insulated from having knock-on effects to full banks, and thus upon the banking system as a whole? These matters did not appear important in the late 1960s, but with the turn of the decade and the rise of other institutions under Section 123 they were to become so.

### Other Institutions

The finance houses continued to prosper, but remained more or less true to their established craft. They were joined at the beginning of the 1970s by a number of quite new institutions, many of whom were by no means exclusively involved in banking. The distinctive features of these newcomers were, first their heterogeneity: their activities included share-dealing, unit trusts, life assurance, property development, property dealing and management, mortgages and second mortgages, purchasing and re-organizing industrial companies, leasing, and financial and investment advice, as well as a variety of foreign and off-shore activities. Secondly, they never stood still, and constantly shifted the centre of their activities to new areas which they thought likely to be profitable – they were the reverse of the staid clearing banks. Thirdly, in style they were quite unlike banks: brash and aggressive in the market-place, self-consciously successful and proud of it, overtly eager to sell their money, their services and their other financial products – again the reverse of the conventional high street or even merchant banks.

Fourthly, they thrived on rapid growth in two senses: they derived their psychological bouyancy and elan from the fact of it – growth rates of over 25% a year were common – but they also grew to depend upon it more and more for their stability as the scope of their commitments grew, and they increasingly used their own shares to purchase other organizations and manage their own indebtedness. As the 1970s wore on they became more and more aware that, although individuals might be suspicious, the market as a whole would not seriously doubt them as long as their profits, dividends and share values grew year by year. Growth was thus more than an achievement, more even than an underpinning psychology, it was the fundamental strategy.

Fifthly, the secondary banks sustained this growth and the confidence of the market by getting extensively involved with the established institutions in a variety of ways: by getting them to purchase their shares, by persuading them to engage in joint ventures, and by getting them to invest very large sums in projects identified by the new high-fliers as the thing of the future. The clearing and merchant banks became involved to a degree, but the principal targets were the newly-rich institutions with vast assets and incomes – the pension funds, insurance companies and most spectacularly of all, that ambiguous organization the Crown Agents.

More needs to be said about some of these characteristics, particularly the last, in explaining the crisis which the secondary banks precipitated in 1974, but before doing so their final common characteristic needs identifying, that is their willingness to grasp every opportunity, every unattached pound in a period of monetary and stock-market boom, without heed for the inevitable subsequent slump. This characteristic was, of course, closely linked with their need for rapid growth. Circumstances conspired to provide ample opportunity for indulgence in this respect.

*The Speculative Bubble*

There was, first, the rise in London in the 1960s of the prime Euro-currency market described above, which brought large amounts of new money into the City, beyond the traditional controls of the Bank of England which were exercised through the discount houses and the discount market. Secondly, there emerged markets parallel to the discount market dealing in such funds as inter-bank loans, local authority debt and inter-company loans. The foreign-based banks participated in both these new markets and brought to them new foreign techniques and instruments, such as the American-devised Certificate of Deposit. Clearing banks, as the main avenue for the control of the money supply and the dominant institutions of the British banking system, began to chafe at their restrictions. Traditionally the Bank of England had imposed constraints on credit by a combination of base-rate changes and requests to restrict lending, which, in later years, had taken the form of requests for special deposits with the Bank. The Bank could also give guidance to the clearers as to where credit was or was not to be directed, and this could also affect the profitability of loans. In addition, the clearers were subject to a 28% liquid asset ratio, higher than that for other banks. The Conservative Government of 1970, elected on the platform of return to free-market principles, was inclined to agree with the clearers' complaints that they were unable to be active in the new and lucrative markets, and that there was a danger that new opportunities would be lost to outsiders, including the foreign banks. The Bank, with the Government's agreement, therefore introduced in 1971 revised arrangements under the general title of Competition and Credit Control, to equalize opportunities. Under the new system, the liquidity ratio was to be 12½% for all banks, and the principal instrument to be used to control the money supply was to be interest rates. This move coincided with the Conservative Chancellor, Anthony Barber's so-called 'dash for growth', as part of which he deliberately relaxed control of the money supply in order to stimulate the economy. The effect was in practice to stimulate the new secondary banks to the point of frenzy.

To the already established new markets providing funds was therefore added the liquidity released by unlocking the clearers' assets under the new rules and the additional cash allowed in to the system by relaxing monetary constraints. The net result was a phenomenal increase in the money supply: M3, the most widely used measure of the money supply, grew at 28% annually in 1972 and 1973, and doubled between mid-1970 and early 1974. The effect of this was to suck in imports and to increase the rate of inflation, but of more immediate interest is that it left quantities of funds with no reasonable outlet. A good deal of this money found its way into the hands of the fringe, who found excellent uses for it in financing their own exponential growth. Sterling bank advances increased 519% and to other financial companies, including fringe banks, 416%.

Property was identified as the golden investment of the early 1970s, a secure hedge against rising inflation. Not only was it unheard of for property values to decline, they had shown a strong growth in post-war years, particularly in the commercial sector for shops and offices. This growth, it was argued, was bound to continue at a healthy rate in prime sites, because it was based on a non-reproduceable commodity, land. This was illustrated clearly in the City of London itself, where new skyscrapers had been built to house the incoming international banks and multinational corporations, all of whom set great store by having their headquarters as centrally-located in the magical square mile of the City as possible, and were prepared to pay for the privilege. Furthermore, the Labour Government's (1964–70) opposition to the effects this produced, i.e. huge capital gains, rising office rents, a transformed London sky-line, the loss of old buildings and increased pressure on services, as more work concentrated in a small land area, was reflected in the ban imposed by George Brown in 1964 on further office development without special permission. Many schemes had been agreed in a hurry before the ban was implemented, but by 1970 the supply of offices from these schemes was running out, and deregulation by the new government released a flood of new schemes. City property rents rose from £2 per square foot in 1960 to £5 in 1968, £13 in 1970 and £21 in 1973.[23]

Property prices too began to rise rapidly, fuelled by the huge injections of cash and expectations of growth, and the affair took on the form of a classic speculative bubble. Clearly the property market could not sustain an increasing growth rate indefinitely without roaring inflation, and equally clearly, once the prime sites had been taken and redeveloped, the let-ability of schemes elsewhere would suffer and, since their value was based on their rental per square foot, it would prove increasingly difficult to put a price on them. None of this deterred the secondary banks, nor increasingly the pension funds and insurance companies, as Tables 5–8 show. The latter moved from investing in secondary banks who were heavily involved in property to, in some cases, co-partnership in property development schemes; all of which generated its own political problems.

The Labour Party was vociferous in its opposition to property speculation, the market became saturated, and office rentals rose to levels even banks quailed at, London being twice the price of New York. Inflation pushed up building costs 7% in 1971, 11% in 1972, 23.5% in 1973 and 25.8% in 1974, so eating into potential profits. The Heath Government felt constrained to reintroduce a ban on further office schemes and a development gains tax to recoup the increased land values consequent upon permission to develop. More telling, however, were the effects of the OPEC oil price increase in 1973 and the Miners' strike of 1973–4, which put the country on a three-day week and led to the fall of the Government.

The bubble burst when interest rates rose from 7% to 13% between June and November 1974, and property companies found that they could no longer service loans with rental income and that they could not sell off their assets at a realistic price. As the clearing banks later put it in a review of the crisis.[24]

In 1972 and 1973 property companies were in fact facing the dilemma with which the local authorities were already familiar. If the rise in interest rates was likely to be temporary, then it would be preferable to borrow short and fund later as the opportunity arose, rather than be committed to higher rates of interest for five or more years ahead. In the event, the rise both in the long and short-term rates was sustained and so proved very expensive. For the property companies covered by the Business Monitor series, debt and interest had absorbed about half their gross income before debt interest in 1972. In 1973 the proportion had risen to about ⅔rds and in 1974 to as much as 90% – a classic illustration of the risks of high gearing.

Property prices in general had risen by 25% in both 1972 and 1973, so distorting the housing market and creating windfall gains for those already in it, but pricing a large number of aspirants out of it. Competition and Credit Control as a means of managing the money supply was a disaster – one which reportedly formed the foundation of Mrs Thatcher's commitment to monetarism. Although bank base rates grew unprecedentedly fast in 1973, with inevitable consequences for the mortgage rate, they would have had to rise to 30% to act as effective controls on the rates of return which were being confidently anticipated on the fringe. Property schemes were, from its point of view, the ideal vehicle for paper growth.

Once a development scheme was agreed upon and the site purchased, the asset was written into the books in its completed or redeveloped and let form, creating a major gain in assets, and allowing for building costs at current prices. Since buildings are traditionally a secure asset they are good for borrowing against, and the fringe and its partners borrowed heavily, sometimes in excess of 100% to allow for professional fees and advice in addition to site and development costs. A further ground for taking such schemes as good security was that their developed asset value was based upon their letable rental, which would be calculated at prevailing rates, yet it was known that office rental rates were rising sharply and hence it could be assumed that, even if there were hitches in the course of development or in finding suitable tenants, when the time came rentals would have increased and extended borrowings could be repaid. What was not reflected upon was that (a) office rentals had to be paid by businesses who could not afford ever-increasing rates; (b) there had in the past been politically-motivated bans on office development, and if it happened again, schemes that had been initiated might well be frozen or have heavy development tax levied upon them; and (c) that given the rate of development, the market would likely become saturated, new offices would become unletable and rentals would fall, as indeed happened in a number of city centres in the mid and late 1970s.

As Tables 5–8 show, the links between the secondary and clearing banks, the insurance companies and pension funds and property companies were substantial in the mid-1970s. Why were these institutions, normally thought of as conservative, drawn into the speculation? As an exhaustive analysis of the identifiable economic factors behind the property boom concluded: 'the major explanation . . . that we are left with, but which is regrettably difficult to test, is that expectations about the future played a vital determining role'.[25] These expectations were evidently widespread and it was not properly appreciated to what extent the frenzied activities of the property developers themselves were feeding on a fundamentally unrealistic rise in the market. But the fact was that while it lasted the rises were real

## Table 5.   Links between Property and Insurance Companies

| Company | Total borrowings (£000s) | Insurance company links |
|---|---|---|
| Associated Industrial Properties | 30 048 | Norwich Union, Guardian Royal Exchange |
| British Land | 96 538 | Prudential |
| Capital & County | 139 313 | Norwich Union |
| Hammerson | 150 059 | Legal & General, Standard Life, Royal London, Mutual |
| Land Securities | 417 983 | Prudential, Legal & General, Pearl |
| Metropolitan Estates | 208 582 | Eagle Star, Prudential, Legal & General |
| Saint Martin's | 58 172 | Yorkshire |
| Star (GP) | 406 463 | Alliance |
| Stock Conversion | 29 483 | Scottish Amicable |
| Town & City | 114 560 | Prudential |

Source: *Investors Chronicle Property Supplement* (Nov. 1973), cited in Counter Information Service, *Your Money and Your Life,* 1974.

enough, and those lucky or astute enough to get out at the peak, or to survive the crash, made handsome profits. The other important aspect of the bubble was that the central actors, the property companies and secondary banks, had no difficulty in obtaining funds to fuel the speculation, both because of the easy-money situation described above, and because of the inherent weaknesses in non-banking institutions which they drew in.

Insurance companies and pension funds have enormous inflows of cash which they are required to invest, and their growth in size is a relatively recent phenomenon: they are the basic security of the salaried population whose numbers have increased dramatically in the post-war years as white-collar workers have come to form an increasing majority of the workforce.[26] The managers of these funds had, and still have, a degree of discretion as to where they place these very large sums of money. Inexperience and pressure to place large quantities of funds in seemingly favourable situations clearly seem to have resulted in close personal links being forged between some fund managers and fringe activists, as Plender has documented in detail in respect of pension funds. More will be said about this in a later chapter. Suffice it to say, that not only does it appear that some fund managers may have lacked experience and been led by glib operators into imprudent schemes, but that, in certain cases, managers became involved in related schemes on their own account, so creating clear conflicts between their own interests and those on whose behalf they were acting as fund managers.

**Table 6.   Holdings in Land and Property (% Total Assets)**

|                      | 1967 | 1968 | 1969 | 1970 | 1971 | 1972 | 1973 | 1974 |
|----------------------|------|------|------|------|------|------|------|------|
| Insurance companies  | 10   | 10   | 11   | 12   | 13   | 12   | 14   | 16   |
| Private pension funds| 4    | 5    | 7    | 8    | 8    | 8    | 12   |      |
| Public pension funds | 10   | 10   | 12   | 14   | 11   | 11   | 18   | 19   |

Source: R. Barras and A. Catalano, *Investment in Land and the Financial Structure of Property Companies*, Centre for Environmental Studies Conference Paper 17, vol. II, Urban Economics Conference 1975. Figures for 1974 from *Commercial Property Development*, HMSO, 1975, Table B, p. 22.

**Table 7   Net Annual Investment by Insurance Companies and Pensions Funds (Present Total)**

|                              | 1965 | 1970 | 1971 | 1972  | 1973 | 1974 |
|------------------------------|------|------|------|-------|------|------|
| *Insurance companies*        |      |      |      |       |      |      |
| Fixed-interest securities    | 71.5 | 29.4 | 53.4 | 31.0  | 40.7 | 19.8 |
| Equities                     | 13.2 | 27.2 | 30.3 | 43.2  | 23.2 | 2.0  |
| Land property and ground rents | 13.6 | 19.9 | 15.9 | 7.9 | 18.0 | 42.0 |
| *Pension funds*              |      |      |      |       |      |      |
| Fixed-interest securities    | 59.2 | 6.9  | 54.0 | -10.2 | 27.9 | 10.6 |
| Equities                     | 37.1 | 47.2 | 46.1 | 67.5  | 27.6 | 12.7 |
| Land property and ground rents | 8.3 | 20.0 | 19.6 | 24.1 | 18.4 | 15.5 |

Source: Department of the Environment, *Commercial Property Development*, HMSO, 1975, Table A, p. 22.

*The Crown Agents*

Perhaps the most extraordinary casualty of the secondary banking crisis, and one indicative of the anomalous state of British financial institutions, was the Crown Agents. The agents had an important role during the Empire as purchasing agents for colonial and foreign governments. As the Empire slowly faded away to be replaced by the Commonwealth, they continued to function, being attached to the Ministry of Overseas Development, by making purchases for foreign and Commonwealth countries. They were, as a financial body, also subejct to the supervision of the Treasury, and of the Exchequer and Audit Department. The small surplus which

**Table 8. Lending to Property Companies (£ million)**

| | 1967 | 1968 | 1969 | 1970 | 1971 | 1972 | 1973 | 1974 | 1975 | 1976 |
|---|---|---|---|---|---|---|---|---|---|---|
| London clearing banks | | | | | | | | | | |
| Parent banks | 242 | 221 | 211 | 184 | 261 | 642 | 850 | 925 | 917 | 855 |
| Groups | NA | NA | NA | NA | NA | NA | 1160 | 1340 | 1414 | 1397 |
| Other banks$_a$ | 103 | 116 | 116 | 159 | 240 | 515 | 1170 | 1494 | 1545 | 1392 |
| Total | 345 | 337 | 327 | 343 | 501 | 1157 | 2230 | 2834 | 2959 | 2789 |
| | | | | | | | | | | |
| % advances to all UK residents | | | | | | | | | | |
| London clearing banks | | | | | | | | | | |
| Parent banks | 5.2 | 4.7 | 4.3 | 3.5 | 4.7 | 8.0 | 7.8 | 7.1 | 7.0 | 5.9 |
| Groups | NA | NA | NA | NA | NA | NA | 9.0 | 8.6 | 8.7 | 7.6 |
| Other$_a$ | 5.3 | 5.4 | 4.8 | 5.3 | 6.1 | 8.7 | 12.5 | 12.5 | 11.2 | 8.4 |
| Total | 5.3 | 4.9 | 4.5 | 4.2 | 5.3 | 8.3 | 10.4 | 10.3 | 9.8 | 8.0 |

NA = not available.

$_a$Excluding London clearing banks' subsidiaries from 1973.

Source: Clearing Banks Evidence to Wilson Committee, Table 61, p. 277.

they made on their operations was redistributed to clients. In 1966 it was decided to end this practice and instead to retain any surplus to build up a reserve fund which was then invested by the Agents on their own account.

In 1968 the Finance Director agreed with the new Senior Agent that dealing on this account could be increased, and it nearly quadrupled in nine months to £200 000 000. Rumours of this reached the Bank and the Treasury, but neither took any decisive action, each thinking it was the other's obligation to do so, though in 1969 the Bank withdrew the Agents' foreign exchange dealing privileges (exchange controls were then in force). The Agents were of course without any substantial experience of investment dealing and, in addition, lacked the internal staff and structure to cope with it, most alarmingly in respect of management accounting, thus exposing themselves to dangerous combinations of risks, without it being properly appreciated internally, let alone communicated to the supervisory bodies. The Agents became known in City circles as a source of easy funds, and were apparently flattered at being treated, not as civil servants, but as substantial men of finance with all the deference and hospitality that involves.

The Crown Agents were eventually shown to have invested in a veritable catalogue of disastrous enterprises: William Stern's property empire, on which they lost £41.2 million and which went bust for £400 million; Triumph Investment Trust, a secondary bank which collapsed into the arms of the Bank of England lifeboat; Vehicle and General Insurance, a cut-price motor insurance company that went bust; London and County Securities, the fringe bank that started the secondary banking crisis by its failure; Israel British Bank, which also went bust; First National Finance Corporation, which survived only with extensive lifeboat support; London Capital Group, John Stonehouse's spectacularly fraudulent banking failure. The Senior Agent protected his Finance Manager, who was at the centre of investment decisions, and seemingly the only one with a grasp of what was happening, and stalled for time to allow things to rectify themselves. Hence it was not until 1971 that the first enquiry under Sir Matthew Stevenson took place, which resulted in a report in 1972, before the disastrous nature of many of the investments came to light, though Sir Matthew did express anxiety about own account dealing, and recommended that the Agents' anomalous constitutional position be dealt with.

By the time the reforms were announced in 1973, the Finance Manager had left the Agents, and serious investigations did not begin until the Senior Agent retired in 1974. In December 1974, the Agents were forced to ask for £85 million of government help, and the Fay Commission was appointed in 1975 to investigate the mess. By this time, losses exceeded £200 million. When Fay reported,[27] he was scathing about the investment policy of the Agents and about Alan Challis, the Finance Manager responsible for it in particular:

> As to financing property, a bank or finance house has broadly two options, one to lend at proper rates on ample security, the other to lend with less security and less or delayed returns on the loan, but as a quid pro quo to take "a slice of the action" by holding a stake in the equity. The former is a banking operation, the latter an entrepreneurial operation. The former has little risk, the latter produces high profits in boom times, and large losses in slumps. The "adventurous" Mr Challis chose the latter course for major investments.

Fay, like Stevenson, identified the source of the problem in the anomalous constitutional position of the Agents. By the time he reported in 1977 reforms had been undertaken and the financial salvage of the Agents under John Cuckney was underway. However, the House of Commons and the Labour government were not satisfied with the lack of detail in the Fay Report: details of who was responsible for the losses and exactly how the various institutions with which the agents had been involved behaved. A Tribunal of Enquiry under Sir David Croom-Johnson was therefore set up, and it spent several years collecting additional evidence before reporting in 1982,[28] by which time the Agents, pruned back to their traditional role as purchasing agents and having lost some of their major customers, were on their way to obscurity once more.

As Moran points out,[29] Croom-Johnson's most instructive aspect is the insight it provides into the way in which banking supervision was exercised. It was not simply that detailed supervision of some 300 institutions by the discount office staff of 15 at the Bank was evidently impossible, but that their style of work was such as to minimize the chance of detecting a weak player, let alone a fraudulent one. Thus, in respect of John Stonehouse's British Bangladesh Trust, whose prospectus was roundly criticized as doubtful by the *Sunday Times* at its launch, the subsequent Department of Trade Inspector's Report discovered that the financial facts upon which the prospectus was founded, which were in some respects untrue and misleading, could have been checked by the Department of Trade before a Section 123 licence was issued, but the procedure for evaluating applications at that time included no provision for an independent verification of the facts. The Bank might have been more flexible, but the Bank was the *fons et origo* of trust as the basis for the relationship among banks and between them and their supervisors. As Moran puts it:[30]

> the failures of supervision revealed by the secondary banking crisis did not, therefore, arise chiefly from the confused state of the law, nor were they mainly due to failures of co-ordination. They arose from the excessive trust placed by the authorities in the independent capacity of bankers to do business prudently. This excess was no aberration of one individual. It served powerful interests by allowing bankers to do business free of close bureaucratic controls, and allowing the Bank of England to supervise the City with little interference from Whitehall or Westminster. In a phrase: it preserved esoteric politics.
>
> The success of this kind of supervision caused its own destruction. Freedom from the close legal controls common in other banking systems gave London a great advantage, so that the history of the money markets in the 1960s and the early 1970s was one of dazzling success and innovation. The consequent economic and social transformation destroyed the conditions which made it sensible to rely heavily on trust. The financial community increased in size and sophistication, but the Bank would not increase its regulatory staff in a corresponding way, for fear of destroying the privacy and informality of its relations with bankers. The result was, that at the very time when the banking community was becoming more diverse, was experiencing fierce competition, and was pioneering new and risky practices, supervisors were forced to place an increasing weight on trust.

This is not to say that legal reform was not made essential by the secondary banking crisis, but to emphasize that administrative reform was more essential, not only in scope but in style. The Bank had ample powers under existing (1948 and 1967) legislation to intervene in so far as it thought necessary and desirable. The problem was that it thought it undesirable to question another banker's word and, this being so, was prevented from evaluating whether it was necessary to do so. The implication of the crisis was, then, that there ought to be more extensive formalized procedures for evaluating banking licence applications and for monitoring activity, involving where necessary more supervisory staff at the Bank and the Department of Trade. However, what was less obvious was that the views of supervisors needed to become much more critical, to the point of hostility if need be, if applicants or supervisees were unforthcoming or devious, as a good many on the fringe were. Under the existing system they often managed to avoid the screening, as is illustrated by the Stonehouse case, with bland exteriors and effrontery.

The other aspect that Croom-Johnson's investigations revealed was the in-fighting between governmental departments, the consequence of which was that none took effective action against the Agents in time. This reflects once again the Bank's desire to sustain its own autonomy. This interacted with its informality to further weaken the co-ordination of essential information:

> The Croom-Johnson Report portrays a world of intense institutional jealousies. Institutions fought subtle battles to control information, to establish jurisdiction and to obtain access to key committees; while the battles were fought, the Agents went their incompetent, imprudent way. Outsiders sometimes imagine that secrecy in British Government is used only against those outside the machine; Croom-Johnson shows that supposed "insiders" can be almost as much in the dark, because control of information is a key weapon in the battles fought in conducting "bureaucratic politics".
>
> In the Bank's case these problems were made worse by the informality which went with esoteric politics. The Croom-Johnson enquiry found that "much of its work was done orally" and that decisions "were either not recorded at all, or were recorded only in a brief manuscript note scribbled on the top of a minute, and often not copied to all concerned". Consequently, "when junior staff who had not been involved in earlier discussions were sent . . . to represent the Bank at inter-departmental meetings, they were not familiar with the background or the Bank's views, and there was no file to which they could turn for a record of the Bank's previous involvement and thinking. Government departments looking for advice from those representing the Bank at such meetings had little idea of how inadequately informed they often were."[31]

It is important to be aware of the pervasive significance of these preocupations, since it is only in this way that it will be possible adequately to assess the reform and its implications for the position and stance of the Bank and other supervisory bodies when it is discussed later. Clearly, if emphasis upon trust and informality persists, and if the maintenance of Bank autonomy is insisted upon, it is liable to frustrate the effectiveness of any reform, no matter what its external appearance is.

It remains to discuss the crisis and rescue operation before coming to the reform. The Lifeboat and its voyage has now been discussed in varying amounts of detail and evaluated from a variety of analytical points of view and there is no need to repeat the detailed account here.[32] The story is certainly a tribute to the skills, both political and financial, of the Bank in mounting the operation and seeing it through to a successful conclusion. The doubts arise about whether such a venture ought to have become necessary in the first place, and whether the need for it has been subsequently removed by reform.

The crisis began in November 1973 when a City banker resigned from London and County Securities only five months after being brought in to reorganize and stabilize it. Small depositors began to withdraw their money in the department stores where the bank had been opening branches, with the opening day sometimes graced with the presence of Jeremy Thorpe, then leader of the Liberal Party and a Director of London and Counties. The share price fell in a few weeks from 305 pence to 40 pence, and it subsequently emerged that the organization's accounts had been artificially inflated by worthless cheques to the extent of £4 million. When the Department of Trade report was completed, it estimated a £75 000 loss for 1972-3, not profits of £2.7 million as L and C had claimed at the time, and pointed out that liquidity was only saved by borrowing £25 million at 13%, which could only be on-lent at 8%. The bank failed at the beginning of December and was relegated by the Bank of England to First National Finance Corporation, another secondary bank with which it had been involved, and which was itself soon to be in trouble.

It was not, however, until 20 December that the Bank of England recognized that a general crisis was developing. The failure of another secondary bank, Cedar Holdings, led to a tense late-night meeting with the principal institutions involved – Phoenix Assurance, the pension funds of Unilever, the National Coal Board and the Electricity Supply Industry which jointly held 23% of Cedar's shares, and Barclays, Cedar's clearing bank.

The Bank of England was adamant that Cedar could not be allowed to sink. However, it took the persuasive powers of leading officials and of the respected liquidator, Sir Kenneth Cork, finally to get the banks and institutions involved to put together the £72 million necessary to rescue it. The Bank was in no doubt that if Cedar failed to open its doors the following day, other banks would soon be in difficulties on the fringe, and if there were a run on their deposits and they were forced to close, the merchant and clearing banks would be pulled down in a widening collapse of confidence. The lesson of Barings in 1890 was well understood, except that in this case the prospect was of a number of failures which would need support.

The following day the Governor of the Bank met the Chairmen of the Big Four Clearers to outline the necessity for a long-term rescue programme, and obtained their agreement to participate. The terms of the arrangement were modified just after Christmas to bring in the three other clearers and to gain the acceptance by the Bank itself of a liability for 10% of the risks. A discreet press statement was made and the Lifeboat was launched. As fringe banks got into trouble in the coming months and years, the Lifeboat Committee moved in to sustain them. At least 25 received help, of which eight went into liquidation, one was scaled down and sold off, and 14 of the remaining 16 were later taken over. It was not made public at the end of 1973 that the banks were aware that a very substantial commitment was being made, and even the banks were then unaware, both of the extent of their eventual exposure and of the length of time the crisis would last. As Tables 9, 10, 11 show, the peak was not reached until March 1975, by which time the clearers had insisted that an absolute limit of £1200 million, which represented 40% of their total capital and reserves, had to be imposed. Luckily for the Bank, the demands began to decline just beyond this point, but not before the Bank was forced to take sole responsibility for the risks in rescuing Slater Walker, which went under in 1975.

**Table 9.  Total Amount of Lifeboat Support at Shared Risk Outstanding at End Quarters**

| End quarter | £ (million) |
|---|---|
| *1974* | |
| March | 390.2 |
| June | 443.4 |
| September | 994.3 |
| December | 1181.7 |
| *1975* | |
| March | 1173.4 |
| June | 1148.5 |
| September | 949.9 |
| December | 913.5 |
| *March* | |
| March | 876.1 |
| June | 827.2 |
| September | 774.5 |
| December | 782.7 |
| *1977* | |
| March | 752.1 |
| June | 731.7 |
| September | 713.8 |
| December | 676.5 |
| *1978* | |
| March | 656.5 |

Source: Bank of England background paper to Wilson Committee, *The Secondary Banking Crisis and the Bank of England's Support Operations*, 1978, Appendix A.

**Table 10.   Trends at some of the larger secondary bank groups**

| Company Year of foundation or coming under new control | | 1965 (unless otherwise stated) | | 1971 | | 1973 | | 1975 | | Share price | |
|---|---|---|---|---|---|---|---|---|---|---|---|
| | | Pre-tax profit (£m) | Gross assets (£m) | Pre-tax profits (£m) | Gross assets (£m) | Pre-tax profit (£m) | Gross assets (£m) | Pre-tax profits (£m) [-loss] | Gross assets (£m) | At peak in 1972 (p) | End 1974 (p) |
| Edward Bates and Sons (Holdings) | 1967 | 0.02 | NA | 0.1 | 24 | 1.5 | 74[5] | -16.3 | 68 | 337 | 201 |
| Burston Group | 1955 | 0.06 | NA | 1.2 | 70 | 1.8 | 100 | — | — | 224 | 16 |
| Cannon Street Investments | 1968 | 0.01 | 0.4 | 0.4 | 3 | 3.5 | 122 | 0.7[6] | NA | 119 | 5.5[1] |
| Cedar Holdings | 1958 | 0.02 | 8 | 0.9 | 18 | 1.9 | 128 | -2.7 | 56 | 99 | 13[1] |
| First National Finance Corporation | 1963 | 0.8 | 201 | 7.5 | 182 | 18.4 | 543 | -83.2 (10 mths) | 417[7] | 139 | 3.5 |
| Keyser Ullmann Holdings[2] | 1962 | 0.6 (1969) | 12 | 0.6 | 13 | 9.0 | 161 | -59.2 | 279 | 385 | 36 |
| London and County Securities Group | 1961 | 0.6 (1969) | 3.6 | 0.7 | 15 | 3.6 | 129 | — | — | 358 | 40[1] |
| Mercantile Credit | 1934 | 2.5 | 12 | 8.2 | 243 | 12.8 | 377 | -10.8 | 355 | 146.5 | 11 |

| | | | | | | | | | | | |
|---|---|---|---|---|---|---|---|---|---|---|---|
| Slater Walker Securities | 1964 | 0.8 | 20 | 16.3 | 280 | 23.4 | 588 | -39.9 | 160 | 309 | 35 |
| Triumph Investment Trust | 1964 | 0.05 | NA | 3.4 | 61 | 6.6 | 203 | -19.4 (1974) | 153 | 150 | 5[1] |
| United Dominions Trust | 1922 | 5.0 | 265 | 11.1 | 466 | 24.3 | 896 | -53.5 | 1095 | 158.5 | 13 |
| J. H. Vavasseur[3] | 1968 | 0.05 | NA | 1.3 | 12 | -16.5 | 52 | -3.9 | 36 | 400 | 3 |

Gross Assets figures over £10m rounded to nearest £1 m. Year is that in which financial year ends.
Gross assets at end of year or period of accounts.
NA Not available.
– Not applicable (see text).

1. Price as at previous supension of Stock Exchange quotation.
2. Except 1975, KUH gross asset figures for holding co. only (Banking co. gross assets £65 m in 1969, £74 m in 1971 and £265 m in 1973). Banking figures included in profits which, for 1969, 1971 and 1973 are net after tax and transfer to inner reserves. Full disclosure and pfts pre-tax 1975.
3. J. H. Vavasseur Group, 1975.
4. Takes into account exceptional and extraordinary loss items as well as provisions.
5. £168 m in 1974.
6. Excludes Cannon Street Acceptances.
7. But £41 m capital deficiency.
Source: M. Reid, The Secondary Banking Crisis 1973-75, pp. 40-1.

## Table 11.   Ownership Changes in Lifeboat Banks

| Banking company | Assets (end 1973) (£ million) | New owner |
|---|---|---|
| Beverley Bentinck | 35 | Bank of Ireland (1978) |
| Bowmaker | 243 | Lloyds Bank (1982) |
| British Bank of Commerce | 59 | Grindlays Bank (1974) |
| Cannon Street Investments | 122 | Nat West (1974) |
| Cedar Holdings | 128 | Lloyds & Scottish (1979)a |
| Edward Bates & Sons Holdingsb | 74 | Allied Arab Bank Bank of England |
| Keyser Ullman Holdings | 433 (Mar 1974) | Charterhouse Group (1980) |
| Medens Trust | 11 (June 1974) | Brown Shipley Holdings (1981) |
| Mercantile Credit | 377 | Barclays (1975) |
| Morris Wigram | 30 | Slavenberg's Bank (1980) |
| Northern Commercial Trustb | 90 | Algemene Bank Nederland (1975) |
| Twentieth Century Banking | 62 | P & O Group (1974) |
| United Dominions Trust | 896 | Trustee Savings Bank (TSB) (1981) |
| J. H. Vavasseur | 52 | Mills & Allen International (1978) |

aIn 1981 Lloyds Bank acquired a majority holding in Lloyds & Scottish.
bOnly parts or subsidiaries of these groups were taken over.
Source: J. Coakley and L. Harris, The City of Capital, Basil Blackwell, 1983, p. 73.

The clearers accepted the importance of defending confidence in the banking system, but their understandings of what they had committed themselves to were not, it seems in retrospect, quite those of the Bank. The objective of the Lifeboat was in principle simple and effective. As fringe banks got into trouble because of the adverse market conditions, they would become subject to a run on deposits. These would be withdrawn and placed in a safer place, usually with the clearers, which would in turn place balancing amounts with the fringe bank, so assuming the risk. The theory behind this recycling procedure was well understood by the clearers to be one of confidence and liquidity. Even they would fail if confidence collapsed and all their depositors demanded their money at once. Indeed, in 1974, at the height of the crisis, the NatWest was forced to issue a statement denying that it was receiving Bank of England assistance – the knock-on effect had penetrated, just, to the Big Four. The point about this arrangement, however, is that it was explicitly concerned with liquidity, not solvency: the secondary banks, given support, were taken to be basically sound, but suffering from the adverse financial climate. This, of course, proved not to be so in very many cases, and instances of imprudence to the point of recklessness and outright fraud became evident as one Department of Trade enquiry into the fringe followed another. The consequence of insolvency, however, was that the clearers would at best obtain almost worthless shares for their risks, and would end up paying through the nose for the rescue of the British banking system, rather than simply providing large-scale support for a limited period on a tolerably commercial basis. Once involved in the Lifeboat, however, they could not back out; they were in no doubt that if the Lifeboat failed they too might become threatened. It was not a welcome discovery and it proved a lesson that they would not forget, whatever the blandishments and authority of the Bank of England.

## Administrative Reform

Not surprisingly, the crisis resulted in changes in regulatory arrangements and practice. In July 1974 the discount office was replaced by a new Banking Supervision Division, and its head given increased rank. The number of staff was increased from 15 to nearly 40 within eight months and to 70 within three years. A month after the new division was founded it began asking for more, and more detailed information, from Section 123 as well as Section 127 banks. The information asked for reflected the Bank's rising anxiety about the length and profundity of the crisis: maturity patterns of sterling deposits, loans to associated companies, and standby facilities. Before the crisis, the Bank had not the close informal relations with the fringe that it had with the clearers and the discount houses and it had little to offer in return for detailed information. The crisis changed all that from the point of view of both sides. The Lifeboat would only work in an orderly way if it was properly informed in advance of problems, and the fringe could only expect its support if it cooperated – and individual terms had to be negotiated for each casualty which could offer a greater or lesser change of long-term survival.

The bank was, however, clearly in a dilemma if it wished to preserve the old system of control. It had to accept that the newcomers were here to stay, even if their numbers were thinned in time by takeovers and liquidations, and it also had to accept that they required more detailed and constant supervision than the established banks. It was straightforward enough to devise a new administrative machine to achieve this, which could process quantities of statistics about them, but the next stage in formalization would, however, introduce an element of rigidity which would not appeal to the bank; that is, the introduction of a series of formal criteria and procedures designed to protect the solvency of all banking institutions and going far beyond the simple rules on reserve asset ratios. It would involve, for example, setting out circumstances which would trigger certain levels of intervention by the supervisors, and specifying procedures to be adhered to if certain misfortunes beset a bank. Ultimately this would amount to a formalization of a code of banking practice which was the antithesis of both what the fringe, as innovators, represented, and what the Bank, anxious that London should remain in the forefront of banking techniques, wished to avoid. Furthermore, it would be liable to be circumvented by unscrupulous or ingenious operators, especially when they came under pressure or wished to take their own route out. Finally, even if the fringe submitted to such procedures, the clearers would not, and different arrangements would have to be made for them. That is indeed what happened, after a working party had reported in 1975 in favour of less onerous supervision for the clearers. Rather than quarterly contact with supervisors, annual discussions were held and these were to have no directive power, any outstanding differences to be resolved by a meeting between the clearer's chairman and the Governor of the Bank. Thus was confidence and mutual trust to be sustained.

For the fringe too, supervision was softened by quarterly discussions with supervisory staff, albeit on the basis of the detailed statistics already provided, but the Bank stressed[33] that in them it sought 'a relaxed, two-way exchange, not an inquisitorial examination'. In the Governor's words: 'it is more useful to seek to influence a bank's policy from the top than to try to monitor its procedures from the bottom'. An informal style was therefore to remain central to the supervisory strategy, but bolstered by increasing levels of formal information flows.

## The Banking Act 1979

Given the fact that administrative reforms were in place by 1975, with the Bank firmly in control, and doing its best to maintain continuity with past traditions, the Banking Act of 1979 seemed something of an anomaly. What interest did the bank have in promoting legislation which would only stir up debate about its powers, responsibilities and effectiveness? Given that a Labour Government was in office from 1974, it might also reasonably fear the loss of some of its autonomy through legislation. The answer lies in several different directions. First, membership of the European Economic Community required participation in harmonizing legislation which took the form, in the case of banking, of the directive of 1977. This legally required that EEC states 'shall require credit institutions subject to this directive to obtain authorization before commencing their activities',[34] and required that member states lay down requirements for authorization. At that time Britain and Holland were the only two members which had no legal requirements for authorizing credit institutions. The 1979 Act met this obligation by requiring deposit-taking institutions to be authorized by the Bank of England, laying down the criteria for authorization and supervision, and establishing a deposit-protection fund. The second source of pressure for legislation was the Labour Government, which was concerned and sceptical about the handling of the secondary banking crisis. The deposit protection fund in particular was regarded as a politically sensible piece of consumer legislation, even though it only guaranteed 75% of deposits up to £10 000.

The Bank had then to reckon with substantial pressure for legislation and was hence moved to influence its shape to protect its own interests. It had also an interest in seeking legislation to secure its powers over the greatly increased numbers of banks for which it was now responsible. The cooperation of the fringe with the new supervisory arrangements might well have been smooth in the dangerous times of the 1970s, but when markets looked up and new opportunities arose, who could say how late and inadequate those statistical returns might become, or how indifferent the Chairman to the advice of the Bank's supervisory staff. The problem for the Bank thus became how to obtain an Act which preserved its discretion and autonomy while entrenching its powers of supervision and control, and at the same time fulfilling the requirements of the EEC directive and political expectation that supervision would be a good deal more precise than in the past. A review of the main requirements of the Act summarized by Cooper[35] demonstrates how effectively the Bank achieved its objectives. The Act reflects the discrimination in supervisory procedures established in 1975 and in Sections 123 and 127 of the 1967 Act, in separating full or recognized banks from licensed deposit takers.

The minimum requirements for a *recognised bank* are that

1. the institution, or in the case of a new institution, its shareholder "enjoys and has for a reasonable period of time enjoyed a high reputation and standing in the financial community". (Schedule 2 para 1)
2. the institution provides, or will provide in the United Kingdom "either a wide range of banking services or a highly specialised banking service." A "wide range of banking services" means all of the following:
   (a) current or deposit account facilities in sterling or foreign currency for members of the public or for bodies corporate, or the acceptance of funds in sterling or foreign currency in the wholesale market;
   (b) finance in the form of overdraft or loan facilities in sterling or foreign currency for members of the public or for bodies corporate or the lending of funds in sterling or foreign currency in the wholesale money markets;
   (c) foreign exchange services for domestic and foreign customers;
   (d) finance through the medium of bills of exchange and promissory notes together with finance for foreign trade and documentation in connection with foreign trade; and
   (e) finance for members of the public or for bodies corporate on investment management services and facilities for arranging the purchase and sale of securities in sterling or foreign currency. (Para 2)

   The Bank of England is given discretion under the Act when determining whether to give an institution the status of a recognised bank to disregard the fact that it does not or will not provide one or two of the services specified in (c) to (e) above; that is the Bank may choose to recognise an institution provided it takes deposits, makes loans and provides just one of the three remaining services specified. The Act is curiously silent on the definition of a "highly-specialised banking service"; and at the time of writing the Discount Houses are believed to be the only institutions to be recognised as banks on this basis.

3. the business of the institution is carried on "with integrity and prudence and with those professional skills which are consistent with the range and scale of the institutions' activities." (Para 3)
4. "at least two individuals effectively direct the business of the institution." (Para 4)
5. the institution has net assets which "together with other financial resources available to the institution of such a nature and amount as are considered

appropriate by the Bank, are of an amount which is commensurate with the scale of the institution's operations." (Para 6)

The minimum requirements for *licensed institutions* are that

1. "every person who is a director, controller or manager of the institution is a fit and proper person to hold that position." (Para 7)
2. "at least two individuals effectively direct the business of the institution." (Para 8)
3. the institution has net assets of at least £250,000. (Para 9)
4. the institution conducts its business in a prudent manner and in particular
    (a) maintains "net assets of such an amount as, together with other financial resources available to it of such a nature and amount as are considered appropriate by the Bank, is sufficient to safeguard the interest of depositors having regard to the scale and nature of the liabilities of the institution and the sources and amounts of deposits accepted by it and the nature of the assets and the degree of risk attached to them";
    (b) maintains "adequate liquidity having regard to the relationship between its liquid assets and its liabilities and also to the times at which its liabilities fall due and its assets mature"; and
    (c) makes "adequate provision for bad and doubtful debts and obligations of a contingent nature." (Para 10)

The provisions for recognized banks plainly allow the Bank to recognize whom it pleases and to refuse whom it pleases. The language of paragraphs 3 and 6, the keys to integrity, solvency and prudence is vague to the point that decisions in practice must depend on the Bank's judgement. The same is the case in respect of the provisions of paragraph 4 which concerns the licensed deposit-takers. True, the Bank had to concede some ground in allowing for appeals against its decisions, but to a Treasury committee rather than to a court.

The Bank did not leave the vagueness of the Act as it stood, however, but capitalized on the advantage offered to initiate a debate with the other banks on liquidity in 1980, leading to a paper on *The liquidity of banks* in 1981 and a final paper on *The measurement of liquidity* in 1982. The intention of this debate was, first, to draw in all the banks to a discussion of the problems of contemporary banking and ensure that awareness of them was enhanced, and particularly to bring into open debate the greatly increased variety of risks undertaken with the emergence of new markets, new techniques, and new instruments. Such was the variety that it was no longer possible to conclude by specifying liquidity ratios, and the intention of the 1982 paper was to establish a common framework of understanding in terms of which liquidity and its problems in banking were to be assessed in the future. The Bank went out of its way during this period to emphasize its supportive and flexible role in relation to its flock, and its acceptance that each institution had its own history and circumstances and was to be treated individually and with repsect, whether a recognized bank or a licensed deposit-taker. Behind this, however, lay a clear recognition that the Act gave the Bank powers which it would use if necessary. As a senior official put it:[36]

I should make it clear . . . that notwithstanding this emphasis, and in my view very proper emphasis, which we put on flexibility and letting management manage, there will always be a point at which the supervisor must be the final arbiter. Hopefully this only arises infrequently and when there is no alternative. It is also important that the arbiter's ruling should be readily accepted.

The implication of this and the preceding comments is, of course, that since the Bank accepts informality in individual case-by-case discussion there are no precise criteria to fall back on, by way of argument against its judgement. The establishment of common frameworks for assessing risk and liquidity was in any case led by the Bank and does not provide unequivocal grounds for objection to a ruling, only the basis for debate before it. In the last analysis, the Bank's discretion remains paramount.

## Johnson Matthey

It remained for this new system to be tested. Would the new mix of increased supervisory staff and practices and a large measure of traditional informal control work? Until a bank again got into difficulties it was impossible to say. That situation arose in October 1984[37] when the banking arm of bullion dealers Johnson Matthey was rescued by the Bank of England.

Johnson Matthey (JM) consisted essentially of two parts, its merchant banking arm JMB and its various industrial interests which included high technology chemicals processing, paints, jewellery and precious metals, particularly platinum and gold. It originated in the eighteenth century with the discovery of a platinum refining process. As a gold dealer it was one of the five privileged members of the London Gold Ring whose twice-daily meetings fixed the price of gold. The Governor of the Bank of England, Robin Leigh-Pemberton, was later explicit that one reason for the rescue was the unacceptability of the failure of a member of the Gold Ring because of its effects on the gold market.

Potential losses were estimated at the take-over at between £100 million and £150 million, and with JMB capitalized at only £100 million this was clearly disastrous. The links with the parent group were sufficiently close to combine the loss of a very well-established bank with that of a key bullion dealer – JM lost its entire £102 million investment in JMB and had to put up £50 million as its contribution to the rescue package. This finally involved the Bank buying JMB for £1 and attempting to get 25 other banks, including the clearers, to put up a £250 million line of credit. The package was worked out at an all-night meeting of all those involved, amounting to several hundred people, and including the Governor of the Bank, reminiscent of the rescue of Cedar Holdings in 1973, but without any suggestion that other banks might potentially be in difficulties. A potential private rescue from the Bank of Nova Scotia failed to materialize in negotiations, because the bank got no firm assurances about the scale of losses. The largest shareholder in JM with 27.9% was Charter Consolidated, the mining and industrials group linked to Harry Oppenheimer's vast South African-based empire. It agreed to inject a further £25 million into JM to secure its future, bringing its holding up to 46% at a share price of 56 pence. JM had been trading at around 240 pence before the crash.

So far, it seemed, so good: the Bank had lost none of its expertise in mobilizing a rescue when it thought it essential. A number of important questions were immediately raised, however, and before long the Bank's ability to marshall support was clearly under pressure. It appeared quite soon that the failure was the result of two large, apparently related, loans to African borrowers; that JMB's loan book had increased by two thirds in 1983–4 from £183 million to £309 million, leaving a grand total of £450 million outstanding at the crash; and that the Bank had been concerned for some months and had held additional meetings with JMB. Furthermore, the accounts had been approved by Arthur Young McLelland Moores only in the summer without qualification. Finally, any loans in excess of 10% of the Bank's capital should have been automatically notified to the Bank's supervisory staff. Not only had something very clearly gone wrong with the supervisory process, but doubts also began to be expressed, both about the necessity for the rescue and its terms.

On the supervisory issue, anxieties were heightened by the implications of the affair in the context of the changing structure of City institutions (see Chapter 4 especially) in which banks were coming rapidly to form the central financial pillar supporting a range of specialist financial services such as stockbroking and commodity dealing: the knock-on effect of a bank failure in the future might be much nastier therefore. The response of the Governor of the Bank that 'I was perfectly satisfied that the systems of the Bank provided us with the information we needed. The difficulty was to come to a judgemental decision based on that information',[38] satisfied no-one, since it only pointed up the fact that it was reliant in effect upon the commercial judgement of the bank it was regulating as well as the auditor. Why did the Bank not intervene earlier?

As time went on the Bank's reluctant partners in the rescue became increasingly articulate in their objections to the proposed terms of their participation. The Bank's technique of negotiating separately with each group on the night of the crisis only contributed further to the dissatisfaction when the participants got together later to compare notes. The Bank committed itself to a £10 million contribution to the rescue, itself controversial since it constituted, in effect, public money. Dennis Skinner pointedly asked the Prime Minister why there appeared to be one set of rules for banks as regards rescues when they became uneconomic, and another for coal mines. David Owen mounted a more sustained campaign claiming that the commitment of public money was a serious political issue and not just one for the Bank. The Chancellor was put in an embarrassing position, having been understood to react to initial questions by saying there was no public money at stake, and took the almost unprecedented step of passing Dr Owen's letters on to the Governor for reply and deliberately distancing himself from its handling of the affair.

The Bank's response to complaints from members of the rescue party was terse: it had agreed to a private takeover of JMB by the Bank of Nova Scotia, but that fell through and there were no other private sector offers. Only in those circumstances did it acquire JMB for a song, and hence stood to gain as outright owner if the rescue turned out well. If the banking community wanted the benefits of ownership it should have bought JMB. This did not mollify the clearers, or the merchant banks, who still felt that, with the Bank contributing only 10% of the rescue package, other participants had some right to any dividend from their much greater contribution, the more so because in most cases they had had no prior links with JMB and were contributing only on the Bank's insistence that confidence was at stake. The emergent issue here was whether the Bank was justified in insisting on rescuing JMB itself rather than only safeguarding the interests of the bullion-dealing side. After all, JMB was a small bank which had, as events increasingly revealed, made some extremely foolish loans: did it not deserve to pay the price? And if the Bank insisted on rescuing a small bank like JMB when there was no suggestion of other failures in the offing, was it not putting itself in the position of underwriting all banks? Such a conclusion was scarcely conducive to prudent banking.

Nor was it only the banks which objected to the rescue. The other institutions, led by the Prudential, which raised its holding to 5%, were not happy with the terms for Charter's injecting £25 million into JM, since this would give it a dominant 46% interest, at 56 pence a share, when JM shares were trading at 135 pence after the crash, and normally an effective takeover like this would require a premium over the current trading price. Agreement was reached before long that Charter would underwrite the whole package and end up with at least a 33.3% holding, but that the other shareholders could subscribe for the remaining shares, so giving them a piece of the action on secure and favourable terms.

The banks, however, demanded tougher terms, and the Bank of England was finally forced to accept half of the indemnity package of £150 million. The stiffness of the resistance of the clearers in particular, who were finally in for only £35 million, rapidly became evident as the full extent of JMB losses was uncovered by Price Waterhouse's investigations. Up to half of the Bank's loan portfolio was doubtful, with losses running to £250 million. Reassurances from the Bank earlier that capital available in JMB of £170 million should have been more or less enough to cover losses, and that the indemnities by the rescuers might well not be called on, now looked hollow. The commitment of public funds to the potential extent of £75 million by the Bank without Treasury approval, inevitably increased political agitation over the affair.

A circular to JM shareholders six weeks after the crash identifying losses showed that extraordinary losses over the preceding 18 months came to £235 million and included losses in JM's businesses as well as at JMB. When these were digested by a stockbroker and redistributed in a circular, the judgement was scathing: JM was 'over-geared, under-capitalised and non-yielding' and the shares dropped to 80 pence and later to 68 pence. The capital injection from Charter Consolidated went ahead, so securing it a reasonable chance of successful future trading, and the affair began to subside as the Chancellor announced a committee to reconsider banking supervision at the end of 1984.

In the meantime delay was the order of the day, a delay which was expressive of the Government's embarrassment and in which doubts and rumours circulated as to the extent of the losses, the reasons for them and the state of relations between the Government, the Treasury and the Bank, and as to whether a proper account of what had happened would ever be published. In consequence the media were keyed up for the announcement of the outcome on 20 June 1985 and it was given extensive and detailed coverage. The Chancellor made a statement to the House of Commons, foregoing a trip to Tokyo for a meeting of the Group of Ten finance ministers to do so, and simultaneously the Bank published the results of its enquiry of the affair as part of its Report and Accounts.

The tale revealed by the Bank is one of almost incredible incompetence, and all but defies belief that there was not deliberate concealment of the problems from the Bank's supervisors as they worsened. These problems derived from JMB lending to two groups of companies run from Pakistan. Having initially entered into loans, each amounting to more than 10% of the Bank's capital, it then increased them by June 1983 to the equivalent of 26% and 17% of its capital, by December to 51% and 25% of its capital and by June 1984 to 76% and 39%. If the size of a debt rises beyond a certain level, the balance of power swings decisively in favour of the debtor, since his default can bring the creditor down. The Bank criticized JMB extensively for its failure to recognize the problems early enough, and for failing to develop adequate internal machinery to manage the rapid expansion of commercial lending that JMB, in common with other banks, indulged in during the early 1980s. More damaging, however, was the Bank's defence of its failure to identify problems in time. The critical report to the Bank was for the period to the end of March 1984, which was not delivered, despite repeated requests, until June, and which omitted one doubtful loan equivalent to 27% of the Bank's capital and understated by half another loan of similar size. On the matter of the need for a rescue the Bank was less persuasive, maintaining that because of JM's position in the London bullion market, the crash of JMB would have brought the parent company down with it, and that in turn would have led to a run on the other four members of the gold ring, possibly precipitating a wider crash, in view of the problems of banking in the USA at the time, where Continental Illinois was in its death throes.

When the Chancellor defended the need to nationalize the Bank, he was naturally treated with some scepticism by the Opposition. Why were the arguments more persuasive for JMB than the textile machinery company, Stone Platt, which was allowed to fail in 1982, or than 'uneconomic' coal mines? The answer was that banks are linked by the need to sustain confidence in their liquidity, but it was not a particularly persuasive answer in this instance, especially as it was accompanied by the Chancellor's admission tha he did not initially know of the £100 million the Bank injected into JMB on takeover, and his statement that he ought to have been told.

Thirty-four recommendations for improvements in banking regulation were made in the Bank's report and a Bill to implement them was promised in short order. Some, such as the further increase in the staffing of the Bank's supervisory provision, could be acted upon immediately. More important, however, was the decision to abolish the division between full banks and licensed deposit-takers established in the 1979 Banking Act. JMB was a full bank, and as such liable to the limited scrutiny which such a status bestowed. Events clearly showed that closer supervision was necessary. In addition, the professional and legal barriers to close consultation between auditors and banking supervisory staff were to be dismantled, so that auditors have an unequivocal duty to pass on the information about banks that threaten liquidity or suggest incompetence or fraud. The Bank was thus forced another significant step towards formalizing and regularizing supervision and gaining constant and unfettered access to banks' books to achieve it.

In the meantime the scapegoats were JMB's auditors Arthur Young who were felt by all parties to have failed to blow the whistle. Whether it was fair to attempt to recover losses from them by legal action, as was intended, when the Bank defended itself against its supervisory failing on the grounds that vital information was delayed and misrepresented by JMB is a moot point. Certainly those losses looked, by this time, to be fairly substantial, although the Government expressed hope of recovering them, at least in part, when JMB was sold back to the private sector in due course. Total losses at June 1985 were estimated at £248 million. Of this, £130 million was met by JMB's original capital, £50 million by cash injection from the parent company and the rest by calls on the indemnity of £150 million finally agreed on a pound for pound basis between the Bank and 23 banks and bullion dealers in the private sector only after much wrangling at the end of March 1985.

What was highlighted by the affair, however, was the potentially isolated position that the Bank could come to occupy because of its historic insistence on its independence and its refusal to depend on the formal bureaucratic methods of monitoring and supervision and preference for informal relationships. The task of the Bank is firmly to encourage prudent banking and to detect failures at an early stage. In this it had plainly failed. Its major difficulty, however, was that because of its persistence in clinging to informality, flexibility and discretion, it had no framework of regulation to fall back on, and say 'well, this one got through the net, but we followed the correct procedures; let us now examine why we failed and modify the procedures accordingly'. The Bank was only too evidently dependent upon its supervisees bringing their problems to it. If they did not, either from ignorance or arrogance, it could be put on the spot about a potential rescue at short notice, which in turn left it vulnerable to outside criticisms as to the wisdom of its decision. What was particularly disturbing was that this episode should occur (a) at a time just after the Bank had completed the revamping of supervision after the secondary banking crisis of the mid-1970s, the Banking Act 1979 and the careful establishment of parameters on risk and liquidity in 1980–82; (b) with a new Governor recently appointed with the clear support of a Prime Minister committed to a highly distinctive and contentious financial strategy; (c) the impending diversification of City institutions with the explicit intention of appealing to small investors and depositors in many cases, and centred upon banks to form new conglomerates; and (d) with the Bank of England emerging, as later chapters will discuss in more detail, as the centre of supervision for City institutions far beyond banking.

## Conclusions

The conclusion to be drawn for the purposes of this book is that the lessons of the influx of foreign banks and new markets in the 1960s and the crisis of the mid-1970s had not been impressed upon an institution which remained powerful enough to resist them, and indeed to capitalize upon its unique position of dominance to extend its formal powers in the City and become identified with the soundness of City institutions in general. Even though, as will become apparent in subsequent chapters, more thoroughgoing reform has taken place in other institutions, the continuing commitment of the Bank to a style based on informality, privacy, flexibility and trusting exchanges of information constitutes essential weakness in reform. It is indicative of the fact that even major scandals and significant market changes may fail fundamentally to influence an institution if it is powerful enough and sufficiently entrenched in its ways. It did not go unremarked in this connection, that the deputy Governor largely responsible for the Lifeboat in 1974–5, Christopher MacMahon, a man very widely respected for his outstanding abilities, was passed over for the Governorship in favour of Leigh-Pemberton, a man from an utterly orthodox establishment background, because he enjoyed the political confidence of the Prime Minister. Where tradition and politics prevail in the face of large economic changes, the danger remains that confidence, so carefully nurtured by reference to traditional values and practices, will be suddenly and dramatically shown to be woefully inadequate in the light of changed circumstances. Reforms at the Bank have been significant and will no doubt continue, but the fundamental challenge posed by past and impending developments has not been met. Enjoying the confidence of the Bank and its staff is one thing; being demonstrably sound and subject to publicly-identifiable constraints to keep within prudent limits is another.

## Notes

1.   For a full account of the work of the Discount Houses see G.A. Fletcher, *The Discount Houses in London,* Macmillan, 1976. A brief account in the context of a review of more recent developments in banking is contained in J. Cooper, *The Management and Regulation of Banks,* Macmillan, 1984, pp. 89—91.

2.   M. Moran, *The Politics of Banking,* Macmillan, 1984, p. 16.

3.   Moran, op. cit., citing M. Lisle-Williams, 'Continuities in the English Financial Elite 1850—1980', paper given to a conference on Capital, Ideology and Politics, Sheffield University, January 1981.

Some of Lisle-Williams' research was subsequently published in the *British Journal of Sociology,* 1984, Nos 2 and 3, and is one of the best sources on the continued cohesiveness and exclusiveness of British banking until quite recent years, particularly in the merchant banking sector. See: "Beyond the Market: the survival of family capitalism in the English merchant banks"; and "Merchant banking dynasties in the English class structure: ownership, solidarity and kinship in the City of London, 1850–1960". Apart from Moran, op. cit., and technical and professional works on banking, the literature on banking is largely informal. While Sampson (see below) is as usual readable and informative, P. Ferris, *Gentlemen of Fortune,* Weidenfeld, 1984 is also helpful in providing a more detailed and personalized account of some banking transactions, on the basis of interviews with major bankers, though it is a work of uneven quality. Finally, J. Scott and C. Griff's *Directors of Industry,* Blackwell, 1984, uses the technique of network analysis to demonstrate the increasing domination of banks and finance capital over the British economy and the sustained role of some families in this.

4.   See T. Heald, *Networks,* Hodder & Stoughton, 1983, Appendix VI.

5.   A. Sampson, *The Changing Anatomy of Britain,* Hodder & Stoughton, 1982, p. 280.

6.   A. Sampson, *The Moneylenders,* Hodder & Stoughton, 1981, p. 32.

7.   For a full account of the technical distinctions between Accepting Houses and other

merchant banks see Cooper, op. cit., pp. 58—64. The main implication of the Accepting Houses as a group is that they have access to the finest rates of interest, the greatest confidence of the Bank of England and constitute an elite among the merchant banks. According to Sampson (*Moneylenders*, op. cit., p. 206) one of the Accepting Houses, Anthony Gibbs, was ejected from the group and lost its privileged status in 1981, when it was taken over by the Hong Kong and Shanghai Bank, on the grounds of the foreignness of the new owner. A full indication of the distribution of types of British banks is provided below in the table taken from J. Coakley and L. Harris, *The City of Capital,* Basil Blackwell, 1983, p. 124.

**Banking Institutions in the United Kingdom Monetary Sector, February 1983**

|  | Number of banks | Liabilities or total assets (£ billion) |
|---|---|---|
| Clearing banks |  |  |
| London | 6 | 96.4 |
| Scottish | 3 | 11.3 |
| Northern Ireland | 4 | 2.2 |
| Total clearing banks | 13 | 109.9 |
|  |  |  |
| Other British banks |  |  |
| Accepting houses | 36 | 20.8 |
| Discount houses and brokers | 11 | 5.6 |
| Other British | 246 | 84.4 |
| Total other British banks | 293 | 110.8 |
|  |  |  |
| Overseas banks |  |  |
| American | 65 | 97.8 |
| Japanese | 25 | 108.5 |
| Consortium | 25 | 17.2 |
| Other overseas banks | 236 | 125.9 |
| Total overseas banks | 351 | 349.4 |
|  |  |  |
| Total in the UK | 657[a] | 570.1 |

[a]Some 54 banks are Channel Islands or Isle of Man subsidiaries of City-based banks.
Source: Bank of England Quarterly Bulletin; own calculations.

8.   Cited in Moran, op. cit., p. 15. The reference is to the Committee on the Working of the Monetary System (Chairman Lord Radcliffe), *Principal Memoranda of Evidence,* Vol. 1, London: HMSO, 1960, p. 52.
9.   Sampson, *The Moneylenders,* op. cit., p. 106.
10.   Ibid., p. 108.
11.   Committee to review the functioning of financial institutions (Chairman the Rt. Hon. Sir Harold Wilson), London, HMSO, 1979.
12.   See Moran, op. cit., p. 25.
13.   According to Sampson, *The Moneylenders,* op. cit., p. 109.
14.   Ibid., p. 111, quoting financial journalist P. Einzig, *Foreign Dollar Loans in Europe,* New

York, St. Martin's Press, 1965, p. vi.

15.   Coakley and Harris, op. cit., p. 66.

16.   Cf. Moran, op. cit., p. 109.

17.   Cited by Cooper, op. cit., p. 274.

18.   Ibid., p. 277.

19.   For a fuller account of the Ambrosiano affair and Calvi in particular, see R. Cornwell, *God's Banker*, A. Deutsch, 1984.

20.   Cited in Moran, op. cit., p. 21.

21.   *UDT* v. *Kirkwood*, Court of Appeal, 1966.

22.   The secondary banking crisis and the Bank of England's support operations – background paper to the Wilson Committee, Bank of England, 1978, p. 1.

23.   This and other information on the property boom of this period is taken from M.J. Clarke, *Fallen Idols*, London, Junction Books, 1981, Ch. 4.

24.   London Clearing Banks' Evidence to the Committee to Review the Functioning of Financial Institutions (The Wilson Committee), Longman, 1977, p. 242.

25.   H.L.I. Neuberger and B.M. Nichol, *The Recent Course of Land and Property Prices and the Factors Underlying it,* Department of the Environment Research Report No. 4, p. 61.

26.   See the major study by J. Goldthorpe *et al., Social Mobility and the Class Structure,* Oxford University Press, 1981, which is presented more briefly in A. Heath, *Social Mobility,* Fontana, 1981.

27.   Committee of Inquiry into the Crown Agents (Chairman E.S. Fay), *Report* HC48 (1977–8).

28.   Tribunal appointed to inquire into certain issues arising out of the operations of the Crown Agents as financiers on their own account in the years 1967–74 (Chairman Sir David Croom Johnson), *Report* HC364 (1981–2).

29.   Op. cit., Ch. 5.

30.   Ibid., p. 94.

31.   Ibid., pp. 91–2.

32.   A brief account is to be found in M.J. Clarke, *Fallen Idols,* op. cit., Ch. 4; the longest account is in M. Reid, *The Secondary Banking Crisis 1973–75,* Macmillan, 1982. Other accounts of interest may be found in Moran, op. cit., Ch. 5, and Cooper, op. cit., Ch. 1. Sampson, *The Moneylenders,* op. cit., Ch. 9 and J. Plender, *That's the Way the Money Goes,* A. Deutsch, 1982. The brief account which follows draws on these and other sources.

33.   Both the following quotations are cited in Moran, op. cit., p. 117.

34.   Cf. Cooper, op. cit., p.246.

35.   Ibid., pp. 251–3.

36.   Ibid., p. 260.

37.   In tracing the development of the Johnson Matthey affair I have relied on the financial press, particularly *The Times* and the *Financial Times* from October 1984 to February 1985.

38.   *The Times,* 4 October 1984.

39.   The announcement of Fraud Squad enquiries into JMB came in mid-July 1985 as this book went to press. This was a further embarrassment to the Chancellor who had, as recently as 20 June repeated his belief that no prima facie evidence of fraud existed.

# 3

## Lloyds: International competition and internal regulation

### Introduction

Lloyds is the clearest case, both in its completeness by the mid-1980s and in its thoroughgoing character, of the combined pressures of international competition and a series of scandals leading to the elimination of informal regulation and the substitution of a formal constitution, public accountability and an externally appointed chief executive with substantial powers. No significant new scandals had arisen by early 1985, as the new regime extended itself in establishing new regulations and standards and hence its effectiveness remained untested. A number of the major scandals of previous years rumbled on embarrassingly however, a constant reminder of the extent of the failures of the earlier regime, and of the deviation from the Lloyds motto 'uberrima fides' (utmost good faith). In order to understand the extent of the changes and the significance of the scandals it is necessary to know a little of the history and traditional practices of Lloyds and the basis of its very considerable financial success.

### The History of Lloyds

The origin of Lloyds[1] lies in the coffee house run by a man of that name in late seventeenth-century London, in which shipping insurers met to do business. Ship insurance, both of hulls and of cargo, was by that time well established as a business, because of the need for some means of offsetting the very large risks involved in shipping. Not only was the capital outlay great, even when shared among a group of merchants, as was usually the case, but the risks of the ship foundering and of its being seized by pirates or by the naval vessels of a hostile state were considerable. Ship insurers, like the owners, also needed to spread their risks, and met to discuss the latest intelligence and to evaluate the risks that they were underwriting. To do this they needed information, first about ships, their cargoes, their backers, their voyages and their crews, that is pre-voyage information, and secondly reliable information as to the fate of ships on their voyages. Two systems grew up side-by-side to cater for this. The Lloyds intelligence system and register of shipping developed over time, particularly under the aegis of an energetic secretary of Lloyds in the late nineteenth century, to provide a worldwide system for monitoring the movements of some 20 000 vessels today, as well as a register of ships of all types and sizes according to widely-accepted specifications and standards of safety and seaworthiness.

It is the insurance rather than the intelligence and registration side of Lloyds that is central to this book, however. This grew in the eighteenth and nineteenth centuries as a reflection of Britain's world naval and mercantile predominance, on the basis of individuals underwriting a percentage of each shipping risk and distributing the rest among their colleagues until the entire risk was covered. The vital decision was the evaluation of the risk by the leading underwriter and it is this which gives Lloyds insurance its distinctive character. Although many of the risks insured at Lloyds are sufficiently routine for there to be a rate for that type, the assessment of the premiums chargeable on a particular risk reflects its unique characteristics. The skill of the Lloyds underwriter lies in charging a rate that will give him a good chance of a return, and this in turn depends upon specialized knowledge of the relevant field. Thus in accepting or declining the offer of a risk the underwriter has to balance what is common to all risks of this kind against the insurance implications of the case in question. From this practice has sprung the Lloyds dictum that there is no such thing as a bad risk, only a bad rate: as long as the underwriter is aware of the current sources of potential losses and of the current and likely future rate of loss, he can calculate a realistic premium and make a profit. As a consequence, the Lloyds market makes its money by the specialized assessment of large, usually commercial risks, risks big enough to generate premiums large enough to finance the time of underwriters carefully analysing the risks. Two prominent recent examples of such insurance innovations in which Lloyds has been central are offshore oil drilling rigs, whose risks in the North Sea are much greater than those in the Gulf of Mexico, where offshore drilling developed earlier; and communications satellites, which involve technologies of a different order from those even of the aviation industry, the insurance cover of which Lloyds played a leading part in developing.

The main points about this kind of insurance business are first, that it is quite unlike the mass retail insurance of cars or household contents, where small premiums are collected from an army of assureds on the presumption that risks can be operationalized by using a few criteria. The essence of this mass market insurance is an effective retailing and administrative system to pull in as many assureds as possible, and to process premiums and claims as efficiently as possible. This, as we will see later, was the basis of the development of the insurance industry in

America. Clearly, it is dependent upon the level of legal requirements for insurance by citizens, and upon the propensity of them to insure other risks above and beyond that. By contrast, commercial insurance is often not only necessary legally, but also to ensure that a technically sophisticated business can remain solvent after a major loss. The implications of commercial insurance for its organization are substantial, and this is the second point. Underwriters need to gather information and discuss it in order to calculate risks and rates – hence Lloyds coffee house – and in a diversified market they need to specialize. Members gradually evolved their information gathering and risk calculation, as well as their specialist capacities, so that by the twentieth century Lloyds had acquired all its contemporary reputation, not only as a competitive market for commerical risks and one upon which risks of enormous size could be covered, but one in which you could find somewhere an underwriter willing to quote a premium on any insurable risk.

This characteristic in turn gives rise to the collegial character of Lloyds. Individual members clearly cannot and never have been able to underwrite 100% of most of the risks the are offered. They must therefore offer them to others, who, if they are to accept them, must have confidence in the ability, financial soundness and integrity of other underwriters. Because of the character of its business, Lloyds has never been free of scandals for long, and each significant one has prompted further attempts to control them and to protect the interests of members and of the insured. One of the earliest steps in this direction was the agreement of 79 members to raise the money to build new premises to conduct their business in and to elect a committee for their self-government: that was in 1771. Even so they remained beset with the problem of lack of rules of membership and the lack of capital of many participants. Where payment of claims depends upon underwriters being able to mobilize the cash at short notice in good times as well as bad, the long-term success of Lloyds was evidently dependent from quite early on upon the financial soundness of its members. There were always those of slender means willing to underwrite risks in the eager expectation of a profit, yet it was not only they who suffered from heavy claims, but others who worked with them on similar risks. Confidence that Lloyds will pay out on claims has been central to its success.

A Parliamentary enquiry into Lloyds in 1810 was followed by the Trust Deed of 1811 which gave corporate status and a degree of control over membership, and provided a basis for requiring proof of solvency – a so-called 'show of wealth' – at least on entry. Financial guarantees were demanded selectively of members from 1850 onwards, and deposits from 1882. The Lloyds Act of 1871 formalized the powers of elected committee over members, improved disciplinary powers, and made it an offence for a non-member to sign a Lloyds policy. Syndicates of underwriters were developed in the 1870s to spread individuals' risks among members as they are today, and to fight off the challenge of the rising insurance companies with their substantial financial backing. Despite difficulties, Lloyds continued to expand, introducing a series of innovations in the types of insurance cover offered and capitalizing on the expansion and consolidation of its ship monitoring system, and the system of local agents who could manage prompt payment of claims by the end of the nineteenth century.

In the twentieth century fraud and scandal were the driving force behind a series of protective reforms. Audit of members was introduced after a scandal in 1908. In 1923 the Harrison fraud, involving hire purchase, left large numbers of insureds exposed, and the membership as a whole rallied round to cover them to the extent of £367000, so raising a principle of collective responsibility. With the Wilcox fraud in 1954 this principle was carried further to cover not just the insureds, but members who could not have been expected to have been aware of the fraud. By this time the elements of the modern Lloyds were in place, including the existence of external or inactive, as well as internal or active, underwriters or 'names'.

## Lloyds Membership

The internal names are the original category of members of Lloyds, those who do the underwriting. The amount of premium they can underwrite is governed by the amount of wealth they can dispose of. Currently the maximum that an individual may show is £300000, and double that amount may be underwritten. A quarter of the wealth shown must be placed on deposit with Lloyds, and 60% must be in the form of cash or Government securities. The minimum for full membership is £100000, although it is possible to be a so-called 'mini-name' for £50000. External names likewise have to show their wealth and deposit part of it, though they take no active part in underwriting, but use their money instead as an investment. From the underwriter's point of view, the external names who allocate some or all of their wealth to his syndicate act as the Lloyds equivalent of the external capital investors in a company, since the underwriter's limits are dependent upon the total wealth available to his syndicate.

The insured are protected from loss by a series of funds and provisions. Normally, of course, the syndicate will expect to make a profit and cover claims from premium income, but it is recognized that there are bad years as well as good, and Lloyds accounts run over a three-year period to reflect this. When premiums come in, they are invested and hence earn income for the syndicate, which at a time of high interest rates may well be an important source of total earnings. At the year-end a proportion of income is assigned to a reserve fund to cover future claims. In addition, there is a contingency fund levied by Lloyds as a whole upon its members, to cover the insured in cases where syndicates cannot cover claims; and finally names, both internal and external, are personally liable beyond the full extent of the wealth shown, down to the last of their personal assets: there is no limited liability.

As perhaps is already evident, membership of Lloyds has decided advantages over many other investments. This is particularly true in respect of income tax relief, and of course the higher the rate, the greater the relief. Losses can and usually are minimized by insuring against all in excess of 10%, which, although costly, may be set against tax; which for many members means that 75% of the premium is paid by the Inland Revenue. Funds transferred to the reserve are also eligible for deferral of taxes. There are a number of other advantages which allow members to reduce particularly their liability for higher rate taxes, for capital gains and capital transfer taxes. Perhaps more importantly, the wealth needed to gain membership of Lloyds does not do day-to-day work like capital invested in a normal business. Even the deposit is invested at interest and the remaining 75% can be redeployed to earn income elsewhere, even while the notional amount is being used as the basis for underwriting, which should yield a profit. How much profit is of course the key question, and losses are by no means unheard of. The highest rate of return in recent years in underwriting profits is around 40% and the average 9%. But the losses of syndicate 895 which closed in 1982 owing £13.1 million and likely to call on £60 000 from the average name were given wide publicity, not only because of the losses, but because of the membership of such sporting names as Mark Cox and Virginia Wade in the syndicate.

Clearly membership of Lloyds does not come cheaply, even if the real value of the £100 000 entry ticket, or even its £50 000 version, has been eroded by inflation. It has remained a requirement that members have substantial means. Membership and changes in it have, however, been closely bound up with the post-war growth of Lloyds, and this in turn has formed an important part of the background which led to recent changes at Lloyds. The post-war record of Lloyds has been sufficiently good to attract increasing numbers of members. The rise has more or less reflected the earnings record. While premium income has climbed steadily from year to year from £126 million in 1948 to £3653 million in 1980, the profits record has been more patchy. The rate of profit was quite good in post-war years, fluctuating between 7.34% and 15.35% from 1948 to 1952. It then declined to 2.26% in 1956 and rose again to 8.73% in 1960. By this time membership had grown from 2422 in 1948 to 4808 in 1960. It rose again to 6062 in 1965, despite a disastrous fall from profits of 8.21% in 1964 to a loss of 3.5% in 1965. No doubt this is why membership stabilized at around 6000 for six years, despite a rapid recovery in profits to 9.61% in 1972. Since then, profitability has remained between 5 and 8%, and membership has expanded very rapidly: 7105 in 1973, 10730 in 1977, 18 552 in 1980 and 21 601 in 1983.

The majority of these names, around 17 000, are external. It is not possible, given the current state of research, to characterize them more precisely, but Hodgson does give a reasonable indication of the provenance of most and the reasons for their membership. Besides the internal names, the active underwriters, and the brokers, who are professionally involved in Lloyds work (see below), Hodgson identifies three other traditional categories of members: those who became members before the expansion of the 1970s – those with historic associations with Lloyds and the insurance and shipping businesses; members of well-established merchant-banking and industrial families; and members of wealthy landed families. The figures cited in the previous paragraph, taken from Lloyds own publication, conceal a membership crisis in the mid-1960s, however. In 1965 Hurricane Betsy wrought havoc in the USA and the Gulf of Mexico, which coincided with the cyclical downturn in the insurance market, and with other losses in oil drilling, which meant a year of disastrous losses for Lloyds, averaging £6000 per name in the whole market and £3000 again in 1966. Applications for membership came to a sudden halt, and there were 295 resignations in 1966–8.

The effect of this was to decrease the capacity of Lloyds to write policies and it was sufficiently concerned to set up a committee under Lord Cromer, a senior member of the Baring family and later Governor of the Bank of England, to recommend ways of reviving numbers. The outcome was a much more liberal attitude to membership of Lloyds, with overseas members being accepted from 1969 (although they were required to show £135 000), women in 1970, and then mini-names. By 1984 there were 4818 women among the 23 438 members and 3366 foreigners, of whom 1694 were Americans. The 6000 traditional members of the pre-1965 era had not deserted en masse, and Hodgson's review of the membership lists led him to conclude that many of the women and some of the other 'new' names were members of the same families. Although those with new and publicly-known wealth like sporting and pop stars are widely publicized as new members of Lloyds, he concluded that the social shift in membership, though significant, was not as substantial as the sheer rise in numbers might at first suggest. Lloyds appears to remain very much part of the system of old money, even if by now it by no means excludes the new.

*Syndication*

Names are organized into syndicates to do business. The number fluctuates with time as new syndicates are formed and old ones merge or are closed, but there are currently over 400. These vary in size from the very large with perhaps two or three thousand names to baby syndicates with half a dozen or less. Names are managed by underwriting agents, more often known as members' agents; syndicates are managed by underwriting agencies, more often known as managing agents. Both of these charge commission on premium income and underwriting profit, which they share between them. Their task is to bring members into syndicates where they will make money, and to supply syndicates with enough wealth to allow them to underwrite policies. There are 12 large managing agencies, each with six or more syndicates underwriting for a 1000 or more names. Some are independent and some are owned by the big brokers. The largest, owned by Alexander Howden, was responsible for almost 10% of Lloyds total premium income in 1982. At the sharp end there are perhaps 50 or 60 underwriters who are the leaders on the main risks. Normally there is little problem in obtaining enough names for a given syndicate, though some have been pushed to seek names, and Hodgson quotes a minimum commission fee of £1000 for scouts introducing new names to Lloyds for this purpose. More important is the independence of the members' agents to ensure that members get disinterested advice on the syndicates they join. In the past (i.e. prior to the Lloyds Act 1982), agencies have been owned by brokers, who have also controlled underwriting syndicates, so producing conflicts of interest; the elimination of these was one of the purposes of the Act (see below).

There are approximately 270 Lloyds brokers who are responsible for introducing business to the underwriters. Whereas ordinary insurance brokers (there are over 3000 in the UK) need only a £1000 capital and solvency margin, Lloyds brokers require £50 000 capital and a £1 million solvency margin. It is the brokers rather than the underwriters who are the dominant financial force at Lloyds, and they provide business for others, not just Lloyds underwriters. To give some estimate of relative size, world non-life assurance premiums (Lloyds does not deal in life assurance, almost the only field it does not touch) in 1980 were $261 billion, of which $131 billion went to the USA (i.e. 50%), 8.7% to Germany, 7% to Japan,

5.8% to France, 5.3% to Britain and 10.7% to Canada, Italy, Holland, Australia and Switzerland, and 12% to the rest of the world. Of this income roughly one third was personal and two thirds commercial insurance. British brokers (acting both within and outside the UK) in 1980 earned about £500 million in fees and commissions. Although 80% of British broking premium goes to non-Lloyds insurance companies, Lloyds is the largest single source of invisible trade income in the City, at about £630 million per annum.

Table 12 lists the 11 largest brokers in terms of 1982 broking commission and fee income only – most of the groups are now considerably diversified. Only one, Bain Dawes, is not listed on the stock exchange as a public company. By 1982 four were controlled by North American Brokers: Bowring by Marsh and McLennan, the world's largest brokers, Alexander Howden by Alexander and Alexander, Leslie and Godwin by Frank B. Hall, and Reed Stenhouse by the Canadian insurers of the same name.

*American Involvement*

Those American moves constituted a relatively recent direct challenge to Lloyds, and its handling of that challenge did not by any means reflect well upon it. In order to understand what happened, it is necessary to know something of the reasons for the overwhelming importance of the US in insurance.

Something has already been said of the difference in style of US insurance business from Lloyds. By the mid-1970s the big US brokers had more or less completed their continental networks of sales outlets, and began looking to the rest of the world for further expansions. Britain was an obvious target, partly because of

**Table 12.    The Largest Lloyds Brokers**

| | Broker | Commission and income (£ million) |
|---|---|---|
| 1. | Sedgwick Group | 176 |
| 2. | C. T. Bowring | 83 |
| 3. | Willis Faber & Dumas | 71 |
| 4. | Alexander Howden | 70 (estimated) |
| 5. | Reed Stenhouse | 59 |
| 6. | J. H. Minet | 56 |
| 7. | Stewart Wrightson | 55 |
| 8. | Hogg Robinson | 36 |
| 9. | Bain Dawes | 34 |
| 10. | C. E. Heath | 31 |
| 11. | Leslie & Godwin | 30 (estimated) |

Note: all these figures exclude affiliates.
Source: G. Hodgson, Lloyds of London: A reputation at risk, Allen Lane, 1984, p. 124.

the complementary nature of Lloyds insurance, based on commercial and specialist rather than mass personal retail insurance, partly because of the size of Lloyds brokers and their established worldwide networks, including the US, which is the source of 70% of Lloyds income, and partly because of the inaccessibility or unprofitability of much of the rest of the world. Many Third World countries do not generate much business and attempt in any case to protect their own insurance companies; Japan is effectively protectionist in this as in other respects, and Europe is dominated by the immense power of two re-insurance companies, Swiss re-insurance and Munich re-insurance, who absorb the excess risk of many European insurance companies and are able to dictate terms in doing so to the extent that what business is left over is not worth British companies fighting for.

The world picture which emerges is thus one in which Britain and the USA, both because of the size of their internal markets and because of the historical developments of their insurance industries, have a position in the world pecking order far greater than that which would be suggested by the proportion of world GNP for which they are responsible, but from the British point of view at leaast there is no escaping the predominance of the US market as the main area of opportunity. The situation which Lloyds was faced with at the end of the 1970s was effectively the terms upon which continued high levels of participation in that market would take place.

Negotiations began in 1973 between Alexander and Alexander and Alexander Howden, and between Marsh and McLennan and Bowring's. What would have become of them is hard to say, but both collapsed with the secondary banking crisis, which hit the stock market hard and sent the shares of the British companies tumbling. A low share price would make the terms for a reasonable take-over or merger difficult to agree and Marsh and MacLennan turned their attention, until the market recovered, to making acquisitions in France and Germany. Bowring already had strong links with Marsh: they were Marsh's chief brokers at Lloyds, and Marsh supplied around a third of Bowring's US business, and a higher proportion of its profit. Bowring's objective was to formalize the link without losing its independence to the American brokers, who were twice its size.

In 1978 matters came to a head. Marsh was offered control of Wigham Poland, a smaller Lloyds broker. It was subsequently bought by other American interests, and was too small for Marsh's purpose of establishing a major British base. At the same time Frank B. Hall was negotiating to buy Leslie and Godwin. Fear of a mass American take-over of Lloyds spread in London, and caused particular alarm at Bowring's; for if Marsh opted for someone else, it was to be expected that Bowring's profitable business with Marsh would suffer. The fear of the Lloyds committee was that if a huge US broker got control of a major Lloyds broker, it would be sufficiently powerful and independent to defy the committee's powers of control. It would not be part of the City of London, let alone the Lloyds club, it would be unfamiliar with City culture, and unwilling to respond to the informal pressures used to manage Lloyds' members and the market. For these reasons the committee imposed a ban on foreign interests owning more than 20% of a Lloyds broker.

Needless to say, this did not go down well in America, and press reaction was extremely hostile. While moves to create an insurance exchange in New York on the Lloyds model had started just before the 20% rule was imposed, it obviously gave considerable impetus to this development, and to similar initiatives in Florida and Illinois. The message was plain that if the British wanted to be insular, America would create rival institutions and compete that way. In fact, American interest in Lloyds-type exchanges had its origins in the damage done by Hurricane Betsy in the mid-1960s, where the lack of US expertise in the required range of commercial cover was exposed; none the less, the publicity effect of the 20% rule was disastrous.

The rule did not last long. By June the Lloyds committee approved a deal whereby Frank B. Hall bought all of Leslie and Godwin's capital, but would own only 25% (not 20%) of a subsidiary which would handle all Lloyds brokerage, the remaining 75% going to the Rothschild Investment Trust. This arrangement was rationalized as fulfilling the overriding criterion that day-to-day control of the broking should be in the hands of people experienced in the Lloyds market. It was a face-saving formula, and was followed by further retreats. In 1980 the Fisher report on the restructuring of Lloyds recommended the abolition of the 20% rule once its recommendations had been implemented, but the committee of Lloyds backed down entirely by the end of that year, accepting a simple undertaking by foreign interests to recognize the committee's authority.

Marsh's embrace of Bowring became ever tighter in the closing years of the 1970s as they supplied them with yet more business. Bowring continued to demur, and finally got cold feet and told Marsh that the merger was off. At this point Marsh struck with a take-over bid priced at 50% above Bowring's current stock market price. Despite an attempt at a legal delay through the New York courts, the outcome was inevitable. In the meantime Alexander and Alexander negotiated with Sedgwicks, the largest Lloyds brokers, but without success, for fundamentally the same reasons that fraught Bowring and Marsh: who was to be in control. Alexander and Alexander were about the same size as Sedgwicks, and the issue of dominance was irreconcilable. In 1981 the talks were called off, and Alexander and Alexander turned back fairly rapidly to Alexander Howden to complete negotiations begun in the 1970s. The pattern of transatlantic mergers and takeovers was completed in 1985 with Sedgwicks' £540 million merger with Fred S. James, creating the second largest broking group in the world after Marsh and MacLennan, with a market value of £1.4 billion and a total revenue of about £600 million.

Alexander and Alexanders' was a merger that was to prove explosive when things were discovered to be seriously wrong at Alexander Howden, but that is to get ahead of earlier important developments. By 1982 the direct American Challenge at Lloyds had been accommodated, and was not as bad as many people had feared four years earlier. Lloyds had proved timid and vacillating, and the latter quality in particular was critical to the other and more sustained aspect of the American challenge. Lloyds depended upon American business for its profitability. That could only be sustained if American confidence in the reliability and integrity of Lloyds was maintained abroad. It was one thing for Lloyds to be stuffy about US control of its members on the grounds of its interfering with traditional ways of doing business, but quite another if the elected committee of Lloyds proved ineffective in controlling fraud and scandal. From the mid-1970s a series of such scandals erupted one after the other, each seeming to involve those closer to the heart of the Lloyds establishment. It was this sequence that led to the constitutional reforms of the Lloyds Act. There is space here to deal with only the major incidents – there were minor ones as well. These were sufficiently large to grab the headlines, and the fairly detailed reporting that they stimulated exposed again and again the inadequacies of the existing regulatory procedures at Lloyds. There are five major scandals that will be considered in some detail: Savonita, Sasse, Fidentia, Minet and Howden. In addition, the role of broker Christopher Moran as a source of pressure for reform and an antagonist of the old regime, is worth nothing.

Before discussing these cases, it is worth emphasizing the reliance upon trust and informal control that particularly characterized Lloyds before the 1982 Act. Lloyds was controlled up until then by a committee elected by members, as it had been since the eighteenth century. The committee's powers proved under court challenges to be substantial, but they were relatively vague and informally exercised, with little emphasis upon public disclosure and day-to-day monitoring of probity and efficiency. Conflicts of interest, which were numerous, were not held to be important because of the professional standing of members and their commitment to fair dealing and 'utmost good faith'. Even after the Act, Lloyds publicity still talked of the

> subtle blend of competition and co-operation which combines with our unshakeable belief in the old insurance dictum of "utmost good faith" to give Lloyds its unique quality. Good faith undoubtedly characterises the relationship between broker and underwriter, who each place a considerable trust in one another. An underwriter's signature on a slip is absolutely binding — in honour if not in law — and the broker can be confident that a valid claim will be settled, even if it were presented before a policy had been issued. For his part, the underwriter knows that the broker will have disclosed all of the material facts accurately and fairly. Without such mutual trust Lloyds would not long survive.

## Savonita

The *Savonita* case began by being about fraud, but ended by being more of an issue of confidence in the committee of Lloyds and the adequacy and fairness of its response to a broker who suspected fraud and refused to press the claim upon the underwriters. The *Savonita* was a cargo vessel which sailed from Italy for the USA in November 1974, with a cargo of 2697 cars, mainly Fiats. They were insured for up to $1 million with S.I.A.T., an Italian company owned by Fiat, and the value above that was re-insured at Lloyds through brokers Pearson, Webb, Springbett (PWS), which owed some of its success to the marriage of Malcolm Pearson into the Agnelli family, owners of Fiat. The story is complicated by difficult personal relationships within and outside Lloyds, but its essence is the response and the correctness of the response of Pearson to suspected fraud.

Fire broke out shortly after the *Savonita* sailed, but it was put out, and the ship returned to port and discharged 301 damaged cars. The damage varied from complete burn-outs to limited damage by water and smoke, but all were declared a constructive total loss and sold for 15% of their new value to a Fiat dealer in Naples. He, by all accounts, set about cleaning and repairing them and then selling them for much nearer their new value. The question was, initially, was there a conspiracy to sell the cars off cheap? This was what faced Pearson when he went to investigate the re-insurance claim by S.I.A.T. for $711 643. Initial reports on the claim were not regarded as satisfactory, and Pearson commissioned further enquiries which revealed that the majority of the cars were being re-sold for around 80% of their new value, and in unusual transactions that looked as though they were intended to defraud the Italian state of tax.

Pearson approached the Chairman of Lloyds as early as 1975 expressing his misgivings in settling the claim, but did not elicit much anxiety on the latter's part. Pearson's report setting out grounds for believing that there had been a fraud was presented to Fiat, but they declined to accept it as adequate evidence and continued to press their claim. Pearson then took advice from leading Counsel John Matthew QC, who, after seeing the report, agreed that there was evidence of fraud and that Pearson was correct in refusing to press the claim because he suspected fraud. He added there was no legal obligation upon Pearson to tell anyone that there was evidence of fraud, though there was clearly a moral obligation to do so, and that Pearson had clearly done.

In 1976 S.I.A.T. tired of Pearson's refusal to press the claim and transferred their business to Willis Faber Dumas (WFD). This was in many ways an important move. Not only was there personal animosity between Pearson and one of the leading figures at WFD in the case, but WFD were large and very well-established marine brokers. As collectors of the claim, they constituted a force underwriters would find it very hard to resist, since behind them stood the promise of a great deal of good marine underwriting business. WFD were indeed effective in not taking the refusal of the leading underwriter on the slip as final, but pressing the rest of those who had signed the slip and so gradually building up a body of acceptances of the claim. In February 1978 WFD formally announced settlement of 96% of the claim, though the underwriters noted that a certain proportion of it was *ex gratia*.

Matters might well have rested there, to the discomfiture of Pearson, but probably not of Lloyds as a whole, but the following month Pearson was contacted by Jonathan Aitken MP, who, on hearing Pearson's account of events decided to use his parliamentary status to press matters further. He went to see the Chairman of Lloyds and was met by a number of members of the committee as well; he went on to talk to leading figures of WFD. His original intention was to use a parliamentary question to prod Lloyds into holding a proper enquiry into the affair, in order to clarify what brokers should do if they suspected fraud, and to try to clear Pearson in particular. He was sufficiently dismayed by the stone-walling of the Lloyds committee to initiate an adjournment debate on the regulation and reputation of Lloyds instead, in which he gave the House of Commons a version of the *Savonita* affair. His determination to proceed was strengthened by his reaction to pressure not to go public from the 70 or so members of Lloyds in the Commons, most of them Conservatives, and including the Conservative Chief Whip. Aitken was highly critical of the Chairman and the committee of Lloyds for their lack of action and called for improvements in regulation.

The debate and the media attention it attracted precipitated action by the Lloyds committee, and a full internal enquiry was set up holding 20 sessions over six months, hearing 50 witnesses and consulting 2000 documents. When the committee completed its enquiry, it strongly criticized Pearson. It took the view that a broker suspecting fraud must either Press the claim, or withdraw from acting for his client. Pearson had done neither, but had effectively deserted his client without explanation. The report gave scant attention to the legal opinion of John Matthew Q.C. which Pearson had obtained and, in default of clear existing guidelines at Lloyds, set much store. Matthew's view was that, if Pearson went to the Chairman of Lloyds, and to the Chairman of the Institute of London Underwriters on behalf of the companies involved, which he did, 'there can be no possible criticism of him' in not pressing the claim. He pointed out that if Pearson were to press a claim, believing or suspecting that it was fraudulent, he was in danger of making himself a party to fraud. The Lloyds enquiry committee pointed out by way of reply that underwriters might still wish to settle even if the claim were doubtful, the allusion here being no doubt to the difficulty of proving fraud in many cases, and the importance of preserving Lloyds reputation as a prompt settler of claims.

In contrast to its tough treatment of Pearson, the enquiry was gentle with WFD, accusing them at most of behaviour in collecting the claim that was on occasion robust beyond the normal standards of broking, and explicitly saying that WFD did not seek to use the weight of their account to settle the claim. When the report was issued the Lloyds committee attempted to refuse responsibility for its accuracy, and tried to get the media to indemnify the Board and the committee for any legal costs arising from publication. The manoeuvre reeked of the caution of a libel lawyer, and it appeared that Lloyds had acted on the advice of a leading practitioner. The public relations effect, however, was disastrous, with the Financial Times telling Lloyds roundly that it should have taken the risks of publication itself, and the sharpest condemnation coming from the Sunday Telegraph: 'The way in which Lloyds of London has mis-handled the Savonita affair has dealt its reputation the worst blow in living memory. Not to put too fine a point on it, Lloyds has succeeded in making itself appear both incompetent and somewhat cowardly.' Whatever the justice of that comment none of Lloyds reaction to Pearson's handling of his anxieties about the Savonita claim smacked of good faith, at the very least in the sense that the authorities at Lloyds were not seen to act promptly, fairly and effectively to deal with them. For an organization that prided itself on the decency, efficiency and realism of its informal methods of self-regulation, this was a severe blow.

## Sasse

The problems of underwriters F.H. Sasse and others first became public in 1977 when syndicate 762 was unsuspended, apparently owing something like $10 million, and with a Brazilian re-insurance company refusing to pay on fire claims from America totalling $2 million. The amount of the losses was contested, but by 1980 it looked like £21.5 million or £195 000 for each of the syndicate's 110 members. Losses to this extent are unusual but not unheard of; nor, as was clear

from the *Savonita* case, are claims held to be fraudulent, which was the implication
of the Brazilian re-insurers refusal to pay. What made Sasse important was that 63 of
the external names in the syndicate decided that Lloyds rules had been broken, and
that the losses were a consequence of this. Hence they refused to pay up and took
legal action against those they held responsible. As Earl Fortescue, a member of the
syndicate, put it in the House of Lords:

> I do not in any way deny that I agreed that my liability should be unlimited against
> normal underwriting risks. However, I never agreed, nor do I now feel like agreeing,
> that I should accept unlimited liability if the underwriter or his agents act fraudulently
> or outside Lloyds rules, or if, in particular, the loss is due to negligence or breach of
> duty on the part of the Lloyds committee.[2]

This division of views, backed by legal action in refusing to pay claims was
unprecedented in Lloyds history, and went to the heart of the principle of utmost
good faith: internally it was being questioned, and externally it was not being lived
up to as far as clients were concerned. Lloyds made strenuous efforts to get matters
settled quietly, but this phase was plainly at an end once the public legal action was
started. As Lord Fortescue's comment suggests, the heart of the matter was whether
the policing of Lloyds was working properly, first in respect of controls on the
introduction of business through agents in North America, which was the source of
the losses, and secondly in respect of the action or lack of it taken by the committee
of Lloyds once they knew that things were seriously wrong with the North
American business. That action was structured predominantly around an attempt to
preserve the public good name of Lloyds as a whole and, in view of the names who
sued, at the personal expense of the members of syndicate 762.

In order to understand how the problems arose, it is necessary to go back to 1975.
Two English insurance agents were introduced to each other in Miami and came to
an important business agreement. Dennis Harrison of Den-Har underwriters of
Miami had access to Sasse via broker John Newman of Brentnall Beard; Ted Smith,
of Inter-Global Re-Insurance Facilities of Houston, had re-insurance arrangements
with Instituto de Reaseaguros do Brasil, with Geoffrey Austen of Austen and Balcon
acting as brokers. Smith wanted to sell direct insurance, while Harrison was
attracted by the availability of re-insurance. The arrangements they reached enabled
them to exchange commissions on insurance and re-insurance, and before long
Smith had a group of 'known sound agencies' operating a business nationwide in the
USA.

There were soon warnings that all was not quite as it should be. Lloyds' American
lawyers Leboeuf Lamb telexed Newman in May 1976: 'Disturbing rumours were
that ???? Den-Har business is produce by John B. Goepfert. Quality of such business
was traditionally been a problem for underwriters.' Shortly afterwards they wrote
to Newman about Smith, warning him off and advising him to confer
with Lloyds' non-Marine Association about him. They also pointed out
Den-Har had not been 'tribunalized', that is officially approved by Lloyds
in London as a reputable agency to get business for Lloyds underwriters. Leboeuf
Lamb noted that retroactive approval of Den-Har's underwriting was requested,
and concluded 'as a matter of sound business practice and informed judgement we
do not favour retroactive approval of any insurance programme'. Since Brentnall

Beard had taken a 20% stake in Den-Har this was not good news. Sasse cancelled Den-Har's underwriting authority in July 1976, but by then a large amount of contracts had been issued, resulting in claims, including a number of fire damage claims in the South Bronx which were investigated by the police. Like Savonita, however, the issue was not just fraudulent fire claims. Here the issue was that Den-Har had managed to do a great deal of business for which it collected commissions, while taking none of the risk, and leaving Sasse with claims.

Later at the trial of Harrison and Goepfert, it emerged that not only did they greatly exceed the limits agreed on underwriting business with Newman, and hence with the Sasse syndicate, but much of their business was low-quality, high risk property insurance, the obtaining of which in quantity was made easier by the use of Lloyds authority and reputation. In addition, Geopfert, Harrison and their associates engaged in straight fraud by billing policy holders for property inspections never carried out, skimming off some of the premium due to Sasse by fraudulent allegations of co-insurance and diverting premium from its proper route through Den-Har to various companies owned by the fraudsters. Altogether, Goepfert was estimated to have diverted $1.7 million and Harrison $900000. This of course takes no account of claims on policies, which were disastrously heavy, if not in some cases fraudulent. Although the policies were re-insured as to 75% through IRB in Brazil, the re-insurers naturally resisted paying claims until a full enquiry was undertaken, once the murky nature of the situation became known. This meant that, where Sasse's premium income had been legitimately calculated on the 25% of the risks that they assumed, they became landed with four times that amount of risk as primary underwriters.

The complaints of external members of syndicate 762 went deeper than attacking the competence of principals such as Newman. How was it, for example, that two Lloyds deputy Chairmen, when told by Newman of the non-tribunalization of Den-Har, allegedly told him to get the policies through the policy-signing office as soon as possible? If true, this implies that Sasse members were to be made to carry the can for the cover-up of improper business in order to preserve the reputation of Lloyds in the public eye. Even if this was not true, how was it that Newman managed to get the policies accepted at Lloyds without tribunalization? And, as if this was not enough, evidence emerged of another relationship between Sasse and a Canadian agency, Deslaurier Wilkins. This was in danger of being axed at the end of 1976 by Sasse, but it was given an extension to 1977 on Newman's information that the 1976 accounts would produce $500000 profit. One outcome of this was that policies under this arrangement were backdated at the policy-signing office at Lloyds as late as September 1978. How was this managed? Where the American fire claims incurred losses to Sasse of £6.8 million, those via Canada amounted to £3.2 million.

When the Sasse rebels lodged their legal claims, they claimed against both Newman and Brentnall Beard for negligence, and against Lloyds for allowing non-tribunalized agents to sell Lloyds policies, and cited the Leboeuf Lamb warnings, the fact that Harrison was not tribunalized, and the allegation that Lloyds' deputy Chairmen condoned this. They also claimed that US agents broke Lloyds rules by writing far too much business, three and a half times the premium limits allowable to 762 on the basis of its members' investment. More importantly, they claimed that the granting of 'binders', that is allowing overseas agents in America and Canada to issue policies binding on Lloyds underwriting syndicates, was contrary to the Lloyds Act 1871, Rule 3 of which states that all business must be transacted on the floor of Lloyds. If this claim were to be upheld, it would not only go some way to forcing Lloyds, rather than the syndicate's names, to pay up, but effectively put an end to most American business at Lloyds, which accounts for about 40% of premium income.

This legal action was followed shortly afterwards by a similar suit by Sasse Turnbull and Co. against Lloyds and Brentnall Beard. The latter was accused of not acting with due skill and care and not disclosing material facts, particularly that much of the business coming from Den Har was known to be 'extremely dubious', and had already cost the American Argonaut insurance company a great deal in losses, and that Brentnall Beard had positively mis-informed them at times over the Canadian binder, Deslaurier Wilkins. Lloyds' deputy Chairmen were accused of condoning and abetting the acceptance by Lloyds of business from a non-tribunalized source, failing to instigate proper enquiries in America on the doubtful aspects of the business, and failing to advise syndicate 762 that they might do best in repudiating these unapproved US policies and the claims arising.

When the cases began to be heard in September 1979, the Judge, Sir John Donaldson, was sufficiently concerned to make considerable efforts to get the parties to go to arbitration, rather than fight it out in the courts, where the cases would be lengthy, the costs would run into millions of pounds, and the damage to Lloyds' reputation, if Lloyds committee members were publicly cross-examined about the detail of how they managed the regulation of Lloyds, would be inestimable. Arbitration was no doubt a sensible alternative, but it was not in the interests of the names, since it would be private and the proceedings informal. The names' strength lay in their capacity to threaten the reputation of Lloyds at trial, and to expose publicly the failings of the committee. But the attitude of the committee throughout was not in doubt: the public reputation of Lloyds as a whole was to be preserved, even if at the price of penalizing the Sasse names, who were receiving bills for hundreds of thousands of pounds in the late 1970s, as more and more of the horrors were revealed. The substance of their claims against the committee was thus twofold: the committee had not acted soon enough, and when it did act it persistently attempted to contain responsibility within Sasse. Hodgson describes the delay in the vital early months as follows:[2]

> Goepfert and his friends did not begin to stuff their "special book of business" into the Sasse syndicate's portfolio through the Den-Har binder until March 1976. The main mass of dubious business did not begin to flow before May. By the end of May broker John Newman said later that he knew that something strange and dangerous was going on, and the board of his brokerage firm Brentnall Beard knew. Tim Sasse the underwriter knew. Leboeuf Leiby and MacRae, Lloyds' general counsel in New York, knew. And, informally at least, the committee knew. It was not until 31st July 1976 that Sasse gave written notice of termination of the Den-Har contract, and even then, he said he would accept business already quoted up to the end of August. And it was not until 29th December 1977 – 20 months to the day after the extent of the mess was known in London – that the Sasse syndicate was suspended from doing business at Lloyds.

Of course, when the committee did act matters were far from clear, but the nature of the action only deferred trouble. Hodgson again:[4]

> The Lloyds advisory service reported to the committee later that it was not until July 1977 that any "meaningful" figures were available. Even then it is hard to see that they could have been very realistic, since no attempt had been made at that point to unravel the Goepfert conspiracy. When Leslie Dew (deputy Chairman of Lloyds) contemplated the situation in late 1976, no documentation and none of the premium received had been sent to the Lloyds policy-signing office in the usual way. Indeed the Den-Har binder had not even been signed. It was obvious that a great mass of poor quality risks having been found, a great tide of claims was about to follow. "We had to batten down the hatches and wait for the storm to break" one of Lloyds lawyers reminisced years later. So in January 1977, on Dew's instructions, the LPSO signed and processed the Den-Har binder with a 1976 date (meaning it would count against the 1976 account). The brokers at Brentnall Beard were instructed to hand over the documentation and such premium as had arrived. It came to just over $1 million gross of commission, $711,000 net. Finally, Dew ordered Sasse to treat the contracts made under the Den-Har binder (cancelled by Sasse in July) as binding on the names.
>
> Dew's anxiety to regularize the position was entirely understandable. So was his concern to make it absolutely impossible for anyone to so much as whisper that Lloyds were welshing on policies that carried Lloyds name. Yet, with hindsight, one can see that the consequence of the dispositions he made was disastrous. In effect, Lloyds had countermanded Sasse's instructions to cancel contracts that were in breach of Lloyds own rules in several respects . . .
>
> By ordering the LPSO to sign the Den-Har business in spite of all the flagrant irregularities, Dew was storing up trouble for the future. Responsibility indeed lies with the committee whose decisions he was presumably carrying out. But in effect he was transferring responsibility for losses due to Lloyds failure to enforce its own rules to the Sasse names.

The dangers of deferring the issue and leaving the pressures on the names in syndicate 762 became evident in 1979 when the names were resisting paying out and their refusal began to backfire on the committee.

> The committee of Lloyds was now in a tight spot and was putting heavy pressure on Merrett (who had taken over the management of the syndicate from Sasse at Lloyds request) to get the Sasse names past the audit. Much more than the future of the Sasse names was at stake as the committee saw it. Every year each underwriting member of Lloyds has to pass the audit or be put in default. When all its members have passed the audit each syndicate then completes a "certificate of underwriting account". And only when each syndicate has passed the audit does Lloyds as a whole receive a certificate from the Department of Trade. This is one of the major requirements the Government makes of Lloyds under statute. To fail to comply was unthinkable. Even any serious delay would be embarrassing.
>
> Late in July the committee was informed that it would not be possible for the auditors to give the Sasse syndicate unqualified audit certificates. Any qualification might mean that Lloyds as a whole would not get a certificate from the Department of Trade. And that would register in every one of the statements that Lloyds must lodge with the regulatory authorities all over the world, not least in the United States. Leboeuf Lamb advised that any qualification in the Lloyds audit because of difficulties with the completion of the Sasse syndicate accounts would be a public relations

disaster of the first magnitude.

The only way out was to arrange a re-insurance in the Lloyds market, limiting the Sasse 1976 losses to a figure estimated by Merrett Dixey. That at least would reassure anyone with any doubts that the losses could not go beyond an admittedly catastrophically high figure. The re-insurance was successfully placed in the market. Even so the submission of the audit certificate to the Department of Trade was slightly delayed.[5]

These same pressures on the committee strengthened over time as the names held firm and pressed litigation. What seemed at the outset a powerful position for the committee became by 1980 a very weak one. Litigation began in February. In March the New York Insurance Exchange, set up to imitate Lloyds, started business and in June the Fisher report recommending the wholesale restructuring of Lloyds and the radical tightening up of regulation was published. By July Lloyds agreed a settlement. In return for the names dropping their actions and bearing £6.25 million of the 1976 loss, an average of £80 000 each, Lloyds would make up the remaining £9 million for 1976 and pay the whole of the 1977 losses of nearly £7 million. Probably the most pertinent comment on the affair came from one of the names' principal lawyers, Leon Boshoff, in a letter to Lloyds early in the dispute. He suggested that it was common ground that 'the Sasse debacle has finally proved that the modern complexities of Lloyds operation cannot adequately be controlled by the outdated regulations and controlling mechanisms now in existence. Lloyds is organised as a club, but operates world-wide in a complex industry[6]

Within two years the Lloyds Act achieving radical reforms would be in place, going much further even than Fisher proposed, and with the active support of some of the external names who had been brought together in the struggle over Sasse. Several further scandals broke before then however, and were important in ensuring its passage and effective implementation.

## Fidentia

Relatively speaking this is a limited affair but it is significant for two reasons. First, it involves two Lloyds underwriters, Raymond Brooks and Terence Dooley exploiting offshore re-insurance, in this case through the Bermuda-based Fidentia Marine Insurance Company, both to make extra money for themselves by special arrangements which eliminated risk, and by engaging in speculative investments with premium income, some of which led to losses. Re-insurance was a problem that came to be seen to pose quite widespread possibilities for abuse at Lloyds. Secondly, the case provides an example in its latter stages of the disciplinary machinery created after the constitutional reform of 1982, and indeed it was the first real test of the new machinery.

Indications that all was not well first came to light in late 1982 when members of Marine syndicate 89 were reported to be considering legal action to force Brooks and Dooley to reveal details of re-insurance contracts over the preceding decade and more. Fidentia was set up in 1970 under the control of Brooks and Dooley. It grew rapidly in size by capitalizing profits from an initial £125 000 to £1.25 million in

1977. Assets reached a peak of £9.4 million in 1976 but fell the following year, when £319000 of provisions were made against unquoted investments and loans to unquoted and un-named companies, and £921000 was paid out in fees to unnamed brokers. In 1974 the company bought residential property in Cyprus, not usual for a re-insurance company, and then Fidentia was sold in 1978 to an unnamed buyer for $896000.

An initial report by Lloyds, after an examination of Fidentia's transactions, was completed in a few weeks and passed on to the Department of Trade. This was reported as showing how brokers Alexander Howden and others moved $20 million from Brooks and Dooley syndicates to Bermuda re-insurance companies and then, once beyond UK control, premiums were passed to Fidentia. It was then claimed that this money was accepted as premiums for re-insurance, so arranged that Fidentia's liabilities rarely exceeded the premiums paid. The commission by Fidentia for the business was more than recovered, it was said, by the risk-free use of the premium income over long periods for investment. Brooks and Dooley were not suspended at this stage, and even in March 1983, when suspension was considered, it did not take place because the pair gave undertakings to disclose all, and that what would be revealed would be only transactions arising in the normal course of business.

At the beginning of October, they were suspended for six months in the light of further information available. What this information was became clear the following month. It was more detailed than earlier reports but only amplified them. The Lloyds enquiry, by a lawyer and an accountant, considered only Brooks and Dooley's involvement and promised a second report later on the conduct of others involved, but the general lines upon which that was likely to run were plain enough. The investigator's main charge was that Brooks and Dooley 'abused their position by procuring quota share transactions (a form of re-insurance) on terms calculated to benefit them at the expense of their seven syndicates'.[7] The use of risk-free re-insurance contracts and long-term free use of premiums for investment, some of which went wrong, was confirmed, as was the fact that syndicate members were not informed. The sale of Fidentia in 1978 was explained as a transfer of it by a complex route to Trusts with Brooks and Dooley as beneficiaries.

The report also identified Lloyds brokers Bellew, Parry Raven (BPR) as central figures. Using Bermuda as a base for Fidentia was the outcome of an introduction to Bermudan lawyers by BPR, and a member of the BPR syndicate helped set up Fidentia, later refusing to give evidence to the Lloyds enquiry. BPR also had a 40% stake in Fidentia's offshore management company, and much of Fidentia's business went through BPR, who earned commission on it. The re-insurance premiums then went on to other companies, two of them owned by Alexander Howden. The enquiry specified that this was a deliberate concealment of Fidentia's beneficiary position. Another intermediary was Midland Re-insurance of Bermuda, set up by BPR, and then transferred to Trusts whose beneficiaries were their children. In several contracts Midland retained some of the money passing through it, which should have involved some accpetance of the risk; in fact deals were risk-free for Midland. Investigators concluded that 'the continued use of Midland may have had much more to do with providing some business to BPR and their insurance company'.

Proceedings against Brooks and Dooley continued in 1984 as a result of a High Court ruling in March that they were subject to the disciplinary powers of Lloyds under the 1982 Act. The pair had contended that they were immune because the events complained of took place before the legislation took effect. The outcome of the disciplinary proceedings was not reached until the end of the year. In the meantime they were no doubt relieved to be informed that the Director of Public Prosecutions (DPP) had decided not to bring a fraud prosecution against them, a decision which fuelled anxiety and anger in some quarters over the apparent ineffectiveness of fraud prosecutions in relation to insurance offences – decisions on the Minet and Howden cases were also eagerly awaited (see below and Chapter 6 for a fuller discussion of the issue). No doubt they were further heartened at the moves to settle their liabilities to names for the £6.2 million by which they had profited through offshore re-insurance against names' interests and without their knowledge.

In the summer, however, one of the names, Christopher Moran, issued a writ against Brooks and Dooley alleging deceit, breach of contract and breach of fiduciary duty over Fidentia, and claiming £10 million in damages. Further, he confronted the names with the choice of supporting his action without contributing to its costs and without being bound by any agreement reached, or being cited as defendants. It effectively put a stop to attempts to reach a settlement informally, which would have involved much less than £6.2 million, let alone £10 million. In early 1985, 1000 Brooks and Dooley names were approached for support for litigation to recover damages over Fidentia, and it seemed likely that this would go ahead. The precedent set in the Sasse case, of external names standing up for their financial interests in a robust fashion, seemed likely to have engendered a long-term shift in attitude away from passivity, and Moran's move was no doubt a catalyst in this.

The outcome of the disciplinary proceedings was published at the end of 1984. Brooks was expelled and had costs of £40 000 awarded against him for his gross conflict of interest over Fidentia, and for giving the 1982 Lloyds enquiry deliberately misleading answers about it. Dooley was suspended for 21 months and had costs of £12 000 awarded against him for a similar conflict of interest, and breach of duties to members of his syndicate. Lloyd's new system was thereby shown to have teeth, and that they were prepared to use them. Consideration was being given by Lloyd's Council to introducing bye-laws to prevent active underwriters owning re-insurance companies, and so creating conflicts of interest. In addition, legal claims were pursued against Brookes and Dooley by names of their syndicates and some money was raised for names by the winding up of the syndicates, and the companies associated with them. Overall, the way in which the Fidentia case was handled seems to augur well for the future of Lloyds, but Brooks and Dooley were not big fish by Lloyds' standards. The resolution of other scandals, to which I will come shortly, was to prove far less easy. Before doing so, however, it is worth recounting more extensively the role of Christopher Moran during this period of scandal and change at Lloyds.

# Moran

Christopher Moran played a role in relation to Lloyds similar to that of Jim Raper in the Stock Exchange (see Chapter 4). He has himself said that he does not expect people to like him, but simply to respect him as a hard but fair player in a tough professional market. He certainly alienated a good many senior people at Lloyds and ended up being expelled, but, unlike Raper, he enjoyed on the whole a favourable press, and successfully retained an image of the tough and enterprising outsider, hated by the establishment at the Lloyds club, and ultimately excluded by them. His wealth was not greatly affected by his expulsion, and in 1983 his private holding company had assets of £20 million and pre-tax profits, excluding his property company, exceeded £1 million for 15 months of 1982–3: a considerable achievement for a man of 35.

Moran's difficulties of one kind and another go back at least as far as 1979, when a report in the *Daily Telegraph*[8] named him and his companies as under investigation by the fraud squad for possible exchange control violations involving transactions with companies based in Holland and Guernsey. The sums involved were said to exceed £500 000 and the main business was re-insurance. Both foreign companies were controlled through nominees. He was subsequently charged with conspiracy to defraud certain members of Lloyds syndicates and bail was set at £100 000 in 1980. When the case finally came to trial in December 1981, Moran and his co-defendent Walker were acquitted on the Judge's direction in what he said was a complex case. The arguments of expert witnesses from Lloyds were demolished by defending counsel and the witnesses failed to agree among themselves on the commercial viability of insurance contracts arranged by the defendants (Walker was awarded costs by the Judge but Moran was refused them).

This capacity to be seen to be within the rules, while openly saying that he was in business to make money and would play hard to do so, was central to Moran's role as gadfly to Lloyds establishment during a period when it was becoming increasingly sensitive about dubious practices, especially those of newcomers. The most embarrassing feature of it was that Lloyds ended up looking arbitrary and oppressive in expelling Moran for discreditable conduct although accepting that he had broken neither the law or Lloyds written rules. Animosity between Moran and senior Lloyds figures pre-dated the argument surrounding his expulsion. He successfully sued the brother of Lloyds Chairman, Peter Green, in the mid-1970s; and his practice of parking his rolls Royce in senior underwriter Paul Dixey's parking space near Lloyds did not endear Moran to those whom he referred to contemptuously as 'the Brownie Club'.

Parallel with police interest in Moran which led to his trial, Lloyds also began internal enquiries in 1979. As a result an *ad hoc* committee was set up by the Chairman of Lloyds consisting of Paul Dixey and three others, which had extensive hearings with Moran and the auditors. The Deputy Chairman, on considering the committee's report, referred matters upwards for disciplinary action, saying:[9]

> I came to the conclusion that the prima facie evidence available to us indicated that
> Mr Moran had been guilty of the gravest misconduct involving the misappropriation by
> the broking company of funds belonging to members of syndicate 566, grave breaches

by the broking company and the underwriting agent of their respective duties to others within the Lloyds community, and behaviour generally which was wholly inconsistent with his continued presence as a member of that community.[9]

Somewhat vague and forbidding language. Steps were taken to initiate arbitration, and Moran was asked to nominate his arbitrator to sit with that appointed by Lloyds. This he failed to do. When warned by Lloyds that their arbitrator would act alone, he sought an injunction to prevent the arbitration on the grounds that the proceedings so far had not been fair, that the report was not supported by evidence, and that various people, including Paul Dixey, were actuated by bias against Moran. In short, Moran claimed that the arbitration would not give him a fair hearing. He lost at the first instance and was rebuffed again by Lord Denning and his colleagues on appeal. The *Times*[10] reported Denning as follows:

> The modern phenomenon was for the man who feared the worst to accuse those who held the preliminary enquiry of misconduct, or unfairness, or bias, or want of natural justice, in order to stop the impending charges against him. It was easy to make such an accusation, which had to be answered. It must go to trial, which meant a dealy of months and months. So the man got that which he wanted most – time. Time to make his dispositions, time to put his money in a safe place, time to head off the day when he had to meet the charge. To his Lordship's mind the law should not permit any such tactics. They should be stopped at the outset.

Denning at least replied to Moran's accusations of Lloyds bad faith by saying that Moran sought the injunction in bad faith. There was little doubt of his support for the Lloyds establishment. He began his judgment by saying that:

> Lloyds was the greatest insurance market in the world. Its existence depended upon its good name, on its reputation for integrity, for probity, for meeting all of its obligations – moral as well as legal – without demur and without delay. Their reputation should be and was jealously guarded by the committee.

More zest was given to the animosity between Moran and Lloyds by his temerity in suing brokers Willis Faber in 1980. Moran had discovered that Lloyds' policy signing office had debited his account without his knowledge and credited Willis Faber's underwriting interest but that the debit notes were forged. The amount involved exceeded £125 000. When Moran complained, the case was heard by Peter Green, who had reason to detest Moran, and Charles Gibbs, a director of Willis Faber. A potential conflict of interest was denied, and the decision was that the policy should be 'cancelled flat' involving no further action. Moran persisted with his suit and Willis Faber settled in full in June 1982 just before the case came to Court.

The arbitration case against Moran proceeded against this background, leading to the unprecedented freezing of the Moran Group in November 1980, with Lloyds insisting on appointing three members of the Board, which Moran resisted. Moran himself was on bail pending trial, and had been suspended from executive duties in August. Clearly, Lloyds was determined to assert itself and was reluctantly accepted by the Moran Group, although it criticized the move as 'unreasonable and in excess of Lloyds powers'.

The background to the case in the words of one commentator,[11] was the:

practice, now apparently stamped out, of gaming on re-insurance policies. In his capacity as Managing Director of Lloyds brokers, Christopher Moran and Co. Ltd (a subsidiary of Christopher Moran Group Ltd), Moran was granted a binding authority to write aviation hull insurance and re-insurance by a Lloyds syndicate. Another subsidiary of Christopher Moran Group Ltd was the underwriting agent for that syndicate, and the leading underwriter (who was also the subject of proceedings) was a director of that company. This appears to be a classic example of the potential conflicts of interest between broking and underwriting, which the Fisher report on Lloyds castigated, and which the 1982 Act will outlaw. Christopher Moran and Co. entered into a number of aviation re-insurance contracts over a period of some four years. The remuneration it received on these was greatly in excess of the expenses and commission allowed for by the terms of the binding authority, and amounted to much more than the profit made on the same contracts by the underwriters. It was found by the umpire that Moran had arranged for this, had concealed the extent of re-insurance purchases from the syndicate's auditors and from the Lloyds committee, and had permitted re-insurance buys at a level of expenses disproportionate to the syndicate's income, thereby exposing it to unacceptable financial risks – the buys were far in excess of what a prudent underwriter would have permitted.

The appeals procedure after Moran's expulsion was not completed until October 1982. The City Editor[12] of the *Times* was then moved to comment that Moran had always remained within the Law, and that perhaps a number of Lloyds brokers and underwriters might be discomfited if they were to undergo the same stringent tests of insurance etiquette. He criticized the vagueness of Lloyds rules, pointing out that thwn Lloyds was a small, close-knit club, such vagueness was less of a problem, but rapid expansion of the market had changed that.

The most singular failure of Lloyds in dealing with Moran was that its leading figures plainly allowed their personal animosity towards him to show, which gave the operation of Lloyds disciplinary machinery the flavour, even if not the actuality, of bias; even worse, the machinery failed in the last analysis to pin anything really heinous on Moran, which could only be taken to mean one of two things: that there was nothing to pin on him and that personal animosity was at the root of the case, or that the machinery was inadequate for identifying wrongdoings. At the very least it was inordinately slow. Either way, Lloyds capacity for self-regulation was shown to be severely wanting.

By late 1983 Moran looked set for a comeback, taking advantage of the reforms. Advised by the redoubtable conciliator Lord Goodman, he believed that the power of the old guard had been broken, and that he might obtain Lloyds consent to return as an underwriter. He was reported as being at 'an advanced stage of negotiating the purchase of a major Lloyds interest', possibly an underwriting agency of a broker required to divest under the new regime.

The last two major scandals at Minet and Alexander Howden are somewhat complex to relate but they share the essential features of earlier episodes. Their most significant danger for the integrity of Lloyds lay in the abuse of the privileged position of internal members of Lloyds, of their responsibilities in managing money put up by external names. In the case of Minet and Howden the dangers were accentuated by the involvement of two of the largest broking and underwriting groups at Lloyds whose leading members played a prominent role in the public political debate surrounding the implementation of the reforms in the Lloyds Act 1982. Further, it was not mere underlings who were accused of wrongdoing, but men at the top of these organizations who were held to have exploited their privileges to make easy extra money for themselves, in some cases directly at the expense of their names, and in all cases in defiance of their fiduciary duties.

Coming after previous scandals, the danger involved was not just that of adverse publicity, which might be expected to die away before long, nor even the embarrassment of the cases arising during and immediately after the passage of the Lloyds Act, and so risking sterner state control of Lloyds, but the division these breaches of trust created between the external names and the leading internal ones. Commentators at Lloyds were afterwards quick to point out that the scandals had little or no impact upon the willingness of names to come forward and invest at Lloyds, but this is to ignore the vital development. The Sasse affair had shown that in certain circumstances the external names could be roused to collective action, and by legal suit make life exceedingly difficult for the brokers and underwriters and for Lloyds as a whole, if not by successful litigation, by creating dissent, delay, disorganization and division. Events at Minet and Howden were further to stimulate external names to see themselves as a separate interest group and, when faced with heavy demands on their assets, to see that that interest is best served by determined resitance and litigation, so establishing within a decade an entirely new pattern of relationships between internal and external names. In the past matters had been governed by the leading internal members, and external names had not enquired too closely as to how their affairs were being managed. The pattern which has now emerged is one in which external names are disposed to see themselves as having rights in the management of their investments and to take collective action to enfore what they see as rights to proper treatment if the need arises.

The specific vehicle for the abuse of privilege, i.e. re-insurance, remained, as in the Fidentia case. Where wealthy and influential internal names had the discretion as to where to direct re-insurance, it proved irresistible to channel some of the business with the lowest risks to re-insurance companies, usually outside the UK tax jurisdiction, in which these same leading Lloyds figures had a financial stake, the value of which naturally increased as a result of the benign increase in business. This was not the only stratagem – baby syndicates involved the similar creation of secure inside tracks to make extra money – but it was the largest and most dangerous abuse, not only because it did not treat external names' interests fairly, but because if things went wrong, as in the insurance recession of the early 1980s, the same re-insurance companies might not be able to take the strain and members' assets would not be protected. The technicalities of the operations, working usually offshore and involving obscure foreign banks or Liechtenstein Anstalts and the like, were no doubt internationally complex, but the idea remained simple: in the words of that financial wizard of the 1970s Jim Slater, 'to make a little bit more for the boys'.

## Minet

The Minet affair came to light in November 1982 when enquiries into re-insurance deals by a subsidiary, PCW, was announced by Minet itself, by Lloyds, and the Department of Trade. The Chairman of PCW, Peter Dixon, 'voluntarily suspended himself'. Ian Posgate, then himself suspended as a result of the Alexander Howden affair (see below), immediately stepped in with a damaging allegation that he had told the Chairman of Lloyds of his suspicions about PCW a year beforehand, but was told to 'go away' unless he could provide proof.[13] His suspicions stemmed from the fact that re-insurances were not handled by the brokers at Alexander Howden, but by Alan Page, then finance director of Alexander Howden and previously auditor to PCW.

A week later it was reported that 1.5 million shares in Minet had been put through the market, days before details were published of the $40 million re-insurance deal arranged by Alexander Howden for PCW. Minet's shares, needless to say, fell on the news. More significantly, the existence of a latter from PCW to 1000 Lloyds names in two syndicates was revealed, which insisted on a new agreement which would give PCW legal immunity far beyond that which was normal. One clause said: 'the agency, its officers and employees shall have no liability whatsoever from any actual or alleged wrongful act, default or omission, including any fraud or wilful misconduct'. So much for *uberrima fides!* One underwriting group withdrew 200 names from the syndicate and Lloyds itself complained, but found itself powerless to act.

Early in 1982, shortly after his retirement, Peter Cameron Webb (PCW), wrote a letter countersigned by Peter Dixon and six other Minet executives, including Chairman John Wallrock, to his friend Sir Peter Green, and asked for Lloyds help 'in stamping out any defamatory stories which may come to their notice'.[14] Behind his concern lay an error in a cover note in re-insurance involving a Monte Carlo based broker Unimar as intermediary and UK broker Seascope as placing broker, in which Peter Dixon of PCW had an interest. Seascope owned 10% of Unimar. The error was identified in 1979 but not rectified until January 1982. Dixon admitted that he should have pursued matters more vigorously. By way of explanation, Cameron Webb told Green that the object was that Unimar should be well-rewarded for generating long-term reciprocal re-insurance business in relation to the £42 million premium income of syndicates 810 and 869. As a result of the way documents were issued and the precise meaning of various terms, the arrangement appeared 'unnatural' in its implementation, even though 'original in its conception'. Unimar repaid £400 000 to the syndicates, but it was accepted that the propriety of the contract and transactions under it was not in dispute.

Despite these assurances that nothing really untoward had taken place, Wallrock, Minet's Chairman, later admitted that he had benefitted by about £2 million from re-insurance deals, and he resigned at the end of November 1982. Wallrock was emphatic that he had not known of any wrongdoings of Minet's, and that when he did learn of them, he took appropriate actions. He told Michael Gillard:[15] 'I had nothing to do with the PCW business. I attended one board meeting a year to pass the dividend. I had 100 other companies in the world to look after. The one company I never had any problem with was PCW.' None the less, Minet sued him for breach of his duty to the syndicate, and its accountants investigating the affair alleged that he had benefitted through several offshore companies to the extent of £770 000. Wallrock admitted knowledge of none. Indeed it appeared that Wallrock, who presented himself as a pillar of rectitude during the parliamentary hearngs on the Lloyds bill, was a minor player in the affair. He told M.P.'s: [16]

> It is the half or quarter per cent in any market writing $2 billion worth of premium per year who will not abide by the rules, and unfortunately as the whole thing got bigger and bigger, the rules got inadequate. I am in favour of every disciplinary rule that Sir Henry Fisher laid down in his report.

The extent of the problems of Minet were uncovered in October 1982 as part of the investigations into Alexander Howden after its takeover by US brokers Alexander and Alexander (see below). Two Minet underwriting agencies, PCW and WMD, had paid some $40 million of marine re-insurance premium to companies in Lichtenstein, the Isle of Man, Guernsey and Gibralta, which seemed to be owned by insiders. This had generated $25 million in profit over five years, which would otherwise have gone to names on the PCW and WMD syndicates. Further, the re-insurance was placed by the broking firms Zephyr owned by Kenneth Grob, Chairman of Alexander Howden and others and APEG, owned by Peter Dixon, the Chairman of the two underwriting agencies and by Peter Cameron Webb (PCW). In addition, Cameron Webb and Dixon had owned 15% of the Banque du Rhone et de la Tamise until just before this revelation, the Bank at the centre of the Howden affair. The involvement of a number of senior Lloyds figures and two of the largest brokers was extremely damaging.

In the light of this and evidence from the Department of Trade, Lloyds dismissed underwriters Peter Dixon, Adrian Hardman and Peter Hill. The sackings left marine syndicate 954, a baby syndicate with only seven members, in the bizarre situation of having the majority of them under investigation and out of Lloyds. Cameron Webb had retired, Wallrock had resigned, Dixon and Hardman, also members of the syndicate, were dismissed. None of this appeared to affect Minet's profits, which in 1982 increased 20% over the previous year to £17.7 million; nor did the affair appear to have an immediate impact upon a large American interest in Minet. The St Paul group, while wishing to remain a minority shareholder, increased its stake to almost 25% of Minet, and these events helped to boost Minet's share price in April 1983 to the level it was before the affair broke.

In the summer of 1984, the Names in PCW and WMD, some 1500 in all, were offered a settlement of £38.17 million by Minet and Alexander and Alexander made up of £25.03 million recovered from a Gibralta trust company and the rest from Minet and A and A. It stood to reduce the names' losses to a maximum of £3000 each, where some had stood to face claims of £125000. Despite vociferous objections that the offer was inadequate, and a refusal to accept it by some, the offer was able to go unconditional in just over a month with 89% of names accepting. They were later offered assistance in dealing with the Inland Revenue, which was claiming back tax of £15.8 million and interest. By the time the offer closed at the end of August only 23 names had refused to accept. As in the case of Sasse, Lloyds too was in a difficult position, since acceptance of the offer was essential to many names passing the annual audit, and only if they did so could Lloyds as a whole receive the certification from the Department of Trade necessary for it to trade internationally. Lloyds set aside £9 million from its central protection fund of £134 million to cover potential defaults, but in the event little of this was needed, with even the Chairman of the names' action committee finally accepting the offer.

Cameron Webb avoided the disciplinary proceedings by resigning just before they had started, but two Howden directors, Jack Carpenter and Alan Page, failed to persuade the High Court that Lloyds lacked jurisdiction because they resigned five days before the proceedings were due against them. In February 1985, PCW's Chairman Peter Dixon was fined £1 million and expelled for life by the new disciplinary committee of Lloyds for misappropriation and taking personal benefit from money belonging to names. He also had costs of £200 000 awarded against him. Three others involved were also sanctioned: Adrian Hardman was suspended from membership for two years and had costs awarded against him but was allowed to continue to work at Lloyds; Colin Davis was suspended from membership for a year and had costs of £40 000 imposed and was also allowed to continue working; and David Hill was reprimanded and also had costs awarded against him. The extent of the penalties, particularly the huge fine on Dixon, were an indication both of the seriousness of the offences and of the extent of Lloyds new powers. The dangers of leading underwriters having personal interests in re-insurance companies to which they could direct business and collect premiums and profits at little risk to themselves, clearly required remedial action. Meantime, Minet continued its suit against Cameron Webb and Dixon for the £13 million still missing from the syndicates.

The affair had less than happy consequences for Lloyds Chairman, Sir Peter Green, who stood down at the end of 1983. He was reported to have been under pressure to go by senior members of Lloyds because he had become associated with the period of scandals which the new regime at Lloyds was attempting by 1983 to consign firmly to the past. In particular, he was criticized for conducting an enquiry into complaints about Unimar and Cameron Webb which was closed in 1982 without decisive action being taken, only to be the subject of later Department of Trade investigations. Further, in August 1983, the Inland Revenue asked for copies of all re-insurance contracts between Sir Peter's Lloyds syndicates and offshore companies, including the Cayman Islands based Imperial set up by Sir Peter's father. These included roll-over policies, a device used to mitigate and defer tax liabilities of syndicate members, whereby syndicate profits are put into an offshore reserve fund and invested instead of distributed as UK profit and taxed. It was reported that, until this point, Sir Peter had lobbied hard for an extra term as Chairman on the grounds that he could act as a bulwark against the outside forces that had disrupted the traditions of Lloyds. Sir Peter wrote to his underwriting members to explain the existence of the £34 million fund in overseas re-insurance companies:[17] 'The problem from the underwriting agent's point of view has been to justify to the Revenue if challenged that reserves for unreported losses are proper reserves, and not tax avoidance.' This letter became public in September 1983. Although Sir Peter was later awarded the Lloyds gold medal for services to the Society, and although part of the problem with roll-over funds and re-insurance abuse was the vagueness of Revenue regulations on the subject, in the atmosphere of 1983, the admission of involvement by Sir Peter was enough to ensure that it was impossible for him to continue as Chairman of Lloyds.

Discussions on roll-over policies continued between the Inland Revenue and Peter Miller, Green's successor as Lloyds Chairman. Miller insisted that the policies, although involving the lodging of premium income in tax havens, were legitimate, though he added, in a letter to Lloyds members reviewing the situation that 'it is likely that agreement in this area would result in the termination of certain roll-over policies for the future',[18] which is close to an admission that all was not as it should have been. The Revenue's view was evident from its demand for records going back ten years: such a position is adopted only where it believes that it has evidence of neglect or fraud.

On the underwriting side, too, the Minet affair seemed to drag on interminably. As the accounts for the period up to 1982 were prepared in 1985 (Lloyds accounts being three years in arrears to cover fluctuations in claims from year to year) it was apparent that the downturn in the insurance industry in the early 1980s had coincided with particularly large delayed claims and produced widespread underwriting losses and an underwriting loss for Lloyds overall for the first time for a number of years. The cyclical features of the insurance industry are well understood, and Lloyds has normally been able to survive them but, coinciding with so-called 'long tail' claims, it was on this occasion to approach disaster, and in doing so to reveal continuing weaknesses in the structure of Lloyds.

Marine syndicate 418/417 run by Stephen Merrett, one of the most respected and cautious members of Lloyds, announced a £17 million loss for 1982 and a £5.6 million loss on non-marine syndicate 421 affecting a total of 2500 names. Merrett admitted that the losses reflected poor underwriting judgement. At the same time marine syndicate 895 announced losses of £18.5 million, and offered a £10.5 million interest-free loan to the 243 names involved to help them out. The biggest losses were those of the syndicates formerly run by PCW and subsequently taken over by Richard Beckett Underwriting Agencies (RBUA), which were estimated at £130 million. Once again, the industry recession and long-tail claims resulting from cover for pollution and industrial diseases, especially asbestosis in the USA, where awards had become unprecedentedly large, were blamed. The same group of names hit by the defalcations of their principals in the Minet affair for an estimated £40 million, and offered the deal that many of them regarded as less than fair, if in the last resort financially expedient, were hence now faced with further massive claims on their funds. Although RBUA maintained that these further losses did not involve impropriety, and were not connected with the earlier ones, the names, like those of Sasse before them, were not satisfied, and held a mass meeting at the Royal Festival Hall under the Chairmanship of Lord Goodman and commissioned Price Waterhouse to investigate with a view to legal action.

In the course of these widely publicized events it became evident that names still felt that they had not been kept properly informed about the activities of the syndicates they had invested in, despite the reforms at Lloyds. Further, it became known that at least some names were at risk of penury if the losses could not be mitigated, and should never have become names in the first place, because they lacked the substantial incomes to place beside their capital and so take advantage of the tax concessions of being a name at Lloyds. Two examples cited were of a secretary earning £100 a week who had become a name on the strength of an inheritance from her father, and of a young farmer with a low income who had used his farm as security. It was asked why 'stop loss' policies to protect names were not more widespread, and whether members' agents had been negligent in failing to recommend them, why re-insurance had not mitigated losses, when the underwriters had first become aware of the extent of the losses, and what particular steps they had taken to deal with them?

Names at Minet facing average losses of £200 000 each and ranging up to £500 000 were not appeased when RBUA successfully pressed for Lloyds to take over the failing syndicates. It was little comfort to them for the Lloyds Chairman to say that names would not be hounded into bankruptcy and for Lloyds to point out that unlimited liability had not yet resulted in such an outcome for any name as far as they knew. Lloyds Chief Executive, Ian Davison, backed up RBUA in saying that the losses were the outcome of normal trading and would have to be met under the normal rules. He pointed out that Lloyds' reserves in its central fund of £176.2 million and its deposits held in trust for underwriting names of £1.47 billion, were more than adequate to protect insureds and the name of Lloyds. He also added that previous problems had not deterred names from coming in and that underwriting capacity had risen a record 29% in 1984 to £6.7 billion. The issue which was less easily dealt with was the further erosion of confidence by external names in the active practitioners of Lloyds who managed their money, and the resulting increased propensity to sue. This had ultimately put Lloyds in a difficult position in the Sasse affair by delaying Department of Trade certification of Lloyds solvency and accounts, and in the event of widespread refusal by names to pay up could do so again. Reform at Lloyds was, it seemed, much more than a matter of changing the rules; the slate might be wiped but it did not easily come clean.

## Alexander Howden

In 1981 Alexander Howden was taken over by the second biggest US broker, Alexander and Alexander (A & A), with a market capitalization of $600 million, in a deal that valued Howden at £160 million. In July 1982, the international accountancy firm Deloitte, Haskins and Sells began a fair value audit of Howden and within a few weeks discovered serious shortfalls in the accounts of Sphere Drake, a Howden subsidiary involved in re-insurance. This was in itself remarkable, in that Sphere Drake's accounts had only recently been filed and signed as satisfactory by Howden's auditors, Arthur Young McLelland Moores.

Deloitte's initial assessment of a shortfall of $90 million was reduced to $35 million after discussions with the directors of Alexander Howden, who were able to point to various miscalculations and sources of funds which Deloittes had not take into account – their investigations were still very much in progress. A & A then came to a remarkably pragmatic deal on 14 August with four of the five directors involved, including the Chairman Kenneth Grob.[19] It was to make an effort to reach such an agreement with Ian Posgate. The terms of this agreement were that various assets should be returned to A & A, and that it in turn would refrain from any legal action, that the agreement should remain secret and, in clause 5, "all disputes arising out of this agreement shall be referred to a sole arbitrator to be agreed by the parties; the arbitration shall be heard in London and conducted in accordance with the English arbitration acts in force from time to time'. The deal had hence the appearance of finality, and A & A announced on 17 August that there was no significant shortfall at Howden. Things rapidly began to fall apart, however. In order to understand why, it is necessary to look at why the directors should have agreed to an indebtedness to Howden of $35 million.

The problems have their beginnings in the censuring by Lloyds of underwriter Ian Posgate in 1970. The reasons for the 'severe censure' were not made public at the time, though it was assumed that it was because Posgate exceeded the limits of his underwriting business in relation to the wealth of his syndicate (in this case 128/9). He was banned from acting as an underwriting agent and from being a shareholder, director, or partner in any underwriting firm at Lloyds. In fact, as Posgate himself later said, his offence was the use of roll-over funds, although he had also been disciplined for exceeding his underwriting limits. The case was regarded as a test of Lloyds' disciplinary powers, but the severity of the sentence was such that it did not really stick. The committee went as far as taking legal advice as to whether it was under a legal obligation to refer the matter to the DPP. It was told that there was no such obligation, and a practical solution was arrived at whereby Posgate joined Howden, under the control of Grob, where the would no longer act as a principal. Grob very soon recognized Posgate's ability as an underwriter, and the expansionist views of both men encouraged a degree of latitude in which Posgate wrote vast quantities of business, ending up with a reputed salary of £700 000 a year, and Howden prospered mightily. The Marine syndicates run by Posgate (126 and 127) were among the largest, with about 3500 names, and the most profitable at Lloyds.

The problem which persisted was Posgate exceeding the limits of business he could underwrite. Howden attempted to deal with this problem by the manipulation of re-insurance; in Posgate's case 75% of his re-insurance went to in-house Howden companies. One result, according to Posgate, was a roll-over fund at Sphere Drake worth nearly £10 million. A & A further claimed that some of the re-insurance premiums, in all about £33 million, were paid to companies controlled by four Howden directors, including Grob, and with Posgate's knowledge, and that about £5.5 million of this was for their personal benefit. The main company, registered in Panama, and not licenced for insurance business, was Southern International Reinsurance. Another Panamanian company was paid £4.1 million in re-insurance premiums in 1982. This was controlled by the four Howden directors and Posgate, and was used to buy shares in the Banque du Rhone et de la Tamise, which was owned by Howden. Posgate firmly denied this connection. It emerged, however, that the Banque du Rhone played a key role, in that the companies involved in the relevant re-insurance deals had connections with it. Thirty five trusts and companies registered in Lichtenstein and Panama were identified as having been set up by the bank, through which benefits, including paintings and a villa in the South of France, passed to the Howden directors. The basis of the 14 August 1982 deal with A & A was that various of these assets, including the villa, paintings and some cash, should be transferred to Howden, and that the directors should explain fully what had been going on via the Banque Du Rhone and the various secretive trusts and companies. It was hoped that this, together with shares and Sphere Drake's and the off shore companies' established obligations to Howden, would fill the gap identified by Deloittes.

When the agreement began to be implemented, problems rapidly began to arise. First the villa, which had been Grob's second home, and was valued at £1.85 million, plus contents of £147 000, turned out to be owned by a Lichtenstein Company. If it sold the villa, French taxes would take half the proceeds. Further, the assets received as the contents of the villa by A & A were worth only £5800. Paintings valued in the agreement had to be sharply written down when received by A & A, and in other cases were not handed over promptly; and shares in an oil company agreed to be worth £1 million, were in fact worth only £380 000. A & A took the view that the other side involved in the agreement were not in fact in a position to hand over assets of the value agreed, and that the agreement was therefore void. They hence took legal action and the matter went public.

Developments came in quick succession, and the air became thick with writs. The committee of Lloyds had asked accountants Ernst and Whinney to investigate Howden in early September, before A & A began its suit against the four directors and Posgate. A full inquiry into Howden was started by the Department of Trade. A month later a special committee was established at Lloyds to deal with the Howden affair. Shortly afterwards Posgate began legal action against A & A and Lloyds. The four directors claimed to have an answer to all A & A's charges and sought to stay A & A's writ. A & A discovered another shortfall of $15 million in the assets of a Bermuda based Howden subsidiary, which with its revised estimate of $25 million for existing deficiencies, brought the total to $40 million. A & A then said (1 November) that it did not anticipate any further deficiencies and expressed confidence in the future of Howden as a whole.

In January 1983 Posgate won a High Court action against his effective suspension by Lloyds the preceding September. The following month the four ex-directors of Howden also won a High Court case in which they pleaded the 14 August agreement was valid, and that disputes over it should go to arbitration as agreed in clause 5. This was followed in May by a suit by Posgate against both A & A and the four ex-directors with the intention, according to Posgate, of ensuring that the matter was publicly aired and of preventing A & A reaching another private agreement with the four. A few days later Posgate was the subject of a suit by the Banque du Rhone which shed further light on the affair, only to produce additional doubts about its orthodoxy. The bank sued Posgate for the interest on loans totalling £1.2 million. In respect of at least £427 000 of this, the exact rate of interest was apparently not specified when the cash was lent. The bank claimed that the terms of the agreement implied that a reasonable rate of interest should be charged. It seems odd that either bank or customer should agree to a loan, the cost of which, in times of fluctuating interest rates, was not agreed.

Doubtless most of the cases mentioned above and others which have also been initiated will be settled out of court – the costs of fighting such cases are enormous and the time taken to mount them considerable. A & A clearly had every interest in bringing the affair to an end as soon as possible, and every reason for its publicly acknowledged regret at signing the 14 August deal. The results of the formal enquiries will provide grist to the mill of Ian Davison in his energetic pursuit of new bye-laws to prevent a repeat of the scandals, and the Revenue will doubtless reach agreements on the tax liabilities of roll-over re-insurance funds and their position when offshore, without sending too many companies into liquidation. The Howden affair has been most important in keeping up the pressure for effective reform after the Lloyds Act was passed in 1982 and the new machinery began to be established, for it is the detail of that machinery that will determine its effectiveness and ensure that Lloyds is subject to a formal, public, bureaucratized examination that can largely prevent collusion, conflict of interest and abuse of fiduciary duty for private (individual or group) gain; that is, whether Lloyds becomes a body like a clearing bank or a nationalized industry, and the old ways of the gentleman's club are finally abolished.

Disciplinary proceedings following Lloyds own and the Department of Trade's enquiries continued through 1984 against Grob, Finance Director Alan Page, other directors Carpenter and Comery, as well as Posgate. Lloyds' disciplinary proceedings concluded on 8 July 1985 with the results of Posgate's appeal against an initial sentence of expulsion. Lloyds accepted Lord Wilberforce's judgment that Posgate be given two concurrent sentences of six months' suspension, so allowing him to return to Lloyds as an underwriter in February 1986, having been suspended during disciplinary investigations since 1982. He was found guilty of failing to disclose hs 10% stake in the Banque du Rhone and of accepting a Pissarro painting as an inducement to place business. He contended that the painting was a gift for past service. Wilberforce overturned the earlier Lloyds committee finding that Posgate's stake in the Bank was also an inducement to place business. Grob, Comery and Carpenter were expelled from Lloyds for misappropriating funds, controlling Southern International Reinsurance of Panama and using it to funnel misappropriated funds to themselves and falsifying Howden accounts.

Rumours and complaints circulated constantly about the imminence of a decision by the DPP on fraud prosecutions in the Howden and Minet cases. Those thirsting for firm action were not impressed with the decision not to proceed against Brooks and Dooley in the Fidentia case, and members of the committee of Lloyds were at one point set on bringing a series of private actions. The situation as regards procescution remained complex, however. First, there was the problem of minor offenders becoming involved, at least by being suspended by Lloyds if prosecutions against major offenders went ahead, which would possibly take many months to complete. Secondly, criminal proceedings might prejudice Lloyds disciplinary proceedings. Finally, if a fraud trial failed, and some of the cases would inevitably be complex, it would leave defendants open not only to return to the market, but to sue Lloyds. There was hence an emergent problem of parallel jurisdictions, but it remained the case none the less that Lloyd's new powers were extensive, allowing for an unlimited fine and expulsion from Lloyds. Much of the press supported calls for the DPP to issue summonses, and such was the intensity of speculation that Davison had at one point to deny a confident press report that he had demanded prosecutions.[20] As will be seen when the issue of fraud prosecution is discussed more fully in a later chapter, criminal proceedings are not necessarily the most effective remedy.

# Reform

It should now be evident that an overwhelming case for the reform of Lloyds was presented by the cumulative impact of the cases presented above. Here we will look at how those reforms were formulated and enacted and how radical and potentially effective they are.

The first step towards reform was the appointment of a representative committee of Lloyds members together with a merchant banker and a journalist under the chairmanship of Sir Henry Fisher, a former judge. The increase in size and number of members of Lloyds, the American challenge, and the Savonita and Sasse affairs showed in the latter 1970s that a serious review was overdue. The commitee began work in 1979 and reported the following year. Its terms of reference were:

> to enquire into self-regulation at Lloyds and for the purpose of such enquiry, to review 1. the constitution of Lloyds, 2. the powers of the committee and the exercise thereof; and 3. such other matters which in the opinion of the working party are relevant to the enquiry. Arising from the review to make recommendations.

The brief was therefore wide, but not open-ended. It was accepted from the start that self- rather than external regulation was appropriate to Lloyds: the committee reported: 'We do not see how (Lloyds) could function in anything like its present form under any other system of regulation.'[21] Self-regulation was, however, showing itself to be increasingly ineffective, even as the Fisher Committee deliberated. The committee's solution was to devise a series of rules, procedures and committees for exercising control and discipline, thereby replacing informal with formal procedure, and more crucially shifting power from the members of Lloyds, who had always been sovereign to the elected committee. Hence, instead of being permanently weakened by having to carry a members' meeting with them in all important decisions, a particularly hard and unpredictable task with the greatly enlarged membership, of whom only a few hundred attend meetings, the committee would for the first time have direct power over members once it was duly elected. Finally, Fisher took up the issue of conflicts of interest in the ownership of brokers and underwriters and of managing agencies by the same organizations and insisted that it was important to divest to end this. Over 50% of the underwriting capacity of Lloyds was directly or indirectly controlled by brokers, and the eight biggest brokers controlled underwriting agents with 59% of Lloyds premium income between them.

Clearer, more effective- and formal regulation was not, in the context of the times, a contentious issue (I do not go into the detail of the proposals here because Fisher was superseded by the 1982 Act); nor was the ending of the 20% rule a foreign ownership, which as we have seen, was regarded by 1980 as an embarrassment. The reforms would, however, require parliamentary legislation for their implementation, and to obtain that the principal measures needed the backing of 75% of Lloyds members. Suggesting that these measures included divestment, with the implications for the earning power of many powerful members, and the transfer of sovereignty from the members meeting, was obviously a risky undertaking. The committee of Lloyds accepted the main proposals of the report, and the need to divest, although it was hopeful that compulsory powers might not need to be used to achieve it. This in itself was a remarkable indication of the pressure Lloyds was under, given that its Chairman Peter Green was not only head of underwriters Jansen Green, but the latter was part of brokers Hogg Robinson, and he would hence be personally affected by divestment. This stage of the reform process, however, went well. The committee sent out a carefully worded letter to members, soft-pedalling on transfer of power and divestment, and asking whether the members would attend the crucial meeting, whether he/she supported the proposals to transfer power to the council and for any comments. Of some 18 000 members 13 587 replied and 13 124 supported the reforms, with only 136 writing to object about divestment. At the meeting only 57 voted against the bill and 13 219 for, more than 10 000 by proxy. It was a considerable consensus on the need for substantial change.

The passage of the bill was less easy. Kenneth Grob, chairman of Alexander Howden, which made profits of £20 million in 1980, was firmly of the opinion that broking and underwriting skills had been developed over the years to a high level by their association in one organization, and this was reflected in the success of both sides of the business, to the considerable financial benefit of external names: 'The whole thing is so incredibly stupid that only Lloyds could do it. By God we're going to make it very difficult before we divest it.[22] Events were to show that things were indeed going to get difficult at Alexander Howden before divestment, but doubtless Grob was not anticipating the sort of difficulties that actually arose – a major scandal – at this time. His leading underwriter Ian Posgate was in favour of divestment but regarded it as largely irrelevant, since a regulatory Act could no doubt establish a framework within which potential conflicts of interest could be prevented from becoming actual, and public anxiety allayed. None the less, he gave evidence in favour of divestment, and was surely aware of its implications for himself. Following his censure by the committee of Lloyds in 1970, he had been deprived of his independent underwriting capacity. His success under Grob at Howden's would be further enhanced if he could take full control of the very large syndicates for whom he now wrote, and it would in addition be a way of vindicating him as an underwriter.

Grob was as good as his word. The major publicly quoted broking and underwriting groups, Alexander Howden, C.E. Heath and Minet Holdings, gave evidence in the summer of 1981 to the parliamentary select committee chaired by Michael Meacher, which steered the bill through Parliament. All were against divestment, and they pointed out firmly that although there had been recent scandals, none had occurred in syndicates controlled by big broking firms. Both Minet and Howden were shortly afterwards to become involved in new scandals. The opposite view was vehemently put by a number of others with painful experiences in the past. Lady Janet Middleton headed the External Names Association, which pressed hard for divestment in the wake of the Sasse affair. She also pressed hard to have a unified electoral system for the Council of Lloyds, against the proposal for external names to elect six members and working names 16 members, voting as separate electorates. On the principle of a unified electorate she was defeated, but she succeeded in raising the external members representation to eight. Broker Malcolm Pearson, who exposed the *Savonita* affair, was likewise believed to favour divestment (though he was strongly opposed to immunity, see below). Clearly, some of the recent scandals played down by Grob were judged to indicate a requirement for real reform by others.

The main objects of the bill can be summarized under the headings Divestment, Divorce, Immunity, Disclosure and Regulation. Divestment has been discussed above, and it was eventually accepted, although not without strong rearguard action by some Tory MPs and among some brokers, which led Meacher to threaten that the bill would be withdrawn if divestment did not go through. The success of its passage owes much to his determination and sharpness of mind in chairing the committee.

Divorce was less significant in that it refers to the requirement that managing agents who recruit names for syndicates should not themselves operate syndicates, and hence that the advice they give names as to which syndicates to join should be seen to be at arms length and dispassionate. The importance of this as an area of conflict of interest was reduced by the introduction of greater disclosure requirements by the new Council of Lloyds, both of members interests and of the accounts and track records of syndicates. The principle and object of disclosure was enshrined in the bill, but the detailed rules which make it effective have been undertaken by the Council.

Immunity gave rise to much more conflict. It was proposed that the Council be immune from legal action for damages by members as the result of actions or statements of its committees or their members. This was held to be important in ensuring that the Council could speak out clearly and boldly when it found cause to do so. It was this argument that ultimately prevailed, though not without opposition and some embarrassment. The Government was at that time considering reducing or eliminating the similar immunities of trade unions from civil suit. And Malcolm Pearson's experience in the *Savonita* affair led to his considerable scepticism about allowing the new Lloyds Council freedom from civil suit for negligence or incompetence, and about protecting Lloyds as a whole from being sued by individual names as it happened in the Sasse affair. Threats by Tory backbenchers to block the bill if there was no compromise on immunity did not materialize.

Regulation was implemented by the new administrative structure of Lloyds headed by the reformed Council. To the 16 elected working memers of the old Lloyds Council the 1982 Act added eight external members and four members nominated by the Bank of England, one of whom is the Chief Executive, a position akin to that of Managing Director of a Company, or as the Chairman of Lloyds, still elected by the Council put it: 'I'm Prime Minister he's the head of the Civil Service'. The Chief Executive is the Bank's nominee, and at £120 000 a year it will want value for money. The first Chief Executive is Ian Hay Davison, formerly a senior partner in accountants Arthur Anderson and Chairman of the Accounting Standards Committee. One of his responsibilities has been in dealing with the media and generally restoring Lloyds' image. From the start he established a style redolent with dynamism, competence and determination, reminiscent of that adopted by John Cuckney when he was appointed to sort out the Crown Agents.

Davison had also been, before his appointment as Chief Executive, chairman of the working party on Lloyds' auditors. It had long been feared by some that the audit of Lloyds' members was too cosy an affair, since the auditors were few in numbers, being highly specialized and requiring approval by the Lloyds Council to be eligible for the work. The working party covered three main issues: disclosure of insurance interests, re-insurance and baby syndicates, all of which had featured in various scandals. The dangers respectively are that re-insurance may be placed abroad and with companies of doubtful reputation, because of the advantages of placing money off shore, where the reserve funds approved by the Inland Revenue for tax concessions may be unduly exploited; that small syndicates may be set up by a few internal members, into which the most lucrative and least risky business is directed, so giving them insiders' privileges and pay-offs in relation to external members. In 1982, one such syndicate included Lloyds' Chairman Peter Green, Kenneth Grob and Ian Posgate of Alexander Howden. The final concern has been that disclosure of members' interests makes appraisal of syndicates easier and prevents accusation of conflicts of interests.

Davison's remit at Lloyds is wide. It is described by Lloyds in the following way:[23]

> He will oversee the establishment of the new self-regulatory regime at Lloyds. He will recommend proposed bye-laws to the Council; setting-up and monitoring of task groups; consultation with the market and outside regulatory authorities on proposed rules; and the setting-up of the necessary machinery to implement new bye-laws. He will also be responsible to the Council for the quality of the new self-regulatory arrangements, both as to the rules and as to their application; and will exercise general supervision over the disciplinary arrangements.
>
> Additionally, Mr Davison will be responsible for the management of, and accountability for, the resources of the society, the overall direction of corporation staff, over-seeing the implementation of the policy decisions of the Council and the Committee, maintaining proper channels of communication and responsibility within the society, co-ordinating the work of the society's various sub-committees, policy boards and other investigatory and advisory bodies, and laying the foundation for the future management of this society and the development of the corporation of Lloyds.

It is hard to see how much more power could be given to a Chief Executive of a society of supposedly equal members. It is clear that his establishment is intended to mark clearly and effectively the end of heavy dependence on *uberrima fides*. Shortly after his appointment a regulatory investigations unit was set up to co-ordinate investigations into[24]

> various alleged "irregularities" in the market . . . The setting-up of the unit and its welding together as a team indicate that the basis of a determined but flexible response to the alleged irregularities has been laid. Much of the work is concentrated on research and enquiry into background information surrounding certain re-insurance transactions . . . Many of the areas under investigation are of a sensitive nature. This however, has not proved a deterrent to the resolve of the unit. As the enquiries have proceeded the unit's ability to carry out its tasks has been strengthened by the enactment of bye-laws by the Council under the 1982 Act.

By 1985, despite announcing underwriting losses for the first time in 14 years in 1984, Lloyds had made considerable progress. Most importantly, the new regime had established an expectation of successful control and continuing reform and so reversed the view prevailing at the nadir of Lloyds fortunes in 1982. On the disciplinary side, proceedings continued against past miscreants, but looked likely to be completed by the end of the year, and the authority of Lloyds had been upheld in two court challenges in which defendants had tried to avoid its jurisdiction. Davison was confident enough to on record[25] as believing that there were no new cases to be uncovered. A flood of new rules and regulations had been promulgated with disclosure as the principal instrument of protection thus far. Underwriting agents have to disclose their interests in insurance and re-insurance companies and accounts are open to public scrutiny. Accounts were brought under the terms of company law for the first time by being required to constitute a 'true and fair view', syndicate auditors were vetted, underwriting agents required to re-register and a standard agency agreement introduced.

The implementation of divestment, however, remained a major task, and the permissibility of underwriters placing business with re-insurers in whom they hold stakes was still under examination. Preferred underwriting or 'baby syndicates' remained possible, although subject to disclosure. Significantly the new Council had the overt confidence of the Association of Lloyds members, representing 10% of members, despite its complaints at the lack of the right of syndicates to appoint their auditors or of names to call meetings of syndicates. It was accepted that the external names had a right to representation and recognition beyond their formal membership of the Council and their determination to assert themselves was evident. Lloyds under the new regime had yet to be put to the ultimate test, parallel to JMB in banking, of severe internal dissension or another major scandal. On the other hand, past scandals had been so substantial and sustained that they had led to very substantial reform, not only in the constitutional substance but in the style of its implementation. It seemed likely therefore that there would be a considerable degree of caution about the conduct of their affairs by active members of Lloyds, for at least a few years, while they digested the detailed implications of the new rules.

## Notes

1.   Lloyds itself publishes a certain amount of useful information which has been drawn upon in the pages that follow, as regards profits, revenues, membership and history. The *Sketch History* and *Global Accounts* are probably the most useful. In addition, Godfrey Hodgson's *Lloyds of London: A reputation at risk*, Allen Lane, 1984, provides a wealth of information on the history and development of Lloyds, and on some of the more recent scandals, notably Sasse and *Savonita*. It also has the benefit of interviews with many leading figures at Lloyds, though the author's journalistic background leads him at times into purple prose and irrelevant detail. For other scandals dealt with later in the chapter, and for additional information, I have drawn upon reports in the business press, particularly *The Times,* the *Financial Times* and the *Sunday Times.*
2.   Quoted in G. Hodgson, op. cit., p. 243.
3.   Op. cit., pp. 258–9.
4.   Ibid., pp. 261–2.
5.   Ibid., p. 269.
6.   Quoted in G. Hodgson, op. cit., pp. 282–3.
7.   Quoted in T. Levene, Fidentia inquiry traces where the money went, the *Sunday Times,* 20 November 1983.

8.   The *Daily Telegraph,* Currency fraud saga rolls on, 3 February 1979.

9.   See *The Times* law report, 1 August 1980.

10.   Ibid.

11.   See the report by J. Birds, *Company Lawyer,* Vol. 4, No. 1, p. 39.

12.   *The Times,* 28 October 1982.

13.   See G. David, Lloyds studies call for more disclosure, *The Times,* 6 November 1984.

14.   See T. Levene, Areas for concern in Minet's investigation, the *Sunday Times,* 14 November 1982.

15.   *The Observer,* 22 July 1984.

16.   G. Hodgson, op. cit., pp. 343–4.

17.   See C. Raw, The tax dodge schemes that threaten Lloyds, the *Sunday Times,* 18 September, 1983.

18.   See *The Times* 10 April 1984.

19.   See the *Sunday Times,* Howden: the Secret Deal, 26 September, 1982.

20.   See the *Economist,* 21 August 1984, p. 18; the *Sunday Times,* 2 and 9 September 1984; *The Times,* 3 September 1984; the *Observer,* 26 August 1984; and the *Financial Times,* 19 September 1984.

21.   Probably the most accessible source is Hodgson's review of the report, from which this quotation is taken. See op. cit., Ch. 10.

22.   See R. Allen, Broker barons prepare for Lloyds battle, *The Times,* 30 March 1981.

23.   *Lloyds Progress 1982–83,* published by Lloyds, 1984.

24.   Ibid.

25.   *The Times,* 5 February 1985.

# 4

---

# The Stock Exchange: The 'big bang' and investor protection

## Introduction

Talk in the City on changes in the Stock Exchange centres on the 'big bang' expected on 1 October 1986, at which point minimum commissions by jobbers and brokers for trading in shares will be eliminated, the distinction between the activities of the two will become optional, and outsiders will be allowed to enter the Stock Exchange, either by becoming members themselves or by ownership of a firm with membership. Nobody in the run-up to the big bang expressed that apparently cast-iron confidence in future success so common in the City, and the closer the climactic hour approached the more the difficulties and dangers ahead were emphasized by commentators – indeed, the one thing that everyone seemed to agree upon was that the hugely increased competition which would ensue would leave a considerable number of casualties before the market settled down into a new pattern of trading. Two things are hence in evident contrast with developments in banking and insurance. First, major changes have yet to be achieved, and hence a full assessment of them is difficult; secondly, those changes are most substantially changes in the market. This has important implications for regulation and investor protection, but so large is the scope of the market changes that as they approached it became more and more the regulatory implications of the new markets that held attention, rather than the deficiencies of regulation under the old system. Thus, although it was the case that a series of scandals tested the regulatory authorities in the later 1970s and early 1980s, and showed them to be inadequate and to require reform, and although this gave rise to the Government reports on investor protection by Professor Gower,[1] the commitment of the Stock Exchange to retaining its traditionally largely informal pattern of self-regulation, and its horror in particular of state intervention on the US Securities and Exchange Commission model was only weakened by the prospect of the big bang and the rush of mergers and takeovers which preceded it.

It might be said then that two parallel processes bringing pressure to bear for regulatory reform were at work. On the one hand, the failures of the established authorities in the face of scandals together with the threat of Government intervention if this were not markedly improved constituted an autonomous development. Behind the insistence of a Tory Government on improved regulation of the stock market lay quite openly its concern to increase public participation in that market, which could only be achieved if public confidence in its probity, and the security of investments made, were established. On the other hand, the Government was strongly committed to free market competition in the City, and antagonistic to the restrictive practices inherent in the select closed institutions at its heart. At the same time, it was recognized by both the Government and the City that American competition was becoming a major factor, and that the pattern of trading in shares worldwide was becoming increasingly integrated. In these circumstances it was necessary to make a choice between remaining a secluded but limited national enclave, and attempting to become a major international trading centre. In order to achieve this, however, reform of the market was necessary, to allow foreign access, to increase capitalization of stock exchange firms to a level adequate to allow them to compete with the large Japanese and American firms, and to establish a market structure broadly compatible with those in other major countries. The Government showed itself as being more determined to achieve rapid progress in reform, both of regulation and investor protection, and of the market, than did members of the Stock Exchange.

A necessary preliminary here is a summary of recent developments, since by the mid-1980s several separate processes were taking place at the same time. Despite the lack of clarity about the outcome, and despite the different interactions between Government initiative, the impact of scandal, and foreign competition, there are important similarities between the Stock Exchange, Lloyds insurance market, and banking.

## Membership

Membership of the Exchange is small, just over 4200 in 1984.[2] Although London is by far the largest trading floor, there are others in Dublin, Glasgow, Liverpool and Birmingham. Members are organized into firms, either as partnerships or as limited or unlimited companies, but in any case the principals or directors trade with unlimited liability. Members elect a Council of 46 members to serve for three years, and since January 1984, five lay members have been appointed to sit on the Council. The Council's Chairman and Deputy Chairman are elected annually by the Council, and they may remain in office for a number of years.

The Exchange also has a number of administrative departments concerned with, for example, quotations, firms' accounts and surveillance. The latter was created as a new division in September 1984 to 'bring together under single executive management work on enforcement which has in the past been done by several departments'.[3] All members are required to abide by the rules of the Stock Exchange, a revised and more stringent version of which was approved in 1984 (the yellow book). The similarities with Lloyds are evident here, and like Lloyds there is a compensation fund to protect clients in the case of a firm's collapse and default. The firms' accounts department receives regular financial returns, with the objective of there being a sufficient degree of disclosure to ensure continued solvency, and intervention by the Exchange in adequate time if firms get into difficulties. This does not, however, prevent firms collapsing from time to time, and a few have done so, or been 'hammered' in the language of the Stock Exchange, in the past few years. The Exchange inspectorate investigates dealing practices, and can instigate fuller investigations, which can lead to disciplinary action. It is fair to say that the zeal and energy which has gone into surveillance and inspection has increased in the past few years. The questions which remain are whether the sanctions available are adequate and used effectively, and whether the level of disclosure of information on dealing is adequate, given the relative privacy of the dealing system as it operates at present.

*Jobbers and Brokers*

In order to understand this it is necessary to appreciate the current peculiarity of the British Stock Exchange in dividing its membership into two categories, jobbers and brokers. In 1984 there were about 3600 brokers grouped into 209 firms, and about 500 jobbers grouped into 17 firms. The essential distinction between the two is that jobbers act as market makers in the range of shares in which they choose to deal, whereas brokers buy and sell shares on behalf of clients. Jobbers' income hence derives from profits on share-dealing, in which they interact only with brokers, not directly with the public. Brokers' income derives from fees and commissions charged to clients for the variety of services which they now offer, including the sale and purchase of shares. In order to attract clients, brokers frequently offer wider-ranging financial and investment advice, and run quite substantial research departments to support this, specializing in particular fields, and sometimes in particular groups of shares. Besides acting for private individual clients, brokers may manage firms such as unit trusts and act for the big institutions – pension funds, clearing banks and life assurance. It is one of the peculiarities of the City that although these organizations have their own fund managers and investment staff, they have up to now also made extensive use of independent stockbrokers, for two fundamental reasons. First, brokers control access to jobbers and hence to the Stock Market – it is a professional closed shop. Secondly, and more positively, stockbrokers vary widely in their size and area of expertise, and investment managers wanting to spread their portfolios benefit from their specialist advice. None the less, it has frequently been the case that investment managers, like private clients, have found it preferable to work predominantly with one firm of brokers, and naturally the benefits of large flows of business have encouraged brokers to develop the capacity to cater to the needs of large clients.

This situation has been one of the principal sources of pressure for reform, for the imbalance in size between brokers, even the larger ones, and the big institutions has been very great, and the tendency for the institutions to develop a high degree of professional expertise in investment has been cumulative. On top of this, the Stock Exchange has always imposed minimum levels of commission chargeable on transactions, in much the same way as other professions have scales of charges, and presumably for the same reasons – that is, overtly to ensure that transactions are always remunerated at a level adequate to allow for sufficient trained time to be spent to ensure that the transaction is of the required standard, and covertly to act as a brake on competition. The problem with minimum commissions became more and more pressing in respect of the institutions, however, because of their increasing dominance of the market and their strong tendency to deal in large blocks of shares. So strong has this tendency become in fact, that if minimum commissions were not addressed, the danger would arise of the brokers and the Exchange being bypassed altogether. As the Exchange itself noted, 25 years ago[4] private investors owned over two thirds of UK companies' shares, with the institutions owning around 20%. Today, private investors own less than one third, and the institutions more than 50%. Further evidence from the New York Stock Exchange indicates the extent to which block trading has grown up and marginalized the normal floor transactions. In New York a block is 10 000 or more shares, and block trading refers to brokers exchanging such blocks by negotiation off the floor of the Exchange, and descending from their offices to the floor only to finalize the transactions. New York does not have the jobber broker distinction, but in Britain the effect of such a practice would of course be to eliminate the jobber, who makes the market on the floor of the Exchange. Much like London, the institutional business amounts for more than two thirds of New York Stock Exchange volume, and block trade as a percentage of the total rose from 17.8% in 1971 to 31.7% in 1981.

*International Participation*

This has by no means been the only pressure on the traditional Stock Market system in Britain. Besides this institutional pressure to abolish minimum commissions, there has been an interlinked range of other powerful forces: government opposition to restrictive practices and a desire for international open-market trading; trading of UK securities abroad and of foreign shares in the UK, which has been made easier by the abolition of exchange controls in 1979; the threat of direct US participation in the UK market; the impending arrival of global trading and financial conglomerates; the diversification of the stock market into separate sub-markets, not all under the control of the Stock Exchange; and the failure of the Stock Exchange authorities to act effectively to control abuses. The cumulative impact of all these pressures has been the so-called 'big bang' due to take place at the end of 1986, by which point minimum commissions will be abolished, and outsiders, including large foreign corporations, will be able to become members of the Stock Exchange and own outright British jobbers and brokers, though the distinction between them is likely to disappear. At the same time, investors are to be protected by a new Act of Parliament.

Without access to ministerial papers, it is very difficult to gauge how aware the Conservative Government was of the likely effect of international changes in the financial and securities markets when it came to office in 1979. What is certain though, is that the policies adopted since 1979 have been such as to propel the City into enhanced participation in such international markets, and in so doing have eliminated traditional protective habits and institutions. No doubt the Government was aware in 1979 of the rise to prominence by that time of London as a major Euro-currency centre, and there seems little doubt that it wished to protect the revenue-earning potential of this. Other considerations must certainly have influenced its decision to abolish exchange controls in 1979, but the easier flows of funds resultant upon this were one measure which enhanced London's attractiveness.

Abolition of exchange controls also made possible a vast flight of British capital abroad in a variety of investments – estimates for 1984 run into tens of millions of pounds[5] – and a considerable influx of foreign capital into the UK, including foreign interest in the UK stock market. One development that exchange control abolition promoted was hence the capacity of foreign investors to buy the shares of UK companies in both Britain and foreign exchanges, and for British investors to do likewise with foreign shares. The deregulation of American pension funds' investment restrictions in respect of foreign investment by the Reagan administration also enhanced this internationalization of share trading. The effect of this was to highlight any identifiable disadvantages for investors in trading on the London exchange. If, for example, an investment manager with a US pension fund wanted 50 000 ICI shares, he could opt either to buy them in London or New York. Similarly, a UK investor can choose whether to work through London or elsewhere, and either buy the same shares as would have been bought in London, or perhaps buy another line altogether. The pattern of such choices by large investors over the medium and long term will go to constitute the new balance of international stock trading, and the determinants of that balance will be, *inter alia*, the quality of investment advice available locally, the fees and commissions charged, the efficiency of the services offered, the willingness to cater to clients' specific needs, and investor confidence in the overall running of the market by the authorities.

## The Office of Fair Trading and the Stock Exchange

It was with the latter points in mind that the Government instructed Mr, now Sir Gordon Borrie, Director General of the Office of Fair Trading (OFT), to investigate the Stock Exchange in 1979, with a view to ending restrictive practices and improving open competition. It was part of a wider Government interest in scrutinizing the restrictive practices of all professions which has given rise to, for example, the legal and accountancy professions allowing advertising of competitive rates, and the ending of the solicitors' monopoly on conveyancing. The OFT began to prepare a case against the Stock Exchange to bring before the Restrictive Practices Court, and collected evidence on the consequences of stock market management and de-restriction (deregulation as it is sometimes rather misleadingly called, referring not to the end of regulation, but to the end of anti-competitive restrictive practices) in America, Canada and Australia.

By 1983 many man-hours and reportedly £1 million had been spent, while the

**Table 1.   The Market's New Alliances**

| Stockbroker (S) or jobber (J) | Financial Institution/bank | Holding |
|---|---|---|
| Akroyd & Smithers (J) | Mercury International Group (Warburg) | 29.9% (£41m) |
| Akroyd & Smithers (J) + Rowe & Pitman (S) and Mullens (S) | Mercury International Group (Warburg) | Market capital of £350 m |
| Buckmaster & Moore | Credit-Suisse | 29.9% |
| Capel-Cure Myers (S) | Grindlays Holdings | 29.9% (plans 100%) |
| James Capel (S) | Hong Kong and Shanghai Banking Group | 29.9% (£25 m) (plans 100%) |
| County Bisgood (J) | National Westminster | 29.9% |
| Fielding, Newson-Smith (S) | Nat West (County Bank subsidiary) | 5.0% (plans 100%) |
| Galloway & Pearson (S) | Exco | 29.9% (plans 100%) |
| W. Greenwell (S) | Samuel Montagu (60%) | 29.9% (plans) |
| Grieveson Grant (S) | Kleinwort Benson | 5.0% (plans 100%) |
| Henderson Crosthwaite (S) (Far East) | Baring Brothers | 77% |
| Hoare Govett (S) | Security Pacific | 29.9% (£8.1 m) |
| Laing & Cruickshank | Mercantile House | 29.9% |
| Laurie Milbank (S) (+ Simon & Coates) | Chase Manhattan | (£30 m) (plans 100%) |
| L Messel (S) | Shearson Lehman | 5.0% |
| Montague Loebl Stanley (S) | Save & Prosper | 5.0% (taking 100% later in 1986) |
| Panmure Gordon (S) | NCNB Corp | 29.9% |
| Pember & Boyle (S) | Morgan Grenfell | 5.0& (plans 100%) |
| Phillips & Drew (S) | Union Bank of Switzerland | 29.9% (plans 100%) |
| Pinchin Denny (J) | Morgan Grenfell | 29.9% (plans 100%) |
| Quilter Goodison (S) | Skandia | 29.9% |
| Rowe & Pitman (S) | Mercury International Group | 29.9% (£16.2 m) |
| Sheppards & Chase (S) | BALL Group | 29.9% |
| Simon & Coates (S)) (see Laurie Millbank) | | 29.9% (£6.5 m) |
| Smith Brothers (J) | N M Rothschild (through Smith Bros) | |
| Smith Brothers (J) | N M Rothschild | 24% |
| Strauss Turnbull (S) | Hambros | 29.9% |
| Vickers da Costa (S) (to merge with Scrimgeour Kemp-Gee) | Citicorp | 29.9% (£20.0 m) + 80% Far East |
| Wedd Durlacher Mordaunt (J) | Barclays Merchant Bank | 29.9% (£30 m) |
| Wood Mackenzie (S) | Hill Samuel | 29.9% (£5.9 m) |
| de Zoete & Bevan (S) | Barclays Merchant Bank Barclays Wedd Durlacher & de Zoete | 5.0% (plans 75%) |

Source: Noel-Alexander Associates.
Note: This table only includes major examples of changes at mid-1985

Stock Exchange on the other hand had prepared its case, refused to concede any points, and professed its willingness to defend its rule book line-by-line in court. The OFT compiled a list of 173 restrictive practices, but its main fire was concentrated upon minimum commissions, the jobber–broker distinction, usually referred to as 'single capacity', and barriers to outsiders having rights to participate in the stock market. In the late summer of 1983 Sir Nicholas Goodison, Chairman of the Stock Exchange, reached agreement with Cecil Parkinson, then Secretary of State for Trade and Industry, and the OFT was called off. Events were moving too fast for legal remedies, and major financial institutions, both British and foreign, were already moving to take stakes in British jobbing and broking firms up to the permitted level of 30%, with a view to a complete takeover when the inevitable happened. A fight through the courts would have taken many months, and only entrenched the Exchange, and although the Government was criticized at the time of the agreement for letting the Stock Exchange of the hook – it will 'only increase the suspicions that the present Government is intent on protecting the pockets of its City friends' was the claim of one Opposition parliamentary spokesman – its assessment of the coming market changes was accurate. In his 1983 Report, Sir Gordon Borrie does not disguise his dismay at having his largest and most significant case halted, but recognizes that the three main areas in dispute were by the in rapid process of resolution:

> At the end of 1983 it was clear that events had moved fast towards eliminating the very restrictions in practices which our litigation had challenged . . .. We could console ourselves with the thought that more substantial changes were being brought about than the Government had required in July.[6]

## Diversification

Following the deal, a flood of mergers and takeovers of jobbers and brokers ensued, so that by 1985 almost every significant firm had a large financial institution waiting in the wings, usually holding the 29.9% currently permitted, with an agreement to raise the stake to 50–100% when the 'big bang' took place. At first it was assumed that the elimination of the minimum commission and access by outsiders would be achieved by degrees, perhaps in stages, and that single capacity or the jobber – broker distinction would be maintained. As the months went by, however, it was evident that this was unlikely, and that once the process of reform was started it would prove uncontrollable. The issue that always had to be kept in the minds of the Stock Exchange Council when deciding on the pace and terms of change was the danger of the complete marginalization of the Exchange. The formal penalty against such a move is a 2% StampDuty on transactions in Stock Exchange listed stocks by non-members of the Exchange, but against this had to be set the size and extent of block trading and the much keener prices negotiable outside the Stock Exchange before minimum commissions are abolished. In addition, the market showed ample signs of diversification in form, and it was essential that the Stock Exchange participate in, if not control, the new markets. But it was not only the giant institutional investor which was introducing change, but the small investor not accustomed to dealing with stockbrokers, and intimidated by the upper class cultural exclusiveness of the City.

The Exchange thus faced diversification in three directions. First, foreign exchanges, following the abolition of exchange control, would be able to compete more directly with London. Secondly, any undue delay in abolishing minimum commissions (the Parkinson-Goodison agreement set a date for the end of 1986) would tend to provoke a parallel market outside the Exchange's control. Thirdly, however, new markets for investors and to some extent for new small investors were growing up. In some of these the Exchange had control, but in others it did not. The difficulty of the Exchange was double-edged. On the one hand, if the market diversified in ways it did not control, it stood to be marginalized, and yet at the same time, if unethical practices took place in new markets it did not control, it could do little about them, but was none the less held vaguely responsible as the principal institution of the relevant financial sector. Further, to the extent that the Exchange either could not or did not control market activities that were detrimental to investors' interests, the State, usually in the shape of the Department of Trade, would be bound to step in to do so, and to the extent that it enhanced its role as a market regulator, it inevitably reduced that of the Stock Exchange, thereby jeopardizing the latter's cherished autonomy and commitment to self-regulation.

Four institutions are worth mentioning in this connection, each with very different limits, statuses and dangers: the Unlisted Securities Market (USM), the London International Financial Futures Exchange (LIFFE), the commodity brokers and the over-the-counter (OTC) market.

*The Unlisted Securities Market*
The USM, has been a modest success for the Stock Exchange. It was launched in November 1980 as a means of allowing smaller companies to trade in their shares publicly without the rigours and now quite substantial costs of a full Stock Exchange listing. There are now over 300 companies on the USM, there have been no serious disasters, and those who have withdrawn have done so mainly for honourable reasons, while the great majority have successfully attracted investors, and so raised capital. For the investor the USM is an interesting forum for speculation, since at least some of the small companies launched on it will become successful, and their shares will increase greatly in value. As it is, shares are relatively cheap on the USM, and hence attractive to the private investor, and some USM companies have attracted research by stock brokers by way of analysis of their potential. So far it is probably true to say that although the regulation of the USM-quoted companies is less stringent than for those with a full Stock Exchange quotation – only three years' accounts rather than five, only a 10% minimum share placement rather than 25%, and far less rigorous disclosure – a degree of informal caution has been exercised by all concerned to ensure that the USM experiment succeeds, even if it means a modest rate of growth in the market. The dangers undoubtedly exist, but not only because of the small size of the companies and the lack of disclosure and long track record required. Most launches are managed by brokers placing around 75% of the shares offered with the institutions, leaving only 25% for general subscription, often only a small number of shares. This means that

USM share prices may respond in a very volatile way to demand and, therefore, fail to reflect at all properly the real value or potential of the company. This is a classic recipe for speculation and for investors to get their fingers burnt.

### London International Financial Futures Exchange (LIFFE)

LIFFE is a fairly technical market trading in currency options, which appeals to large and sophisticated investors and for those who need to buy currency in advance. LIFFE is an independent exchange that operates as a company limited by guarantee with each member having a vote and being required to maintain a net worth of £1 million, £500 000 or £100 000 according to the category of membership and degree of centrality to the market. Currency options do not have to be undertaken through LIFFE, and major banks, both merchant and clearers, offer this service as well. So far LIFFE has been a modest success, though most commentators seem to stress the adjective 'modest', and it remains to be seen whether it will become fully established. While the risks of adequate regulation may become exposed at some future date, especially if LIFFE expands, that does not, so far, seem to be an issue.

### Commodities Broking

Much more open to abuse and political controversy are commodities broking and the OTC market. Both of these constitute an interesting paradox which is indicative of the climate of the times. Commodities are notorious for their price volatility ahd hence for their high risks. Therefore, they are not the place for the small investor. Yet high risk means high potential returns as well as high losses and, as usual in a free market, there is no shortage of brokers willing to claim that they have the skill to ensure gains rather than losses. The following two examples might help to make the three points that:

(a) large losses are not infrequent;
(b) there are a number of unscrupulous, not to say fraudulent, operators in the commodities field; and
(c) there is none the less substantial pressure for investor protection.

This is paradoxical in the sense that if investors persist in entering a known high-risk sector they should scarcely be surprised if they experience losses, especially if they have little expertise and exercise little caution. One such was Brian Jobson, second of a series of cases identified by *The Times*,[7] who lost £19 247 in six weeks to brokers LHW. Although claiming to be 'fairly sophisticated financially', he admitted 'I know very little about individual commodities markets', and complained of the poor advice and high-pressure selling of LHW salesmen. 'The technique includes getting on Christian name terms immediately in my experience, and just keeping up the pressure. I eventually said I would put up £5,000', after virtually daily telephone calls.

> 'A short while later another salesman phoned – precious metals were going up. He phoned solidly for a week and I put in another £15,000 – into gold, silver, platinum and gas oil. I didn't know how my original £5,000 was going because I couldn't decipher the contract notes I received. The salesman was right about gold moving fast, however. It did – in the wrong direction. Three weeks later LHW informed me that the whole £15,000 was gone.'

His conclusion from this experience seems entirely just: 'I think this way of promoting a risky financial product constitutes a danger to the public. There is no doubt that a lot of investors are greedy, and get excited by the prospect of high quick returns, particularly nowadays when new yields on normal secure investments are low.'

At least Jobson maintained contact with his brokers throughout the affair. Those who placed cash with Cornhill Securities, allowing the company to make sales and purchase decisions were not so lucky. Several hundred clients lost contact with Cornhill (no connection with the insurance company of the same name) in 1984, when it seemingly vanished into thin air, leaving only a director based in Kuala Lumpur to whom to direct further enquiries. Cornhill was not alone. Professor Gower's report on investor protection (see below) said that in late 1983, 50 commodity groups were under police investigation (not including Cornhill), and strongly criticized the lack of investor protection in this sector. The response was the formation later in 1984 of the Association of Futures Brokers and Dealers which in due course included the participation of the London Metal Exchange, the main established floor for hard commodities. At the same time brokers LHW were willing to justify brokerage fees of 5% because of the existence of a guarantee that client losses would not be allowed to run above the amount committed by the contract. The director commented that in four years LHW had had clients who had lost £5000 and others who had made £50000; he did not refer to Mr Jobson above, who lost nearly £20000.[8]

*The Over-the-Counter Market*

If commodities constitute the real fringe, and hence less of a challenge to the Stock Exchange, the OTC, managed largely by licensed dealers in securities, demonstrated in the 1980s how much pressure the climate of reform was creating, by bringing even publicly-identified margins within the scope of investor protection and market regulation. There are various pertinent aspects to the OTC market which are best dealt with in turn: the flotation of companies on this market and its regulation; the comparison with the US and its implications; and the stability and probity of the licensed dealers in securities who run the OTC market.

The expansion of the OTC market has been rapid and recent. As *The Times* pointed out:[9] 'in any stock market surge the good, the bad and the indifferent benefit to varying degrees'. OTC dealings in December 1983 rose to about £10 million, compared with £600000 in 1982. By April 1984 around 120 companies were being traded with OTC dealers, working through lists of potential clients who had asked for details of launches and purchases. Some dealers specialize in launches, while others also deal and maintain positions, so creating conflicts of interests when investing clients' money. The market was given a substantial fillip by the Government's Business Expansion Scheme, whereby taxpayers can set investments in small businesses against income tax, so reducing the cost of a £10000 investment to £4000 for a top-rate taxpayer, if shares are held for at least five years. Since companies on the Stock Exchange and the USM were deemed ineligible for the scheme, this concentrated investment in the OTC, with an effective Government subsidy. The dangers of unfettered and unregulated expansion in an environment of widespread change in the financial sector, and in a stock market boom of sustained proportions which had sent the FT index soaring from 300 in the later 1970s to 1000 in early 1985, despite sterling crises, were evident to at least one informed commentator, the managing director of the Industrial Finance and Investment Corporation. He pointed out that

> the latest trick on the OTC market is the company with a five-year trading record with no fundamental change to the business and no forecast of profit, but a projection for the current year of profits increased by more than 100%, and assumptions so clearly difficult to justify that the document even states a risk that one or more of the assumptions may prove to be wrong.[10]

He concluded that:

> if client companies are suitable for sensible investment, they are probably better served by institutions operating in the venture capital and development capital markets. The terms would be no worse than those obtained in the majority of cases from the market-makers in the OTC.... If the OTC is the only available source of funds the company is unlikely to be suitable for investment, and stands a higher than acceptable risk of failing to achieve its trading and profit objectives.
>
> The OTC should perform a valuable function as part of the capital-raising markets, but until the market is regulated it will not do so. A code of conduct and a small staff to vet and approve prospectuses before they are issued, and to monitor practices, would be quite sufficient to overcome the worst of the bad practices. Such a supervisory function would not be very elaborate or costly, but only the DTI [Department of Trade and Industry] can institute that function effectively.

This author clearly held no brief for the National Association of Security Dealers and Investment Managers (NASDIM), which was recognized by the Government as an authority with the right to regulate licensed dealers in November 1983, and which doubled in size in 1984 to 427 members about the time these critical comments were written. The question which arose in respect of the regulation of licensed dealers in the OTC market, was that of the effectiveness of legislation on investor protection as a result of the Gower reports (see p.117–p.119ff). Suffice it to say at this juncture that, at the time of writing in early 1985, it is still an open question whether, even given substantial moves towards self-regulation in the past year or so, NASDIM will prove an effective regulatory body without a very firm State (Department of Trade and Industry) backbone.

The potential importance of the OTC market is plainly evident from the USA where, under the management of the National Association of Securities Dealers Automated Quotation System (NASDAQ), the OTC market has grown to rank in world terms only below the New York Stock Exchange and the Tokyo Stock Exchange. In its review of developments the London Stock Exchange recognized the importance of the new electronic communication system in them.[11]

> Beyond question, NASDAQ has revolutionised the over-the-counter business. Linking dealers together in one wire system capable of providing exact instantaneous wholesale price quotations from all dealers who make markets in important over-the-counter stocks, NASDAQ has virtually eliminated the vast quantity of telephones on which business previously depended. NASDAQ has become, in effect, a new kind of

securities exchange in which the computer and assorted electronic equipment constitutes a nation-wide trading floor throughout the United States, to which securities dealers in some 6,000 offices have immediate access. Internationally, this has developed to the point where there are 8,343 quotation terminals located outside of the USA. Almost 5,000 are in Europe. An equivalent system in the UK would of course mean that regional brokers, Channel Island brokers and London brokers would be dealing under exactly the same terms with no geographical advantage because of proximity to the London floor. Indeed, there would be nothing to prevent brokers based anywhere in the UK registering as market-makers in certain securities; brokers and jobbers based outside London might be expected to register as market-makers in securities and companies local to them.

The review goes on to point out how this automated electronic system is valuable in providing investor protection and, together with the integration of NASDAQ into the investor protection institutions, provides a high level of investor protection and confidence.[12]

Apart from the monitoring of representative spreads the NASD maintain a three-year computer file record of every price movement in stock. It is able to trace the history of a stock second by second, and can identify when changes took place, and who initiated these changes, and what caused them. The computer files provide a complete audit trail, making investigations comparatively easy. In addition, over the years the Securities and Exchange Commission (SEC) have forced on the OTC market most of the regulations that have been imposed on the New York Stock Exchange. Dealers have to make clear on their contract notes the capacity in which they have executed the deal, that is whether as principal or agent. Provision has been made for regular inspection of all dealer organisations by the NASD, and for the filing of regular returns. Salesmen must take much tougher examinations than in the past, and controls have been established to maintain the integrity of advertising and sales literature as well as that of the firm's employees. All of these enhancements, together with the recent introduction of last trade reporting (within 90 seconds) of all deals in national market securities (which will apply to approximately 2,000 securities by 1985), have resulted in NASDAQ having a much higher status than was the case in the past. All members of NASDAQ must be members of the Securities Investor Protection Corporation (SIPC), and accordingly clients have the same protection (for example, the benefit of the compensation fund) as they would if they were dealing on the NYSE. (SIPC was created by Congress in 1970 and is funded by those brokers and dealers who are required by law to be members. There is a maximum limit on claims by clients of $500,000 against loss of security through a brokers default and $100,000 in the case of cash.) The NASD also checks bargain prices against prevailing quotations and monitors best execution, initiating enquiries at local levels when a pattern of suspect dealing is found in the central records.

If it can be done in America, it might be said that it could be done here, but a number of reasons suggest otherwise. First, moves towards effective investor protection have been slow and prompted by public pressure and scandal, and have not been accompanied by the rapid introduction of modern computerized telecommunications by the OTC, and only slowly and under pressure by the Stock Exchange itself (see below). Secondly, the very existence of NASDAQ makes it likely that it would colonize the British market if that shows signs of becoming substantial, rather than the British OTC market becoming a substantial and well-regulated force. This may sound unduly pessimistic, but it might seem more persuasive in the light of the Norton Warburg affair, which was one of the factors that led the Government to ask for Professor Gower to conduct a major review of investor protection. Progress has been made since the affair but has been constantly resisted, as will be further detailed later in this chapter.

## Norton Warburg

At first sight the crash of Norton Warburg (NW) in February 1981 looked more like a media hype than a serious issue for the City. The Group, founded in 1973 as investment advisers and financial fund managers, was only a licensed dealer in securities, not a bank, stockbroker or other established and fully regulated institution; hence those who risked their money for what they hoped would be high returns were surely seeking adventure and could afford risk. The fact that during its first five years NW's main client was the pop group Pink Floyd, and that it also advised other pop stars in reaching a level of £12 million in funds handled by 1981, was plainly confirmation of this and the explanation of media interest; and if the Fraud Squad and the Department of Trade Inspectors were taking an interest, as well as the liquidators, the City had seen the like before with easy-come, easy-go, operations.

As in earlier years, however, the embarrassing features were less what NW may or may not have done that was imprudent or even illegal, but rather the tendency of certain very established city institutions to give success implicit or explicit approval, without either a detailed appraisal of its foundation themselves, or the security of a regulatory institution that would have ensured constant and effective monitoring. Indeed it seemed that the only clear warning was the qualification of the accounts for the 18 months to mid-1977; as the liquidation unfolded the details grew more and more embarrassing.

The first point of difficulty was a debenture issued six months before the crash of the parent company to a new parent company created the same month, which effectively exchanged £1.28 million raised by a private placing of NW shares for paper. More significant were its implications for the creditors at liquidation, for if valid it had prior charge over other creditors and investment clients. The liquidator was appointed by creditors on the general understanding that the validity of the debenture would be challenged. Clearly, even if there were not rules to ensure that fund managers could not make mistakes with their clients' investments, there certainly could be rules to ensure that if such operations went bust, the clients could claim back the value of their investments without the sort of prior charge involved in the debenture. Further, when it became clear who had paid the £1.28 million for NW shares, the implications were disturbing. The company's need for capital was well known in 1979, and a number of enquiries followed, some of them resulting in withdrawal. One, Ronald Shuck, businessman and Chairman of London and Liverpool Trust, said that he did not receive satisfactory answers to his questions. NW therefore sought private placings for is shares and sold £400 000 worth to Save and Prosper, £150 000 worth to Scottish Amicable and others to the Tyndall Group, all of them blue chip city institutions. Clearly, they were satisfied even if Shuck was not; and in any case the sums involved were small in relation to their operations.

Another, though not public indication of imminent danger at NW, was that large round sums were at times shunted from one account to another. Between July and October 1977, for example, £450 000 in all was moved from the client account at Lloyds Bank to a Lloyds Company account and then to a Company account at Barclays. This led in 1982 to the liquidator applying to the Courts for permission to use funds to hand to take action for negligence, Lloyds being the most immediate target. Lloyds' response was that: 'We had no fiduciary responsibility. We were not acting on behalf of NW's clients, only on behalf of the company. We were never party to any arrangement between NW and its clients.' Quite so, and no doubt one implication was that there needed to be tighter regulation of what fund managers did with clients' money, and separate regulation for those who acted merely as investment advisers and those who also went further and managed clients' funds. But there was also the point that here was another institution who ought to have been alarmed at what was taking place through its branches, but evidently was not; it was not after all even likely to appear prudent behaviour on the part of NW, let alone in the interests (technically not relevant to Lloyds) of NW's clients.

There were further embarrassments. In October 1981 the Bank of England made an offer which effectively indemnified its former employees who had invested through NW to up to 90% of the value of monies lost. The bank, in making staff redundant, had allowed NW to discuss investment with them and its pensioners. About 20 pensioners had lost heavily as a result. The terms of the Bank's offer made it clear that it was not accepting liability for NW's losses, but there were other investors who pointed out that the Bank had allowed NW access to its employees as Investment Adviser, which constituted an informal seal of approval that encouraged others to use NW. Also, when it became clear that because of the bifurcated structure of NW some clients who had invested might get half or more of their money back, whereas others, whose cash had found its way into the other side (NW Limited as opposed to NW Investment Management), stood to get almost nothing, resentment of the role of the Bank became stronger.

Finally, the Department of Trade was not free from criticism, for it had renewed NW's licence as a dealer in securities only two months before the crash and, it was said, had had a report concerning NW for some time before then.

Matters were not improved when Andrew Warburg failed to appear for his examination in public for bankruptcy, and a warrant was issued for his arrest in March 1982. Since no extradition treaty for such matters exists between Britain and Spain, whence he had fled, however, it seemed unlikely that he would be cross-examined under oath about his activities at NW. By the second anniversary of the crash in February 1983 things were no more satisfactory. Warburg remained in Spain, and while police seemed confident that they would be able to bring charges, it seemed unlikely that they would ever come to Court. Meanwhile, another former NW director continued to live in some style in Wimbledon, while former Bank of England employee creditors remained sceptical of recovering all their losses. Others, like a widow who invested all the proceeds of her husband's life insurance, lost everything.

Meanwhile, three other licensed dealers in securities, and the commodity brokers, M.L.Doxford, had failed, and along with other pressures this led to the lengthy enquiry into investor protection by Professor Gower at the Department of Trade (D.o.T.). The Department itself has been a good deal more discriminating since the crash. It was reported in September 1982[13] that more renewals for licensed dealers in securities had been refused in 1982 than in the previous two decades. The difficulty of reform, however, lies in the fact that while the rules governing licensed dealers in securities can be tightened in various ways, there was nothing in the relevant 1960 Act that would permit a firm distinction between a dealer who advises his clients and does not administer their funds, and one who manages them on their behalf; hence it was difficult to ensure that the dealer's funds would not become mixed up with those of clients. And even if rules were tightened there was nothing to stop individuals not seeking a licence and continuing to act as "consultants" or using some similar title. Innovations in insurance plans and the growth of sales plans in investment items such as postage stamps and coins suggest that a comprehensive drafting of legislation would be necessary, and hence re-emphasized the importance of Professor Gower's wide ranging review.

Although the Norton Warburg affair indicates how widespread the concern for investor protection became, and the ineffectiveness of the then existing structure of regulatory bodies managing it, it was beyond the specific remit of the Stock Exchange. The Exchange, however, was by no means without its difficulties in enforcing its authority during this and earlier periods. Like the Bank of England and Lloyds it set great store by exercising internal and largely informal control over its members, and this commitment was maintained with great tenacity throughout the period of radical change under discussion, and only finally and reluctantly conceded when the pressures for institutional and market reform and from the Government became overwhelming. Some aspects of the transformation of the structure of the market in which the Stock Exchange operated have now been identified and it remains in the latter part of this chapter to discuss briefly the nature of the new institutions likely to emerge from the reforms. Enough has been said, however, to make plain the extent of public and international exposure involved in the changes, and the likely increase in the scale of institutions and operations.

The entry of large financial institutions as members of the Exchange spelled the end of it as a small gentleman's club run by equals of shared background and outlook. While they constituted effective pressures for a move to a formal bureaucratic and public mode of accountability, and such a move had the increasingly practical support of the Government, despite its constant ritual abeyances to the importance of continuing self-regulation, the effectiveness of the Stock Exchange at coping with current abuses in the late 1970s and early 1980s became an increasing source of embarrassment to those intent on preserving at least the remnants of traditional autonomy and informality in Stock Exchange regulation. There is not the space here to give more than a few examples of the difficulties and embarrassments the Exchange authorities experienced in regulating the market in recent years, but enough can be described to show that those difficulties were substantial and did not enhance the credibility of the existing pattern of Stock Exchange enforcement and investigation bodies.

One of the distinctive features of the stock market is that although certain abuses, particularly the outright frauds, are strongly similar in their form throughout history. Many of the problems which preoccupy the market authorities are the result of the reaction of those active in the market to the existing pattern of opportunities and constraints, which in turn reflect the development of the economy as a whole and the regulations imposed upon it, and upon the stock market in particular. As in other fields in the financial sector, the ingenuity of those in the market in devising new methods of profit maximization is simply diverted when one effective practice is terminated by firm disapproval and regulation. The attention of the regulatory authorities has therefore to be directed with equal flexibility at enquiring into new problems and taking effective but not oppressive steps to control them, a requirement often cited in defence of informal regulation.

## Takeovers and Mergers

In this light it is worth considering the development of what has come to be regarded as one of the most effective of the regulatory arms of the Stock Exchange, the panel on takeovers and mergers. Takeovers and mergers increased sharply in the 1950s and again in the 1960s, under the impetus of governments, with such bodies as the Industrial Reorganization Corporation being specifically created to promote the 'rationalization' of British industry, and to enhance its international competitiveness. It became evident quite early on, however, that takeovers were by no means always of equal benefit to all parties, not to mention the public interest. Perhaps th nadir of such activities was reached in the early 1970s with the property boom, when takeovers became mere collections of assets to be bought up cheap on the market that valued them low because of poor profits, and then sold for a quick profit because they occupied a valuable site. Asset-stripping was clearly a perversion of rationalization, increased unemployment and decreased economic activity and it attracted much approbrium, but it was a phase largely dependent upon a strong property market.[14]

At a much less pernicious level than this, however, it became obvious in the 1950s that the terms on which a takeover or merger takes place reflect the relative strength of the two parties, and that these in turn are affected by the strategy adopted to achieve the takeover. Accounts of contested takeovers often read as though they are the stock market equivalent of rape, and it is important to be clear that in a fundamentally free market it is up to the shareholders to accept or reject an offer by a suitor based upon their appraisal of the value of the company. One danger, of course, is that a predatory offer will be made to eliminate competition, and create oligopoly or monopoly in that sector, with the costs of a good offer to shareholders being recouped later by increased prices. One of the concerns of the takeover panel has been to prevent this, which is ensured by the issue being referred by one of several routes to the Monopolies Commission for evaluation. While ministerial discretion in this matter has at times led to critical reaction,[15] it is not the monopolistic aspect which has caused most trouble, that being largely a matter of public decision-making. Rather, it has been those cases where takeovers have been managed by stealth to the unfair advantage of the covert party. For when a takeover is made public, a premium over the current market price for the shares of the company is almost certain to occur, and there is a natural tendency for a would-be takeover bidder to build up a significant stake in the target company at lower prices before going public, particularly since, if certain key shareholders resist the main offer, an increased one may have to be made, and the last few shares essential to success may turn out to be very expensive.

In short, the issue which has most concerned the Stock Exchange in respect of takeovers is whether shareholders are being made a fair offer, and whether the target company has a fair chance to resist the bid if it wishes (takeover by stealth). An indication of how cautious the Exchange was in acting to try to ensure fair dealing is given by the time scale over which the takeover panel was established – ten years. Under pressure from various quarters at the spectacle of viciously contested takeover battles during the 1950s the Governor of the Bank of England convened a working party and drew up guidance notes in 1959. Because this amounted to little more than a statement of good practice, the abuses continued. Revised notes were issued in 1963 containing, in addition to the previous exhortations as to equality of treatment and disclosure, a warning about insider dealing, in which those who knew the company was to be the object of a takeover bid could buy shares in that company in an uninformed market and sell them at a quick profit once the bid became public. The revised code was no more effective than its predecessor in achieving real probity and continued abuses, coinciding with the Labour administration in the mid-1960s, led to calls for statutory intervention along the lines of the American Securities and Exchange Commission to stamp them out.

This body has always been a particular bogey for the Stock Exchange. It was created in the aftermath of the great crash in 1929 and the subsequent New Deal to reconstruct the economy, and was given very wide legal powers of investigation and court arraignment. By general consent it has been fairly effective in monitoring and regulating the US securities markets, though American practitioners find its practice much less onerous than their British counterparts find the prospect of a British version. It is, however, the antithesis of informal self-regulation, and in 1967 a working party on takeovers was reconvened, and in a short time the Governor of the Bank of England announced the formation of a panel on takeovers and mergers, established under the Deputy Governor in early 1968. It had nine members from constituent institutions, and made it clear from the start that, while it would issue and update the code and be available for advice and consultation, it would also intervene actively in the market to achieve control.

The only problem was that in the last analysis the panel had no teeth, referring serious abuses to the regulatory authorities of the constituent bodies, which proved less eager to take effective disciplinary action in many cases. In consequence, and after further warnings from the Bank that this would not be tolerated, the panel was reorganized in 1969 under Lord Shawcross, with an appeals committee under Lord Pearce and a full-time executive under a director general, with members appointed on secondment from City institutions. The first line of defence was stated to be public or private censure, but behind this now lay the threat of suspension, and the Stock Exchange altered its rules so as to provide that a judgement by the panel would automatically be binding on the Stock Exchange Council, and hence that the member could be suspended from membership. It further contained provision for the panel to request the suspension or even de-issuing of a particular security by the Stock Exchange.

As Rider[16] shows in a well-documented paper, the mettle of the revamped panel continued to be tested in a series of insider-dealing cases in which it did not hesitate to use its powers and its informal authority both to suspend offenders and to order them to pay their ill-gotten profits to charity. Rider's conclusion is that, in its reconstituted form, the panel became moderately effective in this field, though it suffered from two important weaknesses. First, its authority remained significantly informal and extra-legal, and hence a determined offender might well defy it or refuse to cooperate with its enquiries, to an extent which, on occasion, might hamstring the panel. Secondly, the source of information on insider dealing is informal. Because of the jobbing system there is no consolidated transaction tape, still less the store of automated information on transactions developed by NASDAQ. Indeed the marking of bargains, which are the basis of the Stock Exchange official record, were at the time of Rider's writing in 1979 still voluntary. Further, the procedure for investigation by the Stock Exchange was highly informal, private and discretionary, and cases come by this route to the Stock Exchange Council and hence to the panel. The chances of effective enforcement against all wrongdoers are therefore slim. This is not the place to expatiate on insider dealing, which has been commented on extensively elsewhere.[17] It is worth adding, however, that the problems proved sufficiently intractable for it to be covered by legislation specifically outlawing it and imposing criminal sanctions in 1980, and that this has certainly been accompanied by more rigorous action by Stock Exchange in dealing with and publicizing cases which have come to light.

By the later 1970s and early 1980s the takeover aspect of the panel's remit had shown further development under pressure of previous regulatory interventions, and attention was turned away from publicly-contested battles for control in takeovers, though the struggle between Robert Holmes A'Court's Heron Corporation for ACC in 1982–3 attracted much attention, and will be commented on later. Rather, it was takeover by subterfuge and stealth that proved the real problem. The form in which this occurred was through either 'dawn raids', in which a large number of shares are bought up in the early morning buying sprees before the market has time to react, or 'concert parties', in which several parties work together covertly to build up stakes, which are then pooled for the sake of a takeover bid. The complexities of proving concert party activity, particularly if there is determined and articulate resistance, were aptly demonstrated in the Lonrho/House of Fraser saga, in which Lonrho's attempts to gain control were ultimately frustrated, and after enquiries, substantial evidence of a concert party organized by Tiny Rowland was not proven.[18] There is insufficient space here to go into a case as complex as this, and so the difficulties of the panel and the Stock Exchange must be indicated by the rather more clear-cut examples of the St Piran and Consolidated Goldfield affairs.

## St Piran

The central issue in the St Piran affair, which ran from the late 1970s until its settlement in 1983, was the capacity of the statutory and self-regulatory machinery to enforce the requirement of Rule 34 of the panel on takeovers and mergers, i.e. that a company acquiring 30% or more of another must make a bid for the acquisition of the entire company.

St Piran was founded in 1970 to bring together tin interests in the Far East and in Cornwall, where it owned 65% of the revived South Crofty mine. This was rehabilitated after years of decline to the point of imminent closure, on the basis of the greatly improved effectiveness of modern ore processing. One of the many embarrassing features of the affair is that South Crofty, as one of the few industrial employers in Cornwall, was the subject of a £400 000 grant by the Department of Industry and a £2.5 million loan from the European Investment Bank guaranteed by the Department. Its Board membership changed fairly frequently, but between 1973 and 1976 its chairman was James Raper. Other directors, then and afterwards, were also associated with him and his companies.

Matters came to a head in 1979 when shareholders took High Court action to prevent eight companies, thought to represent Raper, from voting at an extraordinary general meeting of St Piran, and then to prevent the directors acting as a Board. However, both failed. Raper was now operating as Chairman of Gasco Investments (Hong Kong), but the allegations were that, despite leaving the Board of St Piran, he had retained substantial influence through nominees; in particular Ruffec, based in Luxembourg, which held 4% of St Piran, and Aerolineas Cordoba, based in Panama, with 3.4%. The takeover panel began an enquiry into the situation in March 1979 to determine whether Raper effectively controlled more than 30% of St Piran, and therefore should be required to make a bid for the rest, and this was followed in December by the announcement of a Departmentof Trade enquiry, after shareholders had failed to identify proxy voters at the AGM.

The panel's report was published in April 1980, and concluded that there was a concert party involved, and that the 34% of St Piran which Raper had held in 1974 'remains substantially under his control through a complex web of companies'.[19] It required that a bid be made by Gasco, Raper's main vehicle, which owned 29.6%, for the whole of the rest of St Piran, at what it judged to be a fair price of 85 pence a share. With the panel headed by Lord Shawcross, a distinguished City and Establishment figure, a trial of strength of uncertain dimensions was clearly on. The issues immediately arising were, first, whether Gasco or Raper could raise the cash to make the full bid as required; secondly, what sanctions would follow if there was no bid, and whether these would be effective or equitable, particularly since the most stringent available to the Stock Exchange was the suspension of the Company's quotation, which would penalize the very minority shareholders it had sought to protect, by freezing them in; and, finally, whether, as Raper complained, the fact that there was no appeal from the panel's ruling was fair, especially given his allegations of, its bias against him.

The evidence against St Piran and Raper was circumstantial, and therein lay part of the difficulties which ensued. The takeover panel reserved the right to itself to form a firm opinion and take consequential action to enforce it, without right of appeal on the basis of such evidence. Some of it, however, seemed clearly to indicate that Raper had rather more knowledge than he admitted of the affairs of St Piran after he resigned, and when he admitted to only holding 1 000 shares himself. The panel's report referred to:

> a former employee of St Piran (who) informed (it) that at least up to November 1979, when the employee resigned, there was a box into which were put copies of letters intended for the chairman of St Piran, other reports and internal memoranda, the fortnightly report by the registrars on the larger share transactions, and the monthly financial statements. Mr Raper's chauffeur collected the contents of the box daily and sometimes twice daily.[20]

By mid-June, however, it was plain that the panel was unable to force Gasco to make a bid for the outsanding 63% of St Piran. In a further statement it referred to Raper as 'unfit to be a director of a public company'. It further noted that Malcolm Stone was Chairman of St Piran and Managing Director of Gasco: 'No doubt Mr Stone will give consideration to his position as Chairman of St Piran and to any conflict to which this gives rise.'[21] This was followed up shortly afterwards by the Stock Exchange imposing a ban on any of its members dealing with Raper, accompanied by a continued suspension of St Piran's shares. Gasco said that it was trying to raise the cash to bid for the rest of St Piran within four weeks. Evidently it proved harder than anticipated, for the bid did not come and matters remained at stalemate.

The next development was at the end of 1980 when the Department of Trade Inspectors published their report. Although their powers had enabled them to search more widely than the Register of Share Dealings, which formed the basis of the takeover panel's report, they were cautious in their conclusions, saying that they could not fully support the takeover panel's claim of concert part.[22] In reply the panel stressed that the circumstantial evidence on which it had formed its view was not disputed by the Inspectors and that a concert party does not require common ownership, which the Luxembourg and Panama basis of the relevant companies ensured that it was unable to prove. Malcolm Stone, not surprisingly, welcomed the difference of view: 'We are pleased that the Inspectors have not supported the take-over panel's view.' None the less, the Inspectors did find that Rule 34 had clearly been breached between 1974 and 1977, when Raper was Chairman of St Piran, since his holdings exceeded 30% and reached 48.5% in 1976, before falling to 29.7% in 1980. The Inspectors concluded that Raper was at all times materially able to influence St Piran's policy.

There were still no significant developments pending the final part of the Inspectors' report concerning potential fraud, which was published in mid-April 1981. On the basis of a detailed analysis of the events of the preceding decade they accused Raper of controlling St Piran, even when not on its board, and of a strategy of controlling companies by acquiring less than a majority holding by putting his nominees on the boards – many of St Piran's directors and former directors were criticized for complicity in this. The Inspectors concluded that the situation was not satisfactory for the majority of shareholders and recommended to the Secretary of State for Trade that it would be just and equitable for him to wind the company up.[23] The buck had thus finally stopped and the challenge of enforcement made. The response of the Under-secretary of State was, however, an immediate refusal to intervene, saying that the law gave shareholders the power to petition for winding up if they thought it to be in their interest.

Earlier in the same week Gasco finally bid for St Piran, but at 50 pence a share not 85 pence as required by the takeover panel. This was followed by a cash and shares bid amounting to 74 pence by Burma Mines which controlled around 17.5% of St Piran, which in turn prompted talk of a bid by Gasco for Burma Mines. Clearly Gasco was the only credible bidder, given its already large holding, and within a fortnight was claiming control of St Piran. It then raised its offer to 60 pence and looked set to pick up the remaining shares. Raper spoke publicly on the issue for the first time for many months, denouncing the takeover panel as a star chamber court which would not admit it may be wrong, and denying participation in a concert party and ownership of more than 30% of St Piran by Gasco until recently. He accepted that he had been influential at St Piran, but pointed out that during his period as chairman its profits had risen sharply.[24]

Two matters now seemed capable of frustrating Raper. The Office of Fair Trading was considering reference of the affair to the Monopolies Commission, and legal action to wind up St Piran was under consideration both by Burma Mines and by Gencor, a South African Mining Corporation which owned less than 1% of St Piran. The object in both cases would be to secure a better price for shareholders on liquidation than any of Gasco's offers.

The Secretary of State for Trade, John Biffen refused to refer the matter to the Monopolies Commission, which provoked further dissension among the regulatory authorities. Lord Shawcross, the takeover panel chairman during the St Piran enquiry, had criticized Biffen for failing to follow the Department of Trade Inspector's recommendation for liquidation. His letter to *The Times* was trenchant in its condemnation of the failure to liquidate St Piran.

> 'This neglect by the Department on what I agree with the Inspectors was its duty in the public interest, has aided and abetted the attempt now being made by Raper and Gasco, no doubt with prior knowledge of the Inspectors' conclusions, to secure for themselves St Piran assets at a share price significantly less than they themselves earlier paid for the controlling interest in the Company'.[25]

St Piran's shares were suspended at 63 pence. Raper justified Gasco's bid at 50 pence by valuing St Piran at 51.5 pence, the fall in price being one adverse consequence of the suspension and allied troubles. Next, Patrick Neill, Chairman of the Council for Security Industries, the supreme representative regulatory and advisory body based in the Stock Exchange, wrote to *The Times* criticizing Biffen for 'letting slip the opportunity for an enquiry into whether the public interest was served by Mr Raper being in control of St Piran and its operating subsidiaries'.[26] Clearly, as *The Times* put it, 'the City and Whitehall have taken differing views of their powers and how they should be exercised'. It seemed that the OFT had recommended no reference to the Monopolies Commission because it could find no grounds for doing so in competition policy. That may have been so, but it left Raper's sustained defiance of the authorities unchallenged, and the authorities in some disarray; so much so that the Chairman of the Stock Exchange, Nicholas Goodison, felt constrained to deny that self-regulation in the City had failed, though he added that statutory regulation was unnecessarily weak, and regretted the Secretary of State's decision not to wind up St Piran.[27]

Matters, therefore, rested with minority shareholders. Gencor pressed its case in the High Court, alleging that St Piran had been managed for the benefit of Raper rather than the shareholders, and that liquidation would realize 80 pence a share against Gasco's raised offer of 60 pence. The case ground slowly into the summer with St Piran strenuously contesting it and Gasco steadily increasing its holdings. Finally Gencor backed out in mid-July when Gasco had over 90% of St Piran. Raper closed the 60 pence offer a month later, when he had acquired 94.17%, and served notice of compulsory acquisition of the remaining shares. Raper claimed that acceptances by 86% of shareholders vindicated the fairness of Gasco's offer, and again denied any part in a concert party. Raper's success was followed up by a threat by South Crofty Tin Mine, which was controlled by St Piran, to sue the Stock Exchange unless its share quotation was restored by the time of the AGM at the end of September.[28]

It seemed that Raper had won hands down, and that self-regulation in the City could be ignored, but events two years later indicated that things were not quite that simple. In August 1983 Raper was involved in a struggle with the Westminster Property Group, in which he had acquired a 30% holding and sought representation on the Board, but was resisted. In addition, however, it lent more than £1 million to a Jersey based property man, David Kirch, in return for a legal charge on his 15% stake in Westminster. This led to a complaint to the takeover panel that Raper had effective control of 45% of Westminster and should, therefore, bid for the rest as required by Rule 34. The panel agreed and further stipulated a price of 35.5 pence, the highest paid by Raper in building up his holding, even though Westminster shares had fallen by now to 19 pence. Raper described the panel's decision as 'complete nonsense' and said that he would appeal (evidently an innovation since 1980).[29]

In early September, however, Raper did a complete volte-face, apologized to the takeover panel along with Malcolm Stone for allegations of bias, and produced a cash bid of 35.5 pence for the rest of Westminster as required. Raper, it seems, was finally persuaded that continued denial of access to City facilities was proving expensive and blocking St Piran's expansion. He spent heavily on legal fees to develop ways round the take over panel's ruling – his lawyer acknowledged that the Jersey deal over Westminster 'may well have owed its complexity to a desire to keep it outside the ambit of Rule 34'.[30] Further, a recent bid by St Piran for house builders William Wittingham, had to be made through a Southend-based licensed dealer in securities, and was unsuccessful. Even worse, potentially, Raper had been forced offshore in financing the St Piran takeover to the Isle of Man Savings and Investment Bank, which by 1983 was in liquidation. In an interview in *Accountancy*[31] Raper admitted that it might have been prudent to back down earlier: 'There's no question of it, the City is very powerful and can make many difficulties.... We are going to have to run twice as hard to make up for the last three years.' But he stressed, 'We may have annoyed the take-over panel and the City, but we're not thieves. There are no directors' yachts and houses and money going astray here and there.' In return for falling into line, the personal ban on dealing with Raper was lifted, and the share quotation of a key St Piran subsidiary, Milbury, was restored.

## Consolidated Gold Fields

This British-based company was regarded for some years as uninteresting in the City. Most of its assets were in South Africa, and its profits record in the late 1970s was unimpressive. But in 1979 and 1980 its fortunes changed dramatically for the better. The price of gold rose very sharply, and management reorganization begun in 1977 looked like paying off in improved dynamism and efficiency. In particular its 46% stake in Gold Fields of South Africa (GFSA) looked like being a long-term as well as a short-term asset of great profitability: GFSA's gold output was expected to exceed that of the giant Anglo-American by the end of the century.

Concern was expressed at the 1979 AGM by Consolidated Gold Chairman, Lord Errol, about the possibility of a 'creeping acquisition'.[32] A pattern of sporadic purchases of its shares, particularly through Brokers, Akroyd and Smithers, was identified, with intervals allowing the share price to fall back after heavy demand. Until mid-February 1980 it remained impossible to identify the ultimate beneficiary. Consolidated Gold finally called for a Department of Trade enquiry under a section of company law permitting the suspension of rights attaching to shares in order to end the continued transfer of unregistered shares. The buyer identified himself as Harry Oppenheimer, Chairman of Anglo-American. His motive, he said, was to preserve the integrity of South African Gold Mining as currently constituted: 'We didn't want a maverick loose in the Chamber of Mines.'[33] This quite failed to allay concern on a number of fronts.

In the first place Oppenheimer seemed likely to have acquired his holding at a significantly lower price than the asset value and recent earnings record of Consolidated Gold would have indicated was appropriate, and lower too than would have been the case if he had made his intention of acquiring at 25% stake public from the start. This raised questions as to whether the market in the shares was not, therefore, a false one. Secondly, the Companies Acts specify that the holders of 5% of a company must declare themselves. Oppenheimer had built up his initial 14% through carefully managed clandestine transactions, using a variety of vehicles and jobbers to achieve it. He was insistent that he had not breached the law. The problem with the law was that it, unlike the takeover panel, made no provision against concert parties, that is groups of separate buyers acting together in a common interest. Yet as long ago as 1973 the Stock Exchange had urged legal reform to end concert parties and 'warehousing', that is the purchase of shares by an agent who holds them for a while for later sale to the organizer of the party. Yet in January 1980 Consolidated Gold's broker appealed to the Stock Exchange to intervene because the market was being abused and the identity of a major purchaser concealed. The Council refused to do so, while accepting that its powers would have enabled it to identify the purchaser if it had used them. Its reason was that it had at the time no firm evidence of impropriety, for its rules define a false market – which is grounds for intervention – strictly as collaboration between buyers and sellers calculated to change a share's price in a way not justified by assets, earnings or prospects. The Exchange concluded that there may have been an ill-informed market and its chairman remarked that company law was frustrated by Anglo's not declaring its interest: 'Adequate disclosure is essential for a fair market', he said.[34]

The Exchange did produce a thorough report on the affair, which was published in July, and detailed how Anglo-American had achieved its success.[35] If anything it only made the regulatory bodies look more ineffective. The acquisition of the major stake in Consolidated Gold by Oppenheimer was discussed as early as the summer of 1979 with brokers, Rowe and Pitman, and the details of how it was to be managed were worked out with Jobbers, Akroyd and Smithers. Rowe was instructed by Anglo's South African Brokers to buy Consolidated Gold shares, and ordered Akroyd to do so. Akroyd in turn bought the shares of Consolidated Gold, which were then sold to Rowe. Hence Rowe acted as a warehouse for Anglo. When the 5% limit at which the holding would have to be declared was approached, Anglo asked other parties, whom the Exchange was unable to identify, to do the same. In this way Anglo acquired 14% of Consolidated Gold. When pressure to identify Anglo became effective in early February, Rowe was instructed to conduct a final dawn raid to bring the stake up to 25%. They began at 8.30 a.m. and spent £100 million by 10 a.m. in doing so. In response to a parliamentary question in the light of the Stock Exchange enquiry, the then Secretary of State for Trade, John Nott, commented: 'I trust that (the Council for the Securities Industry) will have regard to the fact that the strength of a system of non-statutory regulation is its ability to ensure that conduct is governed by the spirit and not merely the letter of the law.'[36]

Clearly something needed to be done, or at any rate to be seen to be done. The Exchange's apologia was lame indeed. It had failed to intervene, to enforce disclosure, and protect the interests of investors, and was apparently content to point its finger at the failure of the law to regulate concert parties, and of its own regulations to include covert partial bids and registration of shares. Its response was a recommendation to change company law on the 5% rule and a series of regulations to govern future dawn raids: the public to be warned in advance, raids to begin from 9.30 a.m. or later, prices offered to be at least the prevailing price, jobbers and brokers to agree deals, and a half-hour suspension of the shares. These were broadly adhered to in the ensuing weeks, with the exception of the last point, on which implementation was avoided because it was felt that suspension would not stop deals outside the market and would prevent an alternative buyer from emerging.

Further pressure came from the Department of Trade Inspectors' report published in August 1980, which was accompanied by a report that the department was working on recommendations to bring overseas investors under the same disclosure rules as UK residents. The Inspectors concluded that 'Anglo-American and De Beers formulated its scheme with the express intention of avoiding the disclosure provisions of the Companies Acts'.[37] They also said that on 26 November 1979 De Beers held 6.3% of Consolidated Gold, and that its defence that disclosure was only an obligation when one person, whose knowledge can be said to be that of the relevant company, knows all the facts was questionable, and asked the Department to consider whether an offence had been committed. The ways in which a variety of companies, including one registered in Liberia, were used to build up a stake in Consolidated Gold were detailed by the Inspectors, but on the dawn raid finale they placed responsibility firmly on the Stock Exchange.[38]

It was the publicity generated by these cases and the number of others with similar implications of inadequacy in the capacity of the existing system to control abuses that led to the Government's calling for comprehensive review of investor protection by Professor Gower. Before turning to this and its outcome, however, it is as well to be aware that difficulties for the Stock Exchange were by no means confined to the large-scale public sphere. There were, in addition, a number of scandals affecting members of the Stock Exchange which, as in the case of Lloyds, called into doubt the effectiveness of existing methods of policing members and more generally the continued insistence upon informal self-regulation. Since the outcome of Gower has been a gradual move away from this, it is as well to be aware of its inadequacies at the personal as well as at the public institutional level in the Stock Exchange. It is also important to bear in mind the Exchange's continuing overt commitment to traditional principles, in much the same spirit as Lloyds. Even in its *1984 Year Book*, the second paragraph of its general introductory statement on the Exchange runs as follows:

> An important element which has made the City of London such a major international financial centre is its code of regulations. This has not been imposed from above by Government. It has grown up through the good practices of those who deal in the markets and who insist on the highest level of fair dealing from the members. The informality and mutual trust is expressed in the motto ''My word is my bond''. A bargain made even by word of mouth is a bargain to be honoured. This is the principle on which the City markets are based. The Stock Exchange as one of the leading market places is an important element, not only within the City itself, but also in helping to finance industry, trade and government, both here in Britain and throughout the world.

## Halliday Simpson

For a Stock Exchange under pressure to police its members effectively this affair had almost all the worst ingredients. It was long drawn out, having its origins in 1978 and only ending in 1983. It involved not only the brash provincial stockbrokers, Halliday Simpson, but Arbuthnot Latham, one of the City Accepting Houses, the most trusted of merchant banks. It also involved risk to Unit Trusts which were managed by Sir Trevor Dawson to the extent of £50 million of investment in 14 trusts, whose units were owned by 41 000 people. The only good thing for the City was that losses to the Unit Trusts turned out to be negligible. It involved two suicides, that of Colin Russell-Jones in 1978 and of Sir Trevor Dawson in 1983; and, finally, it involved behaviour so flagrantly and persistently contrary to the Stock Exchange rules that six partners of Halliday Simpson were banned for life by the Exchange, a sentence of unprecedented severity.

The process by which the affair came to light was gradual and indirect, and the longer investigations continued, the worse the offences that were publicly revealed or hinted at. The story began with the unease of the director of the £15 million Chieftain Unit Trust Group, Malcolm Potts, about the activities of his Investment Manager, Ian Hazeel. Hazeel was responsible for selecting the shares Unit Trust funds should be invested in, and for overseeing the personal share dealings of other Chieftain employees. A well recognized danger is that dealers at Unit Trust Investment Offices may exploit their positions for personal gain. Since Unit Trusts manage £6 billion or so in small savings for 4.5 million investors, their dealings generate huge commission income from brokers – perhaps £2 million a year. The brokers seek that business by researching the merits of particular shares and then arguing their case to the trust manager. The pay-off is the commission earned for sales of shares by the brokers. Cases have arisen in the past where brokers have arranged loans for fund managers to buy shares at a cheaper price ahead of the Trust. This has the effect both of cementing the relationship between fund manager and broker and assuring a continued flow of commission income and boosting the fund manager's personal income at the expense of Unit Trust investors. Neither feature threatens the survival of the Unit Trust, but it probably does decrease profitability and may lead to inefficiency in promoting overdependence on a particular broker – brokers tend increasingly to specialize in different lines of shares. It is plainly an abuse of the fiduciary obligations of the fund manager to the Unit Trust investors.

Potts' concern about Hazeel in 1978 was the result of the Stock Exchange enquiry into Brokers, Burge and Company, the senior partners of which were later criticized after enquiries into the activities of partner Colin Russell-Jones, who was found dead at the foot of Beachy Head in 1978. The Piccadilly Unit Trust Group was also investigated, and the Fraud Squad passed their report on Burge to the DPP in 1981. In 1978 Hazeel was evidently able to satisfy Potts and he remained in his post, but in August 1980 the Fraud Squad gave Potts evidence that Hazeel had dealt in the same shares for himself and for the Trust. Hazeel was fired. In 1981 Potts received further information on Hazeel concerning his personal account dealings with Halliday Simpson, which Potts passed on to the Stock Exchange, which in turn started its own investigations into Halliday Simpson. Its enquiry took ten months to complete, until Christmas 1981.

The senior partner of Halliday Simpson was David Garner, a self-made man who took the Manchester based stockbrokers to considerable success. He had a predilection for the company of the well-connected and titled, and was much involved in show jumping, where he was reported to be one of the three leading organizers of the sport. His financial empire included the insurance, transportation, promoting and sponsorship of horses and show jumping, besides directorships of private and two publicly quoted companies. He promoted Halliday Simpson vigorously, marketing new share issues, many of which were successful, though others went rapidly from boom to bust. The last and most spectacular was Kitchen Queen which went public in 1978, rapidly acquired two other companies, Knott Mill and Moben, and then moved from a profit forecast of £1.5 million to a substantial loss and a bank rescue operation. In Manchester the stock broking firm was a great success, running a series of investment seminars and a share tipping column in the *Manchester Evening News*.

The Stock Exchange investigation eventually showed that these were not the only bases of Halliday Simpson Partners' success. Six partners were banned for life in July 1982 for gross misconduct, three more suspended for several months, and one censured. The key accusation was that Halliday Simpson had maintained an 'open account' to which deals were booked without a client being named and which was used to transfer money to an investment director by inventing non-existent purchases. They were also accused of buying shares for resale to clients at a profit to themselves, misrepresenting the prices at which deals were struck, and distributing open account profits by selling stock at below market price. In sum, they had abused their position as brokers to make money personally rather than for their clients.

It was Halliday Simpson's involvement with Arbuthnot Latham that widened the scandal. The key figure here was the Investment Division Manager, Sir Trevor Dawson, who was responsible in all for some £140 million, including 14 unit trusts. He was the epitome of the blue-blooded banker: Harrow, Sandhurst and the Scots Guards, rising to the rank of Major and very much a public figure at Arbuthnot, though never Chairman. The Stock Exchange enquiry report said that it was the practice for share purchase orders from Sir Trevor to be put on Halliday Simpson's open account. When the share price rose significantly the stock would be booked down to one of the investment funds run by Dawson at a higher price. Dawson was hence evidently as guilty as Halliday Simpson partners of abuse of his position, and far worse, he was at the heart of the City establishment and responsible in a senior position for unit trust investment. The Fraud Squad was in after a copy of the report on Halliday Simpson went to the DPP. At the same time the DPP had on his desk a report from the Fraud Squad about the affairs of Chieftain Unit Trust, where the Halliday Simpson enquiries had started. It seemed that similar irregularities had taken place there and Chieftain began legal proceedings against its former investment manager, Ian Hazeel, claiming damages. There was, then plenty of evidence that existing regulation of small savers' funds in unit trusts was ineffective, and more urgency was given to the Gower Report on Investor Protection commissioned by the Department of Trade and the Stock Exchange.

Sir Trevor Dawson was suspended in mid-1981 along with another Arbuthnot executive, Michael Barrett, and subsequently resigned. What his ultimate fate in the City would have been it is hard to say. He was found dead in his Belgravia home in February 1983 with a plastic bag over his head. A coroner's jury subsequently determined that he had died by his own hand hours before life assurance policies in the favour of his wife were due to expire. The companies agreed to pay out a total of £137500. In letters to his wife, from whom he was estranged, he expressed his concern for their 26 year old spastic son, saying 'I have got no other choice if you and Michael are to have any freedom'.

*Hedderwick Stirling Grumbar*

The merger between the stockbroking firms of Hedderwicks and Quilter Hilton Goodison was announced in March 1981 for implementation the following month. Both firms specialized in private clients' portfolios and it was recognized that amalgamation would give them a powerful position in this sector, with combined business of some £750 million. Discussions on the terms of the merger were to be tidied up, and Touche Ross, the accountants, to report to Quilter in preparation for it. The senior partner in Quilter was, and is, Sir Nicholas Goodison, Chairman of the Stock Exchange.

Hours before the merger was implemented Hedderwick was hammered on the Stock Exchange for being unable to meet its debts. Touche Ross had discovered problems the previous day, which turned out to centre upon a £1.5 million debt owed to Hedderwicks by a Manchester based licensed dealer in securities, Farrington Stead. The crisis arose when more than £1 million of gilt-edged stock, which was being held by Hedderwicks as security for loans to Farringtons, was sold by mistake and the proceeds sent to Farringtons. This was spotted on the Tuesday preceding the Friday when the Hedderwick Quilter merger was due. Quilter gave Hedderwick until noon on Friday to clear the matter up, but it was unable to do so and was, therefore, hammered.

The object of the liquidator of Hedderwicks then became, besides realizing the available assets, to extract the approximately £2 million owed by Farrington. The chances of success were diminished when two of the four shareholders named on Company records filed for bankruptcy in May, and it became apparent that a third was a sleeping partner who had participated little in the dealer's business. The final shareholder was Agnello de Souza, who until 10 April 1981 was Manager of Hedderwick's Gilts Settlement Department. Hedderwick's senior partner confirmed that two of its gilts partners had provided references when Farrington Stead applied for its dealer's licence. Proceedings were started against Souza claiming a breach of duty to Hedderwicks, and an injunction issued over £300 000 held in the Chemical Bank. A creditors' meeting later in May was told that no more than a quarter of the £2 million owed by Farrington was expected to be recovered. However, subsequently de Souza settled the liquidator's claims against him for £375 000. The liquidator initiated an action against Hedderwick's accountants, Ernst and Whinney, for negligence, and remained optimistic about ultimately paying out 100 pence in the £1. A suit against Quilters was also being contemplated, since the liquidator claimed that Quilters had acquired a good deal of business from Hedderwicks as a result of the liquidation. This was finally settled in April 1983 with a payment of £150 000 by Quilter, representing the costs incurred by the liquidators in taking care of clients subsequently taken on by Quilter.

Another £100 000 was obtained by the liquidator in an out-of-Court settlement in April 1982 from a former gilts dealing partner of Hedderwicks, who had left at the end of 1978. After a 15-month enquiry by the Exchange it was alleged that he had acted in 'a disgraceful manner for personal gain' and he was expelled from the Exchange. The claim was that he had made profits on dealing in gilts which were kept secret from the other partners, and it was these monies that the liquidator had sought.

The affair might seem relatively trivial, but it was the first time a major broking firm had crashed since the secondary Banking and Property collapse of 1974, and the close involvement of the Stock Exchange Chairman was scarcely good for his image. The Chairman of Hedderwicks, Wallis Hunt, commented soon after its collapse:

I am sad about what has happened and I feel some resentment. After Ralph Hedderwick resigned as chairman last year someone had to do the job, and there was no reason to suppose that there were any problems. It all happened so suddenly. The best thing that can happen to us as partners is to be cleared to work as employees of

Stock Exchange firms. Then we can help our old clients and have a source of income.[39]

But surely it might be said that there were good reasons to suspect trouble: a gilts partner expelled in infamous circumstances, not long earlier, a current gilts partner with an over-cosy relationship with what turned out to be an exceedingly dubious licensed dealer in securities, and accountants that failed to spot the vital weaknesses. Hunt concluded that 'the moral is that one has got to organise oneself so that one has got eyes in the back of one's head'. Scarcely. The moral for the Stock Exchange, here as elsewhere, was more rapid and continuous disclosure of the activities of those with dealing responsibilities, but it was not a moral the Exchange cared to draw. Far better trust a chap's integrity and judgement.

## Gower

The difficulty in presenting the results of Professor Gower's lengthy investigations in the mid 1980s is that they have been plainly overtaken by events and that what was presented in the report in 1984 as a blueprint for reorganization and improvement in investor protection was in fact a political exercise by the Government, designed to manoeuvre City institutions into recognizing the need for formal public accountability. The Conservative Government, even one led in this sector by such redoubtable figures as Margaret Thatcher and Norman Tebbit, cannot easily afford to take an aggressive stance to the City, yet there seems little doubt that Ministers became convinced that the traditional systems of informal regulation absolutely required elimination and replacement by more effective and more publicly-accountable bodies with State backing. On the degree of State control necessary there seems to have been genuine doubt for some time, but there was no doubt, as was made increasingly public by ministers, that if the City did not reform itself, the State would step in to do the job.

The situation in 1979–81, in the Government's first term of office, was thus one of mounting concern at the ineffectiveness of City controls on abuses and the recognition of and commitment to the internationalization of the City in the banking, insurance and securities fields. It was evident that the traditional closed shops and privileges would have to go, and in the case of the Stock Exchange the Office of Fair Trading suit against it was the first indication of the Government's determination to have real reform. It was, however, a slow remedy, with long negotiations and lengthy preparation of the case by both sides, and events proved too pressing to allow this to remain the chosen instrument of reform. Gower was set to work on investor protection during the same period with, it seems in retrospect, a similar object in view. Before reporting finally, he consulted very widely with all the City institutions, producing an interim report in 1982. The aim of this exercise from the Government's point of view at any rate, was to prompt serious thought on reform and investor protection by the relevant bodies, to gear up public debate, and to mobilize City opinion to consider more than token changes.

It was soon obvious that opinion on reforms varied very widely among the various bodies, that many in the same sector had strong objections to being incorporated into any single regulatory body for that sector (e.g. the Stock Exchange and the

Licensed Dealers in Securities in respect of securities regulation). Most of all, a great roar of commitment to self-regulation went up, with the numbers of potential and actual self-regulatory bodies proliferating by the month. Everyone wanted to manage their own affairs, were horrified at the suggestion that they might cooperate in doing so with vulgar and/or ignorant outsiders, and professed earnest willingness either to improve public disclosure, enforcement and investigation procedures and sanctions if the body already existed, or to form a self-regulating association to do so if it did not. All were agreed that anything was better than State intervention and direct control by some board nominated by the Department of Trade and Industry (DTI). Gower did, however, serve the purpose of the Government who appointed him, since he demonstrated both the cacophony of the responses to regulation in the City, and the impossibility of achieving self-regulation for all, and public credibility in its effectiveness.

The Government increased the political pressure markedly with the deal with the Stock Exchange in 1983, which rapidly gained the fervent attention of City institutions as the rush began to secure a place in the new order after the big bang. This in turn forced a recognition that in this very much larger, more public and internationally-exposed order, traditional self-regulation would have to be substantially modified to achieve public credibility. This left the way open for Norman Tebbit to bring forward the bill in early 1985 to all but create a British counterpart to the SEC, but with the language of the bill still paying lip service to self-regulation and local institutional responsibility.

While Gower reads like a technical review by an academic of investor protection, its function was hence political, as a catalyst to change from informal self-regulation to formal public regulation and for this reason the detail of the report need not concern us here. Gower was in no doubt about the necessity for his reforms:

> unless my proposals are implemented essentially on the lines proposed, further serious scandals undermining public and international confidence are, in my view, inevitable. If they are implemented, scandals would not be wholly prevented, but I believe that they would be fewer and that when they occurred less irremediable damage would be suffered.[40]

The basic principle of his proposals was that anyone involved in the investment business should be governed by a self-regulatory body recognized by the Department of Trade, or be under the direct control of the Department itself, and that the conduct of investment business without registration either with such a body or with the Department of Trade would be illegal. In his interim report he envisaged four such self-regulatory bodies, but this produced such howls of protest by established bodies at the ignominy of being forcibly associated with upstart newcomers that the final report suggested merely working through existing and emergent bodies, and giving an enhanced role to the Council for the Securities Industry (CSI) in monitoring the effectiveness of self-regulatory bodies and liaising with the Department of Trade, which, in default of a Securities Commission, which Gower believed to be the rational solution, would be required to exercise overall supervision.

In a comprehensive report a large number of sensible and needed suggestions were made for amending legislation and regulation to control abuses in a variety of fields, but the essential issues raised for present purposes were the role of the State, either directly or through a statutory commission, and the number and method of working of the self-regulatory bodies. Gower proposed that affiliation to such bodies be determined by the nature of the business conducted rather than the nature of the professional training involved. This shed yet further doubt on self-regulation on the Gower basis as a means of effective control of abuses. With a large number of self-regulatory bodies, albeit now under formal sanctioning and required to come up to minimum standards, there would be difficulty in exercising overall supervision, and the CSI, as an umbrella body formed to govern and enhance the standing of the securities industry in general in the 1970s, but without either teeth or determination, was not an ideal choice politically to exercise a supervisory role. Standards, expectations and capacities in the various bodies would be hence likely to vary from the efficient and determined to the lax and incompetent, and with the CSI standing between them and the DTI, the chances of Gower's optimism in controlling the incidence and impact of scandals in the future seemed slight. If there were to be self-regulation as a result of the acrimony surrounding Gower's interim report and subsequent consultations, it looked as if the necessary framework would have to be very strict and the numbers of recognized bodies small – in short Gower's first proposal for four such bodies was a sensible and practical one. If this was unacceptable, as was the case, the solution was not, as Gower then proposed, to let a hundred self-regulatory bodies bloom (or moulder), but greatly to reduce their significance, and to enhance the role of the State, whether by a commission or directly through the DTI.

This implication was made the more plain by the consequences of the deal on the Stock Exchange in 1983 and the impending big bang in 1986, and it would seem that it was increasingly born in upon Norman Tebbit as he revised the drafts of his white paper on investor protection in the latter part of 1984. During this time increasingly unequivocal statements were made by DTI Ministers to the effect that, if the City did not police itself, it should be in no doubt that Government would step in decisively to do the job. When the white paper came, it did not resolve the issues, but looked more like a calculated risk, with perhaps sufficient reserve powers to act decisively in the future if necessary. As in Gower, existing self-regulatory bodies were to be recognized and given formal status, but supervision of these bodies was to be exercised by two State boards, The Securities and Investment Board (SIB) covering securities and The Marketing of Investments Board (MIB) covering life assurance and unit trusts. They are, however, to be housed in the same building, and the Government was explicit that it would not object to the merger of the two boards in the future if appropriate. Membership of the boards was to be of relevant practitioners, but both the Bank of England and the DTI were to have rights to vet members.

A number of criticisms were made of the detailed provisions of the white paper, for example, that it explicitly excluded investor protection for some items which had been the bases of recent abuses, such as leasing, and collectables such as postage stamps and gemstones, but as in the case of Gower, what is of concern here is the overall balance of proposed control. A good deal of the undergrowth in Gower seemed to have been cut away, and substantial powers of supervision, intervention and investigation given to the SIB and MIB, with the State able to exercise control of membership of these boards, and so ensure their competence. It looked, at least in prospect, not unlike a British SEC, but commentators were quick to point out that the flexibility of the new arrangements left a great deal of responsibility upon the shoulders of chairmen of the boards, and especially upon that of the SIB.

Not only would the chairmen have to be alert to new abuses and to any laxness on the part of the bottom-tier self-regulatory bodies, but they would have to manage political relations between the State board or boards and the self-regulatory bodies, know when to exercise polite but firm pressure for them to come up to scratch, and when to realize that improvement was unlikely and so take thorough and determined action independently through the board. This political relationship had another side, and it is there that Norman Tebbit's calculation is displayed. For if a self-regulatory body is persistently inadequate at its task, it stands the risk of direct intervention by the Board, the DTI or the Secretary of State, and hence would become less and less significant. The judgement in the white paper would thus appear to be an attempt to give self-regulatory bodies enough scope to gain public (and board) acceptance if they are vigorous and effective as defenders of investors' interests, but to allow the boards enough powers to condemn them to oblivion within a few years if they are inert. True, the OFT will have power to vet the rules of new self-regulatory bodies, and promptly announced the formation of a new unit to do this, a move which did not endear it to City institutions in the throes of re-organizing their rules to prepare for the big bang. Whether the new regime as a whole will work, however, will depend upon the ability of the boards to monitor self-regulatory agencies properly, which will depend in turn on adequate funding and staffing, adequate levels of competence, and determination among members of the boards, and determined, perhaps even zealous, leadership by the chairmen. The pattern proposed is not nearly as radical as that which overtook Lloyds, in large part because the market is much more fragmented, and the Stock Exchange itself is only one forum in it. The risks of the reformed system falling apart, and the problems of monitoring success are hence proportionately greater, and they are made greater still when the challenges of the institutional and market changes following the big bang are considered, which is yet to happen.

When the choice of the first Chairman of the SIB was announced a few weeks after the publication of the white paper it was given some acclaim even by exacting commentators. Sir Kenneth Berrill began his financial career as bursar of Kings College, Cambridge, moved into investment trusts, and then into Whitehall as head of the Government Economic Service, and then to the Central Policy Review Staff (think tank). In 1981 he became Chairman of stockbrokers Vickers da Costa, and effective manager of the £2 billion Universities pension fund. He also became a nominated member of Lloyds Council after the reforms there.

The most important of these posts for his new job was undoubtedly his position at Vickers da Costa, which was taken over by the major US bank Citicorp in 1982 in one of the earliest moves by an American institution to position itself for participation in a reformed stock market. Citicorp also took over the major brokers Scrimgeour Kemp Gee, and in February 1985 took over the discount house of Seccombe Marshall and Campion, the Bank of England's brokers for 60 years. It was an indication of the scale of penetration that the Bank was allowing for outsiders, and also of the scale of activity that was contemplated by Citicorp. Berrill's expectation at the time of the Vickers–Citicorp deal was that expansion on the share dealing side would result in a worldwide non-stop 24-hour operation which would involve massive investment in expertise and technology.[41] The scale of these developments and the market advantages they are expected to bring are likely to reduce the number of main London stockbroking firms from 80 to 20, probably only 10–12 of them expanding while the rest remain small and specialized. At a Phillips and Drew seminar in 1983 the Chief Executive of the Natwest Bank echoed these views, saying that financial diversification, with securities dealing, retail and merchant banking, and other financial services, such as unit trusts and life insurance, being managed by large financial conglomerates with banks at their centre would spread worldwide, and then only 10 to 12 global entities would survive and become profitable.[42] Walter Wriston, until 1984 the Chairman and much the dominant figure at Citicorp, was similarly in no doubt.

> I couldn't say strongly enough that the global marketplace has moved from rhetoric to reality . . . the marriage of telecommunications and computers has really created something new under the sun . . . what it means is basically that there is no place to hide. There is no separation between foreign and domestic markets . . . it is a matter of almost total indifference to our chief financial executive whether he raises $200 million in London or New York or any other good place. That was not true as recently as five years ago.[43]

While allowing for small firms to survive as specialists, Wriston clearly gives pride of place to the 'big hitters' who can adapt and invest and compete, and prophesied a considerable number of casualties in London after the big bang.

Wriston was by no means alone in his views, even if perhaps he was more forceful in expressing them and drawing his conclusions than others, and it was in recognition of the truth of them that almost every jobber and broker of substance in London sought protective association in one large financial institution or another in the months after the July 1983 agreement on the Stock Exchange. The fallout, however, will be considerable, and whether or not it involves large numbers going out of business, it will certainly involve a great deal of restructuring of businesses and job mobility, and it will result in the creation of altogether new organizations trading at a great intensity with very high turnovers. The point for Berrill to note as Chairman of the SIB is hence that the impending changes do not just involve better policing of the old institutions, but dealing with the period of reorganization in 1986 and thereafter, and policing new institutions which combine activities that have up to now been largely separated among specialist companies, so creating a variety of conflicts of interests, and trading at a level of financial turnover that would rapidly magnify to very great proportions any significant undetected errors or improprieties.

Some of the early consequences of this were apparent even in 1984 and 1985. There was evident concern by employees of brokers and jobbers about their job security, and equal concern among incoming big banks to buy up prime talent to try to secure their competitive position. Analysts and specialists left brokers not in singles but in teams, and the salary figures on offer increased dramatically. At the same time, three of the main clearers bought stakes in stockbroking firms, with the implication that in due course securities business would be channelled through them as subsidiaries, so cutting out the range of brokers who had in the past picked up some of this business. Lloyds, the odd one out in not having bought a broker, started the process by axing 100 brokers from its lists, some of whom had worked for Lloyds and its customers for years.

In the meantime the Stock Exchange itself remained for months deeply divided over the new rules for membership after 1986, and in particular over the costs for membership. What was in fact happening was well identified by leading stockbrokers, one of whom said: 'This is getting ludicrous. What is being asked is just how much we need to pay to bribe the minority so that we may open the Exchange to outsiders.' Another commented that smaller brokers 'will find the climate (after 1986) very cold, and some may decide to close, which is why they are holding out for what amounts to a once-and-for-all redundancy payment'.[44] The way in which this was to be exacted was by existing members allocating their shares and vote to the new members at a substantial price. Given the need, as at Lloyds, for a 75% majority vote on the new rules, those who felt themselves in a marginal position under the future regime, were in a strong position to exact favourable terms.

The terms eventually recommended to the Stock Exchange Council for approval in mid-1985 divided each member's share into five and required existing members of the Exchange to hold at least 50 new shares and newcomers to buy 100. The Exchange intended to exercise taps, so that a maximum price of £2000 a share would operate, though supply looked likely to greatly exceed demand. As a lump sum entry fee for newcomers an absolute maximum of £500 000 was proposed, with most paying far less than this. None of these arrangements amounted to an insurance policy covering the likely demise of weaker firms when the big outsiders gained membership. The response of the Exchange has continued to be one of preoccupation by members with the defence of their established interests and privileges, and its reaction to the big bang one of internal dissent and anxiety.

This was plainly evident in the votes on the Reform of the Exchange in June 1985. Outside membership of the Exchange was overwhelmingly approved by 3248 votes to 681, but the second vote on the method recommended by the Stock Exchange Council to admit outsiders was approved by 2890 votes to 1035, a majority just under the 75% required to make a constitutional change. The consequences of this success by what came to be known as the rebels, who believed their Stock Exchange shares to be worth more than the maximum £2000 each allowed in the terms of the proposal, were almost inevitably limited to causing confusion, however. The Exchange, having accepted that outsiders should be admitted, had to pitch its terms so that they would seek admission, and with every passing month developments took place which increased the attractiveness for the big American players of operating outside the Exchange. Three months before the vote the merchant bank of Robert Fleming was dealing in over-the-counter stocks, concentrating in electricals. With prices on British Telecom identical to those on offer on the Exchange, but net of commission and having paid the penalties of stamp duty and differences in VAT liability, there was a clear, if so far limited, challenge. With more than 60% of trading in ICI shares said by mid-1985 to be taking place outside the Exchange, the challenge was also a potentially substantial one. The lesson from the deregulatory big bang in the United States some years earlier was that commission rates went into a devastating downward spiral, which left little room for the small specialist operator traditionally characteristic of the British Stock

Market. This was a lesson increasingly impressed upon members of the British Stock Exchange.

Perhaps the greatest visible challenge, however, came from the speed with which competition to provide price information systems for the Stock Market increased. The Stock Exchange's own attempts to introduce its computerized instantaneous price display system, SEAQ, referred to above, proved costly to develop, and was largely responsible for the Exchange's 1984 profits falling to £400 000 from the 1983 level of £5.2 million. With the second stage development costs of the system likely to be £30 million, and the prospect of competition from Reuters and from the US service Instinet, as well as from NASDAQ, the risks of going it alone in automation were formidable. Just how formidable became evident shortly after the muddled vote on constitutional changes, when Reuters and Instinet announced that they were negotiating, to join forces. Both sides said that, if they did not reach agreement, they would compete for the UK market. Given the Stock Exchange's lack of experience in the field and the international dominance of the others, the large costs of setting up the system, the need for it to be both reliable and as good and comparable in range and quality to those in the US, and the clear danger of the Stock Exchange losing its dominant position in the UK stock market if rival automated quotation systems became established side by side, some accommodation by the Exchange seemed the only prudent course.

Things look much more promising at NASDIM, with membership rising rapidly and expected to double over 1985–6, and with a view of the new market and investor protection legislation that was largely positive. As a rank outsider only a few years previously, NASDIM in 1985 was desperately keen for respectability, and prepared to pay the price in terms of strict supervision and disclosure. Not only does the new NASDIM require all members to pass a fit and proper person test of membership, encompassing professional training and experience and financial soundness, but enforcement of membership rules in the new regime is stringent. Members are required to maintain a client account, adequate financial resources on a scale laid down by the association to protect against market downturn, and professional indemnity and employee fidelity insurance are required at a minimum level of £250 000 or three times annual revenue, whichever is the greater. As an additional protection to clients, a compensation fund is managed by a levy on members. Most striking, however, are the provisions for enforcement, which include not only an initial demonstration of soundness on entry and an annual check that a firm is in compliance with NASDIM rules by the firm's auditors, but submission to random checks on compliance by auditors and specialist inspectors, and, on top of that, the possibility of further random checks on compliance at any time by a NASDIM officer and a specialist inspector.

Meanwhile, the Exchange itself struggled on in 1984 and 1985, cajoling agreement on new rules, introducing a new surveillance division to consolidate and improve the monitoring of deals, and pressing ahead slowly with the great technical revolution of the Stock Exchange automated quotation system, which, in its complete form, should give a level of computerized accessibility and monitoring capacity close to that of NASDAQ. More will be said in a later chapter of the implications of the new financial institutions, the range of which has not been fully identified here. For the present the task of the new investment boards will be a stiff one, for they will have to cope, not only with improving on past habits in the securities industry (and there is little likelihood that fast operators will disappear during a period of rapid change and expansion and a bullish stock market), but also with the short- and medium-term fallout of the big bang and its likely casualties, and with the long-term challenge of new trading patterns which pose problems that are not only partly unknown and unexplored, but which carry greater risks because of the much increased scale of operation over those in the past.

Attempts at the reform of securities regulation and investor protection have involved a good deal of muddling and fudging and a great deal of resistance to effective public regulation, which the white paper does not unequivocally break with. Everything depends, therefore, on the willingness of the new boards to exercise their supervisory powers effectively and to demand additional ones if necessary, and upon the Government to grant them. The conditions have been laid by the variety of developments since 1979 for the real reform of the Stock Exchange and the securities industry, and a potential institution for achieving reform mooted. Whether real reform ensues is a political matter for the future, but if it does not, it seems certain that the scale of future scandals will dwarf anything seen in the recent past. This is a matter to which we shall return in a later chapter.

## Notes

1. *Review of Investor Protection*, Command 9125, HMSO, 1984. Gower's earlier working paper, *Report on Investor Protection*, was published by HMSO in 1982.
2. See *Stock Exchange Year book*, 1984.
3. *Stock Exchange Quarterly*, December 1984, p. 8.
4. *Stock Exchange Quarterly*, September 1984, p. 23.
5. According to T. Congdon, Why Britain's foreign nest egg quadrupled, *The Times*, 14 December 1983, net assets increased from £17126 million in the fourth quarter of 1979 to £56838 million in the first quarter of 1983.
6. *1983 Report*, HMSO, 1984, p. 10.
7. *The Times*, June 1984.
8. See the *Sunday Times*, 19 August 1984.
9. *The Times* Business News, editorial, January 1984.
10. *The Times*, October 1984.
11. *Stock Exchange Quarterly*, September 1984, p. 20.
12. Ibid., p. 21.
13. T. Levene, Dealers licence rules o.k., *Sunday Times*, 12 September 1982.
14. For an account of some aspects of this see M.J. Clarke, *Fallen Idols*, Junction Books, 1981, esp. pp. 112–20.
15. See, e.g. N. Green, Crisis in the Monopolies and Mergers Commission: Anderson Strathclyde and other recent developments, *Business Law Review*, 1983, p. 303.
16. B.A.K. Rider, Self-regulation: The British approach to policing conduct in the Securities business with particular reference to the role of the City panel on takeovers and mergers in the regulation of insider training, *Journal of Comparative Corporate Law and Securities Regulation*, 1978, pp. 319–348.
17. A discussion and further references may be found in, e.g. M.J. Clarke, *Fallen Idols*, op. cit., p. 199 ff., in B.A.K. Rider, op. cit. and in D. Sugarman, The regulation of insider dealing, in B. Rider (ed.) *The Regulation of the British Securities Industry*, Oyez, 1979. Although the contemporary evidence clearly indicates the ineffectiveness of the Stock Exchange's

self-regulatory machinery, this is not to suggest that matters had always been thus. For an illuminating account of the strength of stock market self-regulation in the mid nineteenth century see R.B. Ferguson, Commercial expectations and the guarantee of law: Sales transactions in mid nineteenth century England, in G.R. Rubin & D. Sugarman (eds.), *Law, Society & Economy 1750–1914: Essays in the History of English Law*, Professional Books, 1984.

18.   See D. Milman, The Griffiths Report: invitation to a concert party, *Company Lawyer*, Vol. 5, No. 6 pp. 284–5, and *The Times*, 10 August 1984. Also of interest in this connection is Rio Tinto Zinc's attempt to buy Enterprise Oil when it was denationalized in 1984. See J. Davies, The shares coup that stunned ministers, *The Times*, June 1984.

19.   See *The Times*, 2 April 1980.

20.   See the *Sunday Times*, P. Wheatcroft, Takeover panel in trial of strength, the *Sunday Times*, 6 April 1980.

21.   *The Times*, 12 and 13 June 1980.

22.   *The Times*, 5 December 1980.

23.   *The Times*, 18 April 1981.

24.   *The Times*, 30 April 1981.

25.   *The Times*, May 1981.

26.   *The Times*, 9 May 1981.

27.   *The Times*, 1 May 1981.

28.   *The Sunday Times*, 6 September 1981.

29.   The *Sunday Times*, 1 September 1983.

30.   The *Sunday Times*, 11 September 1983.

31.   *Accountancy*, November 1983.

32.   R. Pullen, Goldfields: Mr Oppenheimer shows his hand, *The Times*, 13 February 1980.

33.   *The Times*, 14 April 1980.

34.   *The Times*, February 1980.

35.   J. Bell, Dawn raids: The City fails to police itself, *The Times*, 13 July 1980.

36.   *The Times*, 22 July 1980.

37.   *The Times*, 5 and 6 August 1980.

38.   For additional comments on the affair, see S.R. Coxford, The problems of regulating substantial acquisitions of shares, *Company Lawyer*, Vol. 3, No. 5, p. 200.

39.   The *Sunday Times*, 17 May 1981.

40.   See report of the press conference on publication and summary of the report, *The Times*, January 1984.

41.   See his comments in *The Times*, 9 November 1983. Mark Weinberg, Chairman of Hambros Life Assurance, was appointed part-time and unpaid Chairman of the organizing committee of the Marketing of Investments Board in March 1985. The contrast with Berrill, who became full-time, and the initiative to establish only an organizing committee was another clear pointer to the likelihood that the two boards, which shared the same premises, would in due course be amalgamated into one. Weinberg was not likely to be short of work in his new job, however, with considerable acrimony surrounding the commitment of the Government to forcing disclosure of rates of commission by insurance brokers. This was particularly difficult because rates traditionally varied widely and were calculated differently as between companies using tied brokers and those working with independents. Sorting out a clear and publicly intelligible set of rules when insurance is involved as an aspect of so many other financial transactions – personal loans, mortgages, investments, pension plans – looked like being formidably difficult. For a more detailed review of the issues, see R. Thompson's article in the *Times*, 1 May 1981.

42.   See the *Sunday Times*, 20 November 1983.

43.   *The Times*, 14 December 1984.

44.   *The Times*, 13 February 1985.

# 5

---

# Other Reforms: Tax avoidance, insolvency fair trading

## Introduction

The last three chapters have looked at recent reforms in three areas of the City conveniently circumscribed to a large extent by traditional City institutions. I have argued that three sorts of pressures have coincided to achieve change: scandals, changes in the market for the services involved and, especially, increased international competition, and government enthusiasm for reform and 'modernization'. In addition, I have maintained that the traditional City practice of managing the regulation of their own affairs privately and informally among members has, to a substantial extent, given way to formal and public modes of accountability, although with varying extents of success, and there has been substantial resistance to these changes. I would be misrepresenting the scope of change, however, if I confined myself to the three prominent examples of banking, Lloyds insurance and the stock market. Similar changes have been taking place in other areas also, which are less easy to categorize immediately as part of the reform of the City, but which are none the less important aspects of it. They should be understood as part of the need for a government committed to the extension and entrenchment of free market principles and to a wider participation by the population in the institutions of capitalism to ensure, as I have argued earlier, that those doing so particularly for the first time and on limited means are protected against undue risks and fraudulent exploitation. More generally, this can be expressed as the requirement for the new participants to experience the acceptable rather than the unacceptable face of capitalism and to draw therefrom the desired conclusions that the system is benign, rational and personally and more widely rewarding, rather than that it is a jungle infested with predators large and small, of infinite ingenuity and total lack of scruples.

Of the four topics considered in this chapter, two deal with this issue directly, while the others deal with some of the new means employed to achieve and sustain public confidence. I shall deal first with tax avoidance, traditionally a preserve of the rich, which by established convention in Britain allows those particularly with landed wealth to pass on their fortunes substantially intact, despite the provisions of income and capital transfer taxes. Here two key political developments have led to major changes in the legal administration of tax avoidance. First, the Rossminster tax avoidance schemes, developed in the 1970s, helped to make avoidance available to those whose wealth was less great, and promised to set a very bad example to those newly enriching themselves by 'entrepreneurial' activities. Secondly, the Vestey family, having made its fortune in the latter part of the last century and the early part of this, and subsequently having avoided paying all but minimal taxes upon it, won what might be called a traditional avoidance case in 1979, and were given wide publicity as a result of a detailed investigation of their remarkable tax-free history by a *Sunday Times* journalist.[2] Important changes in tax law followed, not only in plugging the loophole the Vesteys had taken advantage of, but much more remarkably by the Law Lords in a series of decisions introducing a policy change on the appraisal of tax avoidance schemes, which makes their legal acceptability generally much more doubtful. A clean-up, then, to prevent the hoi polloi usurping the privileges of the rich, as well as an embarrassed curtailment of the excesses of one super-rich family.

The second area requiring government attention, insolvency, has proved much more diffiult to deal with. The problem here has been sustained publicity, perhaps most easily identified with the BBC's successful investigative series *Checkpoint*, which identified rogue directors of companies as predators upon unfortunate customers, creditors, partners and employees. Yet the government has been anxious to encourage the formation of new businesses, and has explicitly suggested that redundancy payments be used for this purpose. It has therefore been reluctant to circumscribe the traditional freedom and privacy of the limited liability company for fear of discouraging worthwhile initiative, while at the same time feeling constrained to do something to curtail villains who move from company to company leaving trails of debt and distraught creditors. Its answer was to commission a major report from a respected liquidator, Sir Kenneth Cork, and in the fullness of Parliamentary time, to legislate – but as we shall see this has not proved at all easy, and a solution looks no nearer in the mid-1980s than it did when the government came to office.

The third topic is the Office of Fair Trading (OFT), a body which has been mentioned on several occasions already in connection with reform, and which has prospered as the government's chosen instrument for improving competitive practices, for the investigation of restrictive practices and taking them to court, and generally seeing that the public gets free market value for money. The OFT, under the able leadership of the Director-General, Sir Gordon Borrie, has played an effective role in various respects. In publicity terms it has come across as the champion of the public interest in ensuring fair trading practices and value for money. It has mounted a long series of investigations detailing and bringing to light restrictive and unfair practices, not only in such obvious targets as the second-hand car trade, but in the professions as well. Finally, it has come to play an increasing role as a public authority in, for example, exercising a formal surveillance over the rules and practices of self-regulatory bodies in the City securities industry, as mentioned in the last chapter.

The final topic is the so-called institutions – pensions, unit trusts and life assurance – which have been referred to in earlier chapters but not fully discussed. It has already been suggested that it is through these bodies, even if in an abstract and distant way, that large sections of the public in post-war Britain have been brought into touch with the City and its workings: for example, interest rate changes are now immediate headline news because of their impact upon mortgage rates. More needs to be said, however, about the implications of the size of the new institutions, their role as guardians of the public – or at any rate, their large and diverse members' and clients' interests – and about their place in the City as institutions representing a mass public of limited means, in contrast to those traditional institutions which have largely comprised the interests of a limited public of substantial means.

## Tax avoidance

Some general comments by way of introduction to this topic have been made above. The importance of it and of the changes in the legal evaluation of avoidance schemes recently can best be appreciated by an account of the Rossminster and Vestey affairs.

*Rossminster*
Rossminster was important for a variety of reasons: first, the extent of its operations, which were estimated potentially to have cost the Inland Revenue £1 billion; secondly, the unprecedented vigour with which the Revenue reacted both in its famous raid in 1979 and in subsequent hearings in the courts and before special commissioners; thirdly, the momentous change of attitude in the Law Lords judgment of March 1981 towards tax avoidance; and finally the involvement of senior members of the Tory party, some of them part of the government, with the threat that they might be called as witnesses at the fraud trial of the principals which threatened for a long time. It is perhaps just to conclude that after Rossminster tax avoidance and inland revenue enforcement will never be the same again.

The central figures in Rossminster were accountants Roy Tucker and Ronald Plummer. After experience in the early 1970s in avoiding tax on behalf of clients, they formed the Rossminster partnership in 1973. The initiative was founded upon a recognition that the imposition of such taxes as capital gains and capital transfer (the substitute for death duties) by Labour governments in the 1960s had created a large market of rich individuals and cash-laden companies eager to outwit the taxman. In the past, tax avoidance had been relatively gentlemanly on both sides: the taxpayer had taken the best advice, and a package was devised to suit his particular circumstances; equally, the Revenue, while it carefully probed the legitimacy of such arrangements, did so through a restrained and decorous procedure, making a sharp distinction between avoidance, that is the management of one's affairs so as to minimize tax liability, and evasion, where fraud was necessarily involved. Avoidance schemes might well be questioned, and if they proved faulty the taxpayer would have a large bill to pay, but this was not taken as implying wrongdoing on his part.

In order to set up novel schemes, tax advisers needed the cooperation of banks, lawyers and an administrative machine, which traditionally they applied for in the appropriate quarters *ad hoc*. Tucker and Plummer's innovation was to create a tax avoidance enterprise that would do the job without outside aid, except for the advice of leading counsel. Then, having perfected a particular scheme, it could be sold not just to one client, but to as many as those whose circumstances warranted it. It became an attractive proposition for all concerned. The client could leave everything to Rossminster, just supplying the details they required and complying with the complex procedures they led him through. His security lay in the high reputation Rossminter acquired for effectiveness, the opinion of leading counsel that Rossminster obtained that the scheme would work, and the commitment by Rossminster that it would provide up to £50 000 to take a test case through the courts if need be. The advantage to Rossminster was up to 20% of the tax saved. The advantage for an increasing range of people in the tax advice field was the commission Rossminster paid them for introducing clients.

Eventually Rossminster produced 13 schemes servicing about 2000 clients, both corporate and individual. They were all ultimately challenged by the Inland Revenue, and Rossminster complained that the Revenue, by demanding strict proof of each document and close adherence to procedure, was dragging out hearings over an average of six weeks each, which implied it would take 120 years to clear them all. This process of slow strangulation, which Tucker complained of in 1980, developed after two spectacular events which brought them into the public eye and which severely weakened Rossminster.

The first was the analysis in the *Sunday Times* in 1977 of one of the early schemes, commodity carry. Lorana Sullivan, in a review of Rossminster in 1979, explains it as follows:[2]

> The aim of the idea was that if you enjoyed an exceptionally high – and therefore penally taxed – income one year, you should theoretically blow the lot on a disastrous commodity speculation. This, needless to say is a sacrifice. In fact the client purchased what are known as commodity straddles, that is the buying and selling of matching commodity futures where any risk should be notional. The major marketing tool for this scheme was leading counsel's opinion provided by Peter Rees Q.C. Ironically, Rees is now Minister of State at the Treasury with special responsibility for personal taxation.
>
> Administratively the star of the show was Tom Benyon (Tory MP for Abingdon), then a founder member of Rossminster with a 2½% intake. To put through the complex performance with its usual discretion Rossminster bought control of an established firm of commodity brokers. Benyon duly went on the board of the firms concerned, E. Bailey & Co., E. Bailey & Co. (Holdings) as well as Avon-grange, the English nominee company which held Bailey for Rossminster's Isle of Man interests. More particularly Benyon was the other partner (together with the client and two

cardboard companies) in the commodity partnerships set up as part of the mechanism of the deals.

As is apparent in this description, the schemes involved a mass of highly intricate and usually temporary relationships between comapnies bought or set up for avoidance purposes, the procedures involved being both an effective smokescreen and essential to achieving technical legality. Sullivan says that the *Sunday Times* looked at some 600 of 1000 or more in compiling its review. Rees and Benyon were not the only Tory MPs connected with Rossminster. More senior in government though less closely involved was John Nott. He was a paid consultant to E. Bailey while it was under Rossminster's control, and a shareholder in an associate company – both matters were recorded by him in the register of MP's interests. His brief was to advise on risky commodity business on the basis of his experience in that field with bankers, S.G. Warburg. Nott said in 1980 that he had no idea, at the time of his work at Bailey, that transactions taking place were part of a tax avoidance scheme. When Nott took up 10% of the Bailey subsidiary it was as part of a reaction to pressure to distance the firm which dealt in sugar, from Rossminster, and after the commodity carry scheme had been reviewed in the *Sunday Times*. He therefore knew about it by then and only took the shares on condition that tax planning be eliminated from future dealings by the company.

The reaction of the Labour administration to the revelations about the scheme was decisive. It introduced retrospective legislation in the Finance Act to ban it, hence giving Rossminster further notoriety.

By this time the Inland Revenue were also alerted, and apparently spent the next two years amassing evidence to deliver a knockout blow. The Revenue applied for search warrants under the 1976 amendment of the 1970 Taxes Management Act which allowed forcible search where fraud was suspected on reasonable grounds by the commissioners, and at 7 a.m. on Friday, 13 July 1979, 60 revenue officials and 30 police officers raided the homes of Benyon, Plummer and Tucker and then went on to Rossminster's offices: they took away 12 van loads of documents. Plummer and Tucker appealed in the High Court that quite irrelevant material such as children's cheque books and passports had been taken, and that the raids involved an abuse of power. They also complained that nearly £2 million had been withdrawn from Rossminster in a month, and withdrawals were still occurring at a high level. The High Court did not agree, and Tucker and Plummer appealed. Lord Denning presided over a court specially convened out of term to hear the case in August. The court decided in Rossminster's favour, with Denning's well known dislike of excessive state power apparently being decisive. It was front page news.[3] He said there had been no comparable case since 1763, when the King's messengers arrested John Wilkes, the prominent radical politician, and seized his papers, and that the revenue had not given enough information as to what the charges were, and a suspected person was entitled to know what he was suspected of. The major problem was that the warrants for the raids only quoted the very general terms of the 1970 Act, and were granted because there was reason to believe that unspecified offences had been committed. The information had been given to the circuit judge who issued the warrants, but the court deciding Rossminster's appeal had not had these facts. Denning also pointed out that the 1976 Amendment to the Act under which the operation had been carried out had been passed (by a Labour administration, M.C.) by a narrow majority, and opposed by some as a possible infringement of the rights of the public. 'Once great power is granted there is a danger of it being abused.'

As happened frequently with Denning's judgments, the Lords did not agree on appeal, and found for the Revenue. By a 4:1 majority led by Lord Wilberforce they accepted[4] the court's obligation to supervise critically, even jealously, the legality of any purported exercise of the powers (in the Acts 1970/6).

> They were guardian of the citizen's right to privacy. But they must do that in the context of the times, i.e. of increasing parliamentary intervention and of the modern power of judicial review. Appeals to eighteenth century precedents of arbitrary action by Secretaries of State, and references to general warrants did nothing to throw light on the issue. Furthermore, while the courts might look critically at legislation that impaired the rights of citizens and should resolve any doubt on interpretation in their favour, it was not part of their duty, or power, to restrict or impede the working of legislation, even unpopular legislation; to do so would be to weaken rather than advance the democratic process.

Evidently Denning's attempt to act as a constitutional court in the absence of a written constitution did not hold up.

In the month between the court of appeal and the House of Lords hearings the Revenue had, as instructed, returned Rossminster's documents. With the success of the final appeal it demanded them back, as Rossminster had been warned it would have a right to, and most were returned. Tucker however failed to return his desk diaries for 1974-7, producing only that for 1978, and it appeared that they had been thrown away in error by a new secretary. For this he was fined £1000 for contempt of court, it being accepted that there was negligence rather than contumely.[5] The importance of the diaries was indicated by Revenue counsel. Since they detailed Tucker's actual movements in the years in question, they could be checked against company records which indicated the dates of meetings of the many Rossminster companies, the minutes of which indicated his often-essential presence. The evidence of the 1978 diary showed that there were a number of cases when Tucker was elsewhere than at such board meetings.

From there on it was downhill for Rossminster. In 1980, besides protesting at the length of time the Revenue was taking to deal with cases, it was forced to issue a letter to all its clients on the 'advance interest scheme', by which tax was avoided by the shuttling of effectively fictitious loans on which equally fictitious interest was paid, saying that the £35 000 fighting fund set up to test the scheme in the courts had been considerably exceeded, and that clients were now on their own. In December the following year a test case involving a former Rossminster employee who had used the scheme came to court and was decided in favour of the Revenue. With these sorts of developments the attractiveness of Rossminster's guarantees to clients of the security of their schemes was badly damaged.

The major blow, however, came in March 1981 when the House of Lords decided unanimously in favour of the Revenue in W.T. Ramsay v. Inland Revenue and Inspector of Taxes v. Rawling.[6] This involved an avoidance arrangement sold principally to about 50 wealthy landowners. What was significant about the Lords' judgment, however, was not that it rejected the scheme on its technical details, but that it attacked the principle of schemes designed solely to avoid tax by artificial means, thus distinguishing between aranging a taxpayer's affairs so as to minimize tax liability within the rules and deliberate artifice to manipulate the rules to avoid liability.

This was an important change to established procedure. In the words of one well-qualified commentator:

> The tax avoiders have traditionally relied on the canons of construction as applied to taxing statutes. The intention of such Acts is found by examination of the words used. Only if a clear intention is found can tax be imposed. There is no equity about tax. Accordingly, it is said, no-one is bound to leave his property at the mercy of the Revenue if he can lawfully escape their grasp.[7]

This strict constructionism and refusal to consider the intention of Parliament in legislating on tax matters was also challenged for the first time by Lord Wilberforce in citing two American cases in his judgment, 'not as authority, but as examples expressed in vigorous and apt language of the process of thought which seems to me not inappropriate for the courts in this country to follow'. This 'process of thought' can be traced back to a Supreme Court decision which looked beyond the literal terms of the tax provision, to apply it only when a business purpose could be identified for it, thereby rejecting the legal form for the sake of reality. This approach in turn was possible in the USA because of the greater freedom allowed to courts there to give weight to the intent of the Legislature as expressed in reports and debates where the Act itself is not clear.[8]

Concurring with Lord Wilberforce, Lord Fraser said that the essential feature of both schemes was that they did not result in any actual loss to the taxpayer. The apparently magic results of creating a tax loss that would not be a real loss was to be brought about by arranging that the scheme included a loss which was allowable for tax purposes and a matching gain that was not chargeable. Lord Wilberforce insisted that the complex series of transactions needed to achieve this must be seen as a whole, and that if they were they plainly resulted in no losses or gains other than payment of fees and expenses to Rossminster, and pointed out that Rossminster's letter to Ramsay was explicit in that it stated that 'the scheme is a pure tax avoidance scheme'.

Although Tucker denied that Rossminster's other schemes would necessarily be threatened, it was clear that the new principle was very wide ranging in its implications. In retrospect, it almost seemed that Rossminster, by turning tax avoidance into big business, had managed to provoke a reaction that would in future make all avoidance much harder. Lord Wilberforce all but explicitly confirmed this: 'While the techniques of tax avoidance progress and are technically improved, the courts are not obliged to stand still. Such immobility must result either in loss of tax, to the prejudice of the tax payers, or to parliamentary congestion, or (most likely) to both.' Such willingness to take initiatives is not common among the Law Lords and still less on tax matters. And as Tucker pointed out, the peculiarity of the consequences of the decision was that it provided a new principle by which to evaluate existing schemes and was thus similar in effect to retrospective legislation. Not that Tucker and Plummer personally had anything particularly to worry about.

At the time of the *Sunday Times* review in 1979, Tucker was in no doubt that Rossminster would not be a lasting affair, and had taken steps to secure his personal fortune: 'We thought it right to get out while we were doing well.' He was not at risk from the 1981 decision, though he admitted that 'it will have a severe effect on a lot of people caught up in the middle', as a result of using Rossminster's schemes.

The matter which remained in doubt for a long period was criminal prosecutions. The raids in 1979 had been undertaken on the basis of suspected fraud, and the Director of Public Prosecution's (DPP) office was substantially involved. No doubt the Revenue saw its main task as eliminating the Rossminster schemes, and was well pleased with the Lords' judgement in Ramsay. Whether it stood to recover much of the £1 billion in tax avoided is unclear. In 1982 rumours appeared in *Private Eye* that a decision on prosecution was imminent, and the magazine looked forward to the cases eagerly, since it seemed likely that Benyon and Rees would be called as witnesses, and conceivably also Nott. As time passed it became more and more evident that little progress towards a decision was being made. Certainly a criminal trial would have been embarrassing to the government, though it is also likely that the complexity of any likely trial, and hence the time and cost and the risk of failure, were significant matters in inclining the DPP to caution.

Although it looked as though Rossminster was both down and out as a result of the moves against it, it recovered sufficiently by 1985 to hit back at the Revenue and the Metropolitan Police. Freed from the problems of defending itself against criminal charges following the Attorney General's statement in June 1983 that none would be brought, Rossminster had evidently devoted its energies to attempting to recover some of its losses. Roy Tucker, commenting on the writ by Rossminster and by himself, Plummer and Benyon, who had stepped down as an MP because of the affair, for £7 million in lost business plus exemplary damages and interest, said that the fight was both for the cash and the principle, because of the gross abuse of executive power by the Revenue (*The Times*, 17 May 1985). Whatever the chances of success of the Rossminster case, there seemed no chance of reversing the underlying change in hostility by the law, the Revenue and the Government to tax avoidance schemes. Legislation to outlaw bond-washing, a somewhat arcane procedure involving the rapid sale and purchase of Government securities, which enabled higher rate taxpayers to obtain liability for Capital Gains Tax at 30% rather than Income tax at 60% on their transactions, was even attacked (by *The Times Business News* editorial, 19 June 1985) as unduly oppressive of the individual and appropriate in its strigency only to institutional dealings, yet it was a measure of the extent to which the Chancellor had given his clear commitment to limit as far as possible tax avoidance schemes.

A further consequence of the Rossminster affair was a government committee chaired by Lord Keith to review the enforcement powers of the Revenue.[9] The Report appeared in 1983, and although it recommended safeguards to protect the public and prevent abuses, and the issuing of search warrants by circuit judges rather than magistrates in cases of tax fraud, it generally supported the powers of search, entry, scrutiny and seizure by the Revenue and Customs and Excise. It also recommended greater cooperation between officers and between the two branches, and greater publicity both for Revenue powers and the safeguards limiting them, and for the naming of tax fraud offenders – traditionally this had been kept private, provided offenders agreed to pay what was owed. It is unclear how many of the detailed Keith recommendations will be implemented and how far this could be done without legislation, but it is plain that, despite the government's predilection for social security fraud, as evidenced for example in the notorious Operation Major in Oxford in 1983,[10] enforcement against tax avoidance has taken on a permanently different complexion as a result of the Rossminster affair. This should not, however, be taken as suggesting that efforts at avoidance have become any less vigorous or even numerous.

Although the Inland Revenue commissioners celebrated their victory in 1981 by vowing to use the decision to attempt to extract capital transfer tax from the estate of Charles Clore, which had been transferred to Jersey rather late in the day via a company called Stype investments, the decision was no panacea. To cite two prominent later examples, the Duke of Devonshire was reported in November 1983 as having been successful in reaching agreement with the Revenue for the establishment of trusts which would ensure the continuity of his estate and provide a model for other members of the landed aristocracy. And in the same month the chancellor intervened with regulation described as 'simple, neat and effective' by *The Times* to eliminate the so-called offshore roll up funds that had been widely used by high taxpayers to covert income into capital, on which the capital gains tax chargeable was much lower than the highest rate of income tax, the main operator of these arrangements readily admitted defeat, but simultaneously Barlow Clowes, a Jersey based investment advisers company, offered a new scheme which it said would achieve the same object. It was scarcely to be expected that Rossminster would be decisive in controlling tax avoidance. The Lords emphasized their support for the long accepted principles of freedom to arrange affairs to minimize tax in their judgement. But it did have the effect of setting down limits and firmly preventing the free for all for which Rossminster had looked like providing the vehicle.

*Vestey*

Coinciding as it did with the Rossminster affair, Philip Knightley's lengthy inquiry in the *Sunday Times* into the long tax avoiding career of the Vestey family in 1980, and its continued defiance of the Inland Revenue, can only have added to the embarrassment on that score. For by the 1980s, far from being men of newly made fortune, as were many of Rossminster's clients, the Vesteys were at the heart of the establishment, on good terms with royalty, particularly through polo and hunting, members of London clubs, owners of substantial estates and reputed to be Britain's wealthiest family. Knightley's claim was that, although the family's fortunes had been founded upon Victorian ascetic entrepreneurship, they were sustained in more recent years by a successful refusal to pay taxes on the greater part of their incomes and wealth.

The Vestey fortune was built up in the latter years of the nineteenth century and the early years of the twentieth on the basis of an early recognition of the revolutionary potential in marketing of cold storage. Before the days of large capacity freezing, meat, poultry and eggs had a brief shelf life and could not be kept safely even over a weekend. Hence their distribution was patchy and reflected more the problems of transportation and storage than the costs of production and distribution. By the 1890s there was a substantial British market for these products, but the major sources of cheap supply in Russia, China and Latin America were too far away to be exploited, except by canning. The Vesteys, already well established then as now in the meat trade (they own the Dewhurst chain of butchers), invested first in freezer plants both in Britain and Argentina and then elsewhere, out of which grew the giant Union Cold Storage. They then invested in refrigerater ships, giving rise to the famous Blue Star Line, and were able to take advantage of cheap supply and therefore satisfy market demand. Most importantly they ensured in time that they owned plant for every stage in the marketing process–abattoirs, docks, freezing plants, warehouses, ships, retail outlets–and that they spread themselves widely wherever cheap meat and eggs could be bought for sale in Europe or the USA. At the same time they maintained ownership and control strictly within the family and were very secretive about the management of their companies' affairs, trusting only a few close but usually very able advisers. The First World War further expanded the Vestey fortunes, with British troops eating up to a million pounds of meat a day.

In 1915, however, the family was challenged by changes in the tax laws, due to war pressures. Company taxation, income tax and death duties all increased; even company earnings abroad not remitted to the UK became liable for tax. William Vestey calculated that for every £100 profit he would have to pay 40% profits tax, income tax at 6% and super tax at 4/6 leaving only £28.10s which, after death duties which he regarded as merely deferred income tax, would be reduced to £17.2s. He put these calculations to the Treasury in the expectation that the government would see reason, particularly in the light of fierce competition from America, and given that foreign companies did not have such a heavy tax burden. To concede Vestey's argument would have been to open the floodgates to other claims and so it was refused.

The Vesteys reacted by setting up an American company to which their British counterpart agreed to cede the use of all Vestey's overseas assets. In return the US company paid the British one enough to meet its costs and pay dividends–around £250 000 p.a. It was the US company which hence received profits from Vestey's worldwide operations, and hence they were not subject to UK tax. But the profits did not go to the US company, so avoiding tax there, but to the Vesteys, who moved to Argentina where there was no income tax.

The subsequent history of the Vesteys was by no means without difficulty. Their near monopolistic position in the meat trade in Argentina was abused, and in 1934 the Argentine government began to investigate the workings and profits of the company. This was adamantly resisted for fear that inquiries in Buenos Aires might lead to inquiries in London, for by this time the Inland Revenue and the Treasury were well aware of the Vestey problem. In his evidence to the Royal Commission on Taxation in 1919 the head of the family had made no bones about his rooted objection to paying income tax and his removal to Argentina to avoid it. Nor were matters improved when, allegedly after paying Lloyd George £20 000 for it, he was given a peerage in 1921. King George V was outraged and wrote to complain to Lloyd George. That a wealthy man should desert his country in the dark days of the war was bad enough; that he should profit extensively from government contracts while avoiding paying any tax was worse; but that he should be given a peerage for his efforts was outrageous.

By 1921 the Vesteys were UK residents again, thanks to a carefully arranged operation which in essence has enabled them to remain almost free of tax liability to the present. The arrangements were complex in detail, but their essential elements were as follows. They leased most of their overseas operations to their British company, Union Cold Storage. The lease specified that Union would pay £960 000 a year for 21 years for the use of Vestey plant worldwide to three French residents, all well known and trusted by the Vesteys. By the terms of a family trust settlement the income was to be held in a fund and invested by the trustees, the income from this being divided into half to accumulate for 21 years for the benefit of the two brothers who headed the family. The funds were then to be used for the benefit of the Vestey family, which still draws much of its income fom this source. The problem with trusts is that they are invalidated if they permit the people establishing them to benefit from them. The Vesteys circumvented this problem by nominating themselves as the persons authorized to direct where investments should go and then having large sums sent to the Western United Investment Co. in Britain, for which the trust received interest. Western in turn acted as bankers to the Vesteys and neither charged nor paid any interest on their accounts for debit or credit balances. This in turn was possible because the Vesteys owned the only four shares in Western with voting rights. The other million had none.

The problems with the Argentine authorities in the 1930s never resulted in disclosure of their affairs in Europe, though they came close to doing so. None the less, the Revenue was extremely interested in pursuing the Vesteys, and in 1942 succeeded in bringing mattters to a head, by imposing huge assessments on the estate of one of the brothers who had died in 1940, and on the other who was still living. The revenue demanded more and more information, and further increased demands for back tax, amounting to more than £6 million. The long and bitter case was only concluded in the House of Lords in 1949. The Vesteys lost before the special commissioners, the High Court and the Court of Appeal. In the latter, Somerwell LJ said:

> There was a finding which was not disputed before us, that the main purpose of the creation of the £960 000 rent and its transfer to the settlement was the avoidance of the U.K. taxation. Looking at the arrangement as a whole, it seems to me that the Vesteys were receiving benefit in the shape of loans without interest . . . The result is that in my view, the whole income of the transfers has to be deemed the income of the Vesteys.

The Vesteys, however, won their case in the Lords and it is instructive to see the differences in the tenor of the argument between their case in 1949 and that on Rossminster in 1981. The Lords explicitly construed the Vestey trust deed 'without regard to the fact that (it) is part of a scheme of tax avoidance'. They then applied the terms of the Finance Acts of 1936 and 1938, which formed the basis of the Revenue's case, to determine if they made the Vesteys liable. Section 18 of the 1936 Act was directed at tax avoidance, and particularly at the transfer of money by UK residents out of the country, as a result of which income is payable to people domiciled outside the UK. It specified that if a UK resident then acquires the power to enjoy that income, and if it would have been liable to tax if received in the UK, it shall be taxable. The Lords found however that neither of the two Vestey brothers had an individual power to enjoy the income from the Paris trust, only a joint power. Further, even if the brothers enjoyed interest free loans originating from the Paris trust they were not taxable. 'To say of a man that the trust income should be invested in a loan to himself, that he has the beneficial enjoyment of that income is a misuse of language . . . the words point to an out and out disposal of an income for the benefit of some person or persons and are wholly inappropriate to an investment by way of a loan.' The general perspective of the Lords on the case is plain from Lord Normand's judgement:

> Parliament in its attempts to keep pace with the ingenuity devoted to tax avoidance may fall short of its purpose. That is a misfortune for the tax payers who do nothing to avoid their share of the burden, and it is disappointing to the Inland Revenue, but the court will not stretch the terms of the taxing acts in order to improve on the eforts of parliament and stop gaps which are left open by the statute.
>
> Tax avoidance is an evil, but it would be the beginning of much greater evils if the courts were to overstretch the language of the statute to subject to taxation people of whom they disapproved.

It certainly gives new clarity to such notions of enforcing the spirit and the letter of the law, and to seeking to determine what parliament intended. It was also a decision out of line with what became the leading case, Congreve v. Inland Revenue of 1948, in which it was decided by the Law Lords that even if tax avoiders exploited the income of foreign based trusts not for themselves but for their children or other relatives – so called passive beneficiaries – they were still liable for tax. This decision was regarded as an important bulwark by the Inland Revenue and was thought to be effective in deterring other tax avoiders. After losing the Vestey case in the 1940s, it took the Revenue until 1979 to mount another one. The Vesteys were extremely secretive about their affairs. The accounts of the Paris trust were kept in Uruguay and only produced after the imposition of a legal notice under the 1970 Taxes Act. The Revenue's assessment indicated that, in a period of four years in the 1960s, six members of the Vestey family were due for income tax on £4.3 million and surtax of £7.3 million. The Lords decided in November 1979, as they had done earlier, that the Vesteys were not liable, and went further in deciding that Congreve in 1948 was bad law and to be overturned, and that passive beneficiaries were not liable for tax. They called for an urgent reconsideration of the law to close the loophole, which informed estimates subsequently suggested could involve £1 billion in lost taxes. The Revenue's claim was dismissed as based on bad law, 'arbitrary, unjust and fundamentally unconstitutional'. It was this decision that stimulated the *Sunday Times* researchers; the publication of researchers; the publication of their work in autumn 1980 prompted the Chancellor to pledge that he would act to end such avoidance.

It was not until March the following year that any action was taken however, in strengthening the 'power to enjoy' benefits derived from overseas trusts, and so restore the Revenue to the position they thought they had established with Congreve. The Treasury was also reported as having gone further in examining proposals for a wide-ranging anti-avoidance law, along the lines of those in existence in the USA and W. Germany, and in which the intention behind a scheme would become important – if that intention was avoidance then it would not succeed. What contact there was, if any, between the Treasury, ministers and senior judges is not known, but it was in March 1981 that the Ramsay decision was handed down by the Law Lords over a Rossminster avoidance scheme that achieved this purpose without legislation. It was no doubt significant that it was Lord Wilberforce who headed the court, as he had in the 1979 decision letting the Vesteys off. The key power which the judges now said they could exercise was to consider, at any rate in some cases, the intention behind a scheme. The principle that it was no business of the courts to try to determine the purpose of a tax scheme, only to see if it conformed to the rules, 'does not compel the court to look at the transaction in blinkers'. The Ramsay ruling was taken as an indication by other judges that highly artificial avoidance schemes should be ruled unacceptable. The Vesteys had made it from nouveaux riches to the centre of the establishment in three generations, and such figures traditionally secure financial privileges, but their immunity from taxation in the 1980s, coinciding with Rossminster's brash operation to provide a mass market service to the nouveaux riches of today created enough pressure for a move to more universal control. It remains to be seen how the Vesteys will fare when their affairs reach the House of Lords again; it will be interesting to see if the Revenue can manage to achieve this in less than another 30 years.

Lesser mortals at any rate were left in no doubt of the substance of the Law Lords' changed view of tax avoidance by a further decision against a modest scheme to defer tax in 1984.[11] In Furniss v. Dawson, Dawson had sought to defer paying tax when selling shareholdings in two small family companies and took advantage of a special provision of the 1965 Tax Act to do so. This provides for exemption from Capital Gains Tax when shares in a company are transferrd to another company, which thereby gains control, in exchange for shares in the transferred company. Capital Gains Tax then becomes payable when the shares in the second company are sold or the company liquidated. The Court of Appeal, in finding for Dawson, was persuaded by the fact that if tax was levied when the shares were exchanged,that would not exclude the possibility of a further Capital Gains claim when the shares in the second company were sold, so creating the danger of double taxation. The House of Lords, however, decided that because the transfer had no business purpose (i.e. only a fiscal one) it failed on the Ramsay principle; and the fact that it was a deferral, not an avoidance scheme, that it was modest, involving only some £155 000, and that it involved only one contentious transaction and that that transaction itself was not wholly artificial but did have a business effect (i.e. on the company with which Dawson exchanged the shares), none of this should be construed to allow exemption from tax.

In response to this decision there was widespread consternation among tax consultants and accountants, since it was seen as giving the Revenue a means to attack a wide variety of schemes commonly used by companies to defer to minimize tax and, even worse, to give the Revenue wide discretion as to when to invoke Furniss v. Dawson and claim that a step in a scheme had no business purpose and that the scheme was therefore invalid as a whole.[12] A more measured view came from Roger White, a tax partner with Peat, Marwick and Michell:[13] 'It is an important decision, but a part of emerging law which follows from cases such as Ramsay. It curtails the most aggressive tax planning but then, most of the totally artificial schemes which arose in the 1970s have now gone. However, we do need a statement from the Inland Revenue on what it considers acceptable and on the instructions it has given to Tax Inspectors.' In default of which, not only would companies trying to minimize tax be in difficulty, but so would those advising them, since clients are not likely to be keen to pay good money for advice that concludes: 'That is what I recommend, but I cannot be sure it will work.' To the ordinary wage-earning or even humble self-employed citizen, however, such a curtailment of discretion to manipulate personal and corporate circumstances to avoid tax might well seem entirely welcome.

## Insolvency

This is a topic that is likely to be the source of enduring embarrassment to a government committed to free market principles. One of the bastions protecting the integrity of such a market must be the law on bankruptcy and insolvency, for it is essential to free market competition that only the fittest survive and that the unfit and the unlucky fail. It is important that if bad luck or bad judgement drives them over the edge of solvency they should be prevented as far as possible from continuing to trade and from being led into frauds on creditors and others. Equally, it is important that bankruptcy law be used sparingly to recover as much as possible for creditors where an individual is genuinely beyond redemption, and not be available for aggressive creditors to oppress an individual in temporary difficulties over a modest debt.

In fact, the present law works – by which I mean it is often administered so that it works, not that it necessarily or by legal intention so works – in precisely the opposite way. Bankruptcy law may well oppress the modest debtor and insolvency protect the unscrupulous entrepreneur, and there is little doubt that the rich and well-advised are liable to escape financial crises virtually unscathed where the poor and ignorant are given a drubbing. That all was far from satisfactory became evident in a number of different and well-publicised ways in the latter 1970s and 1980s.

The celebrated cases of William Stern, Freddie Laker and DeLorean, all in their different ways indicated defects in the system as it pertains to the big fish. In the case of Stern, the difficulties arose directly out of the property boom and crash of the 1970s, in the course of which Stern built up a large base in association with his father-in-law and then struck out on his own, expanding at an astonishing rate during the peak of the boom by buying up blocks of flats in London and the south of England with money borrowed from banks and, as we have seen, other fringe institutions, most notably the Crown Agents. Stern appears to have been carried forward upon his own optimism and his success thus far – the various lending institutions did little to enquire into the substance of his empire, which rapidly became heavily over-geared and dependent upon the property boom continuing. In almost all cases the lenders were willing to accept Stern's personal guarantee, and as a result when the crash came and Stern's companies disintegrated, these guarantees were shown to be wildly in excess of his personal assets, even though these included a sumptious house in London, for which his wife borrowed £457 000 to furnish it from Stern's main company, Wilstar. When the receivers were called in at Wilstar's crash in 1974 the clear prospect was that this debt to the company would be recovered and force the sale of the house. Stern, however, managed to stave off a formal declaration of bankruptcy until 1978, during the initial period of which he worked as a consultant to the receivers, Cork Gulley, at a salary of £15000 a year. Stern's father bought his son's house contents and wife's fur and jewellery later in 1974, and because the bankruptcy declaration did not take place until 1978, William Stern was able to invoke a clause in the 1883 Bankruptcy Act which held that any sale of assets at least two years before bankruptcy should be allowed to stand.

He continued to live in the house and applied for his discharge five years later in 1983. At that time he testified that even after his bankruptcy his annual outgoings were around £30000. He continued to run three cars, applied for planning permission to build a £15000 games room in 1979, spent £15000 on a reception following the marriage of his daughter in 1982, continued to maintain a chauffeur and to educate his children privately. Commenting on his application, the presiding judge remarked: 'The transactions over the house do not redound entirely to his credit' and that 'as matters stand it would not be wise to release him on the business world'. None the less Stern's discharge from bankruptcy was granted, suspended until September 1985. Stern's own comments on his bankruptcy are perhaps even more telling than those of the judge. Counsel for the creditors remarked at one point: 'It strikes some people as very odd that a man who has gone bankrupt for a hundred million pounds should go on living in a pretty susbstantial mansion.' Stern replied, 'Yes, of that I am acutely aware. It raises a severe public relations problem. But the value of the house is not an issue before the Court. If it had been worth ten million pounds or fifteen million pounds it might have been different.'[14]

These are not sentiments which would appeal, for example, to Michael Riley, a British Rail engine driver who was made bankrupt by a finance company for a debt of £641 despite owning a house worth £30000 at the time, and utlimately faced with a legal bill in consequence of over £8000. Nor would it evoke sympathy from solicitor Arne Asirwatham, precipitated into financial crisis in 1977 as a result of the rent on his office being doubled, and thence into bankruptcy over a deficiency of £2000, after falling out with a friend who had offered to tide him over by guaranteeing the loan from the bank. Asirwatham had his house sold, lost thousands in fees to the liquidator and had to go as far as the Ombudsman for a judgement that he had been overcharged, and was still debarred from legal practice by the Law Society even after his discharge from bankruptcy.

What emerges from the researches of those such as Aris, and of the BBC's *Checkpoint* team,[15] is that not only does bankruptcy law operate as a relentless and extraordinarily expensive juggernaut against the weak and guileless, leaving them shattered not only financially but often psychologically and physically, but that its law in practice is sufficiently lax to allow a network of predators to operate. These cowboys, who do not need any professional training or formal accreditation to operate, descend upon companies in difficulty and offer to 'help'. In fact, they charge extortionate fees, defraud the creditors, and get additional kickbacks by arranging to sell off the assets cheaply either to associates, or in some cases to the managing director, allowing him to restart in business again.

This is not the place to go into detail on the criminal activities of rogue liquidators, nor on the activities of company directors whose capacity to rise, phoenix-like, from the ashes of one debt-ridden company to restart trading under a new name in another company has become notorious. So rampant has this practice become as to be given the now quite well known tag 'Change the name, the game's the same'. The *Checkpoint* programme at one point demonstrated that it was possible to buy a new company off the shelf from an organisation specializing in such matters for £105, in a transaction taking 15 minutes.[16] Once installed behind the protective legal framework of limited liability under the Companies Acts, personal property is protected from creditors, and only the assets of the company may be sold if it becomes insolvent. It is therefore extremely easy for a reasonably sophisticated entrepreneur to move from business to business, avoiding personal liability, failing on each occasion, and leaving a trail of unpaid creditors and often employees, and often transferring assets from the dying company, both financial and material, to the next venture. The chances of successful prosecution for fraud are limited, because of the difficulty of obtaining proof where small companies are operated by a single individual, and even disqualification as a director after repeated failures can be circumvented by installing wives and children as nominees.

The point about these forms of exploitation is not that they are new – they derive from companies and insolvency legislation whose framework has altered little since its construction in the latter part of the nineteenth century. What has changed in recent years has perhaps been the incidence of abuses or perhaps the incidence of particularly flagrant abuses. But this is not certain, since substantial records which would allow a proper evaluation are not kept. What has certainly changed is the level of publicity about such cases provided by investigative journalists, particularly those working for the Sunday papers, but most notably by broadcast consumer programmes. Esther Rantzen's *That's Life* made its name in the early 1970s by exposing some abuses and by the natural drama of demanding answers to consumer complaints in public, but has since moved away from this format.

In the latter 1970s investigative reporting, specializing in its early years on small entrepreneurs and their depredations was taken a bold step further by Roger Cook in his radio, and later TV, *Checkpoint* programme. This achieved very wide and positive publicity, not only for the standard of reporting, but because of Cook's ability to present himself as the dogged and frequently physically battered champion of the public against the seedy and unscrupulous entrepreneur. It is a format and style later copied elsewhere, though without the same panache, and it was of course just the message the Tory government least liked to hear. At a time when the Secretary of State for Employment was telling the redundant to invest their redundancy pay in setting up in business, it was a public relations disaster to have the BBC providing endless examples of the sharks waiting to exploit the novice entrepreneurs, and scarcely likely to bolster naive confidence in them by their potential customers. Worst of all, the abuses, both by liquidators and by entrepreneurs, were going on with no effective remedy: rogues were making a good living, and when the law caught up with them conviction only took place in the most flagrant cases with any certainty. Sentences were not long, and the villains soon returned to their old habits under new names.

The message that something needed to be done, and that it required a substantial overhaul of the bankruptcy and insolvency laws, got through in the mid-1970s to the Labour administration, who appointed a redoubtable liquidator and public figure to review the whole of the law on the subject – Sir Kenneth Cork, head of W.H. Cork Gulley, one of the largest firms of receivers and liquidators. Cork was never in any doubt about the need for radical reform and took his task seriously, reporting in 1982 with a long, comprehensive list of recommendations. By this time, however, the government had changed and it was much less interested in radical reform. It had not been able, given the publicity and the head start Cork had had by 1979 when it came of office, simply to scrap Cork and ask for a quick report to eliminate the most obvious abuses. As Cork later remarked, this could have been done in a year and a half. It contented itself with shuffling off criticism as a result of publicity about abuses during its first three years in office on the grounds that it was 'waiting for Cork', and that it would be wrong to act prematurely. After 1982, while giving an almost openly cold smile of welcome to the report, it managed to delay another two years 'studying the report', i.e. deciding how to get away with not doing what the report recommended. Cork himself was not going to let his report[17] follow those of many other worthy investigators onto the shelf, and showed himself ready to give interviews and to make public statements fiercely defending the enactment of the whole package of reforms in short order. What then, did Cork recommend?

There is not the space here to review the very extensive details of the proposals, but the main ones, which have become the basis of controversy, can be identified briefly. Cork proposed to reserve 10% of the assets of an insolvent company for the liquidator to use to pursue claims against debtors of the company, so ending the situation in which creditors have to put up further money of their own to try to recoup their losses through legal action, and most, if not all, of the assets go to the preferred creditors, the banks, who have a charge on the company assets, the Revenue, the VAT office, and the liquidator for fees and expenses. Secondly, the 'Change the name, the game's the same' operators would be attacked as follows:

> If a director of one company that comes insolvent becomes the director of another company within two or three years, and if that other company becomes insolvent, the director would be permanently liable for the debts. They would also be guilty of fraudulent trading and that would bar them from being a director of a company for a considerable period.[18]

In addition, the concept of wrongful trading was introduced, which was to differ from fraudulent trading in being a simple matter of fact and not requiring fraudulent intent, which is hard to prove. This meant that if the company continued to trade while insolvent, the directors would be guilty of wrongful trading, and would become personally liable for debts incurred, which would also act to discourage under-capitalization of companies and stimulate directors to inject more of their own funds. In general, Cork intended to promote the realization that 'Limited liability is not a right but a privilege, which would be taken away from those who abuse it.[19] On the bankruptcy side, Cork recommended a specialist court to deal with insolvency and the creation of an administrator to act more like a receiver to try to save companies, rather than a liquidator to close them down and sell off their assets. All liquidators and administrators would in future have to be trained and properly accredited.

Cork's view was that the government would be 'mad not to implement it all now',[20] which might seem a rather aggressive stance for the Chairman of a Government Committee of Inquiry, but events showed it to be well justified. It took the government two years to produce a White Paper, followed in late 1984 by a Bill.[21] The government's proposals on the bankruptcy side, whilst more limited than Cork, were broadly in sympathy with him, accepted the idea of an administrator, and suggested a streamlining and simplification of procedure, whilst removing the official receiver, the most expensive current institution for the bankrupt, from all cases involving deficits of less than £15000, and making it impossible to be made bankrupt for less than £750. The Government, however, abandoned Cork's provision for a special Insolvency Court to operate five days a week all year round, not just in the legal terms, to streamline bankruptcy proceedings. This omission was strongly criticized by the Institute of Chartered Accountants.

The government concentrated on insolvency, and here the differences from Cork were significant. Automatic disqualification for two company failures was 'too far-reaching', and whilst curbing 'the activities of the delinquent director, it would at the same time deter the genuine entrepreneur from risking his capital in a further venture', a view which Cork dismissed as 'a lot of bloody tripe'. Instead the government adapted Cork's concept of wrongful trading to allow for the possibility of prosecution and loss of limited liability on conviction of directors who knowingly allow their company to continue trading while insolvent. Cork conceded that this 'might do the trick', but it is weakened by the need not only to show that the company was insolvent when trading, which is often hard to prove in small companies where accounts are poorly kept, but to prove that the directors knew this was the case. Cork, in contrast, placed the onus upon them to have a duty to know, as the price of being protected from personal liability. As to the 10% of assets to be retained by the liquidator to fight for the creditors, it was turned down flat by the government. Where the government seemed to be innovatory was with the proposal that companies should suffer penalites if they went into compulsory liquidation rather than taking earlier action for voluntary winding up. The government proposed that directors of companies compulsorily liquidated would be disqualified from being directors for three years. Cork, however, was scathing in his comment on this:

> They [the government] are not doing this as a discipline on directors. They are doing it because Maggie and the boys think that the private sector should do everything. By cracking down on directors whose companies go into compulsory liquidation they think they will encourage people to go into voluntary liquidation and thus take the load off the shoulders of the official receiver and shove the business into the private sector where they think it belongs. But it won't. In fact the reverse will happen. Creditors will try to blackmail directors. Those who think they have been hard done by will now have every incentive to go for a compulsory liquidation in the hope that the directors will pay up and thus avoid disqualification. So instead of having fewer compulsory liquidations as the government hopes, you will have more – precisely the opposite of what was intended.[22]

On the issue of liquidators' qualifications the Bill appeared tough in making it a criminal offence to act without being qualified, but failed to clarify what the qualifications consisted of. It was clear that the various bodies such as the Accountants and Insolvency Practitioners' Association would be allowed to exercise their own judgement on the matter and that provision would be made for at least some unqualified liquidators to continue in business. 'It's the old story' remarked Cork, 'there is always pressure from those who are running a business to be allowed to continue as before.'

Despite Cork's evident cynicism about the government's intentions of achieving real reform, it was soon evident that it was having to contend with strong pressure against even its limited proposals. The White Paper was published in March 1984, and by May the Institute of Directors (IOD) had mobilized itself as the main focus of opposition. A delegate from the venture capital arm of the Midland Bank at an Institute of Directors' conference entitled 'New Legislative Threats to Directors' revealed that its lawyers had advised it not to put its representatives on the boards of client companies for fear of disqualification if they went broke, and pointed out that the problem could be very serious in the case of management buy-outs of their own companies, a solution to difficulties much applauded by the government, where the failure rate in the first six months is high, and experienced outside directors can give invaluable advice. Further, directors felt much threatened by the insistence in the White Paper on collective responsibility based upon what directors know or can reasonably be expected to know, a responsiblity not to be escaped by resigning, and the penalty for which, it decisions taken turned out to be the wrong ones, could be conviction for wrongful trading. By the summer the government seemed to be backtracking, accepting a 28-day period to allow directors to appeal to a court before disqualification could take place, but when the Bill was published at the end of 1984 it conceded no substantial ground.

If the government thought that after the initial round of opposition it would get away with reasoned and technical debate by introducing the Bill through the Lords it was much mistaken. The IOD found plenty of supporters in the House, and a former Bank of England industrial adviser moved an amendment virtually removing the distinction between voluntary and compulsory liquidation, and confusing the issue of personal liability of directors for wrongful trading. The determination of the IOD and its allies to kill off the notion of civil liability for wrongful trading was made wholly explicit during the same period in submissions by the accountants and the IOD to the government arguing that rogue directors should be subject to criminal prosecution, and strongly against automatic disqualifications for directors of companies compulsorily liquidated. Not to put too fine a point on it, the government was in a mess. Notwithstanding the possibility of reinstating some of the original clauses when the Bill was debated in the Commons, the chances of anything susbstantial by way of reform of insolvency coming out of it looked slight.

The topic is likely to continue to cause the government some anxiety. If it does not fight and succeed in achieving what it can at least lay claim to being significant reform of insolvency, its propaganda in favour of the entrepreneurial spirit and the healthiness of the free market will ring very hollow. If it does, it will still find itself subject to attack by Cork and the investigative journalists for not going far enough, and the journalistic publicity machine will be doubly alerted to test the efficacy of any new system, and to proclaim its failings. It is an example of a more general difficulty which is implicit in efforts by the state to clean up capitalist institutions, to which I will return in increasing detail in later chapters. Suffice it to point out at present that insolvency had all the appearance of a cleft stick for the government from which they were unlikely to benefit much whichever way things went.

## The Office of Fair Trading

If in these rather dismal circumstances there was an institution likely to keep the government's spirits up, it was the Office of Fair Trading (OFT). Under the leadership of Sir Gordon Borrie, now in his second term as Director General, and rewarded for his efforts and ability by a knighthood, the OFT has changed its political scope and significance under a Conservative government to become a central instrument in the campaign to improve competitiveness and secure consumer interests. The OFT was founded in late 1973, and was shaped in its early years by a Labour administration strongly committed to consumer protection, but its role was politically a minor one because of the much larger Ministry of Prices and Consumer Protection headed by a Secretary of State. The Ministry had a central role in managing the government's anti-inflation policy by enforcing government restrictions on price rises and taking steps to identify and protect consumer interests. For a Labour government, these were worthwhile and important interests in their own right, giving rise, for example, to the Fair Trading Act 1973, under which the OFT has recourse to its own investigative powers and to the courts to seek assurances about unfair trading practices, and the Consumer Credit Act 1974, under which the OFT issues and revokes licences to provide consumer credit, but price control and consumer protection were also a means to a greater political end. The long struggle with the trade unions over the size of wage increases and their effect upon inflation was the dominant element in the lives of both Labour administrations of 1964–70 and that of 1974–9. A variety of tactics were adopted to attempt to control wage rises: legislative proposals, most notable Barabara Castle's 'In Place of Strife', which was rejected after much dissent in 1968, a variety of statutory and non-statutory policies on wage restraint, culminating in the 'Social Contract', which faltered through the mid-1970s, a complete lack of any restraint in 1974–5, which resulted in inflation soaring up to 25%, and a commitment to price restraint and consumer protection as a *quid pro quo* for wage restraint. The latter was part of an argument redolent of fundamentalist Labour thinking: if greedy capitalists, particularly monopolists and oligopolists in the consumer goods and services sectors, could be prevented from putting up prices at will and making fat profits, and if smaller unscrupulous traders could, by a combination of coercion and persuasion, be prevented from ripping-off the public in such fields as second-hand cars, dry cleaning, double glazing and home improvements, the trade unionists would accept that the inherent evils of capitalism were being kept in check and would themselves exercise restraint in pressing wage demands. It was a view which displayed a characteristically generous view of human nature, and which was finally destroyed with the collapse of the Social Contract in the so-called Winter of Discontent in 1979, which preceded the collapse of the Labour administration.

Consumer protection and competitions policy have quite a different place under a right-wing Conservative administration. The Department of Prices and Consumer Protection was, not surprisingly, scrapped and there were no doubt many who expected the OFT to succumb to the axe in the successive rounds of purges of publicly funded public-interest bodies that became known as 'Quangos' (quasi-autonomous non-governmental organizations). Yet the OFT not only survived but grew under the new regime. It started life with a staff of 183 in 1974, stabilized at 293 in the following year and remainded at 295 in 1982. By the end of the following year it had grown to 329, and further growth seemed likely with the advent of its responsibility for oversight of the rules of self-regulatory organizations under the Investor Protection Bill (see Chapter 4). A staff of just over 300, however, is very small by government standards, and while the key to the OFT's success under such different governments in one respect no doubt lies in the quality of its staff, a large part of the answer lies in two other directions.

Clearly, the OFT and consumer interest generally have little part to play in the Thatcher government's anti-inflationary policy. Tight monetary restraint and deflation have been the instruments here, and trade unions, so far from being constant bargaining partners, have been ignored and battered into submission by ever-rising unemployment, a series of legislative initiatives to strip them of their privileges, curtail their freedom of action, and cut into their finances, and by a series of well-chosen, well-organized and hard-fought strikes (strikes are made, even if not technically called, by employers and governments as often as they are by trade unions, and all parties to them are aware of the importance of not fighting on ground chosen by an adversary). It has not been the employee but the self-employed and the employer, those much-lauded generators of wealth and jobs, who have been seen as in principal need of support. Why then should competition policy, which is surely designed to expose the struggling entrepreneur to the full rigours of the free market, be important to a market-oriented government? And even more so, why should consumer protection be an issue at all, when surely the market can be relied on to ensure that although a thousand products and services are offered, only the sound and worthy ones are bought long term?

It is a measure of the Thatcher government's recognition of the limits to which a free market can be introduced, and of the importance of consumer protection as an important political aspect of citizenship, that it has backed state enforcement of consumer standards firmly. One of the major political achievements of post war economic growth and the emergence of Britain as a mass consumption economy was the acceptance by all parties that in an ever-increasing variety of fields the consumer is entitled to protection against dangerous and shoddy products. The movement began on unassailable ground with moves to protect the public against impure foods and unsafe drugs, but expanded into new territory in the 1960s with the foundation of the Consumers' Association under the sponsorship of that able political entrepreneur Michael Young (now Lord Young of Dartington). The ground the Consumers' Association took up was to insist that all goods offered on the market be safe, even if subject to limited abuse (for example by children); that they be of adequate quality and do the job claimed over a reasonable life span; and that in the event of failure the customer be entitled to free repair or replacement. In general terms, which were rapidly accepted politically, this amounted to a claim that the customer was not required to take risks in making a purchase, that there was to be no longer *caveat emptor* implicitly stamped on goods, but that all were to be of 'merchantable quality', and that institutions should be established to allow for the enforcement of consumers' rights to this. The OFT has played an important part in achieving this at national level, with its stream of research into different areas, its agreements with trade associations over codes of practice, and its increasing powers of enforcement of them under various Acts. It has its counterpart for the individual customer in the Trading Standards Office run by each local authority, which can investigate consumer complaints, and in the Small Claims Court, through which easy and cheap redress has been available to consumers since the 1970s.

The incoming Conservative government in 1979 was committed to promoting the virtues of the entrepreneur. However, while urging as many as possible to put their skills and energies to the test as businessmen, the government recognized that its own election depended not upon the entrepreneurs but upon the votes of the employed. It was critical therefore that while creating a climate conducive to enterprise and initiative and allowing for additional rewards from it, it should carry the great majority of the non-entrepreneurial population with it, so that the creation of an economy fit for business to generate new wealth and jobs was not experienced by the rest of the population, who are the customers and clients of those businessmen, as an economy marked by a lack of protection for them, or of recognition of their interests. This view was given further backing by the ready recognition that while much might be achieved on a small scale in the home market, the real test lies in the international one. For that reason, it is essential to ensure that goods and services marketed widely are of sound quality and that there is effective machinery to ensure that this remains so.

Competition policy, then, becomes the handmaiden of the free market and the consumer, by ensuring that the latter gets value for money and that exploitative monopolies are not established, and simultaneously trying to ensure that access to markets is kept open to newcomers and that cartels are not formed to close off sectors of the economy. The role of the OFT in consumer protection and competition policy has, from the point of view of the Conservative government, been reinforced by both the conviction of economic principle and by realistic political appraisals. It has been a particularly important public instrument for demonstrating the determination of the government to protect the interests of the unorganized general population as consumers as well as an attempt to spread the purifying air of free competition as widely as possible in the interests of international trade advantage and fairness to all entrepreneurs at home.

In pursuing this policy, the OFT has been encouraged to move far beyond the conventional limits set for it under the Labour administration. Most notably, it has taken on the service sector in general, and the professions in particular, as particularly pernicious and self-serving clusters of restrictive practices, oppression of the rights of consumers, and poor value for money. The interest in this area goes back to the early days of the OFT, as its research record shows, but it was only with the following kind of support from ministers that it could yield fruit: 'The sharp end of industry, like the car and steel workers, know all about competition; they've lost thousands of jobs. Competition needs to be extended throughout the professions, which are part of our increasingly important service sector'.[23] The attack on the professions was doubly acceptable.

On the one hand, it was very easy to mobilize public opinion against the self-protectiveness, high fees and charges, impossibility of redress against negligence, pomposity, stuffiness, obscurantist jargon and self-importance of professionals, and it was notable that the government found a willing ally in its efforts in the shape of Austin Mitchell, MP, whose Private Member's Bill ending the solicitors' monopoly on conveyancing, a government strongly supportive of home ownership found it impossible to oppose in 1983–4. On the other hand, as we have seen, pressures in the City from international competition were building up dangerously in the 1980s, and reform of traditional professional practices and division of labour was plainly necessary to obtain the requisite restructuring of institutions, streamlining of practice, and improvements in accountability necessary to survival. Hence the OFT's remit to mount the restrictive practices case against the Stock Exchange. But this should not be seen in isolation from moves against other professions.

Accountants, for example, have been under sustained pressure to reduce and rationalize the number of their professional bodies and certification systems, to improve the monitoring and enforcement of ethics, and to agree common, enforceable accounting standards for audit, while at the same time being forced to recognize that their business is rapidly changing – audit is only 40–60% of the work of big firms now. Increasingly what is on offer is competition for management consultancy, insolvency, tax advice and special efficiency reports, especially in the public sector. Lawyers will be aware that tax advice is a profitable activity, lost by them not so long ago to accountants, and with conveyancing, the bread and butter of many solicitors' practitioners, now under threat, and fees earned for it cut by around 30% by rising competition already, new alternatives, perhaps by closer integration with estate agents or by working with new organizations offering financial services, are called for.

In brief, the OFT has been at the centre of major shifts in the organization of work by the professions and of a sharp increase in competition between professions for business and for public standards of accountability. Sir Gordon Borrie's 1983 report, looking back over ten years of the OFT's work, indicates a clear awareness of these issues:[24]

> The loosening of restrictions on competition now taking place in the Stock Exchange is a telling example of what my Office has been achieving – and will continue to seek – in manufacturing and service industries generally.
>
> Several major reports, each initiated by Government and each relating in some way to competition policy or to consumer/investor protection, are currently being discussed: Professor Gower's Review of Investor Protection; the National Consumer Council Report on Banking Services; and the Cork Report on Insolvency. Each in its own way is questioning long-established institutions and pratices. The Office's efforts to persuade the professions to relax their unduly restrictive rules against advertising seem at last to be bearing fruit and the promise of a Government Bill to liberalise house conveyancing is a further sign that the professions are not to be sheltered from competition policy.
>
> Many of the restrictions on competition that prevail among the professions are said to be justified as necessary to protect the public. The question then is whether

protection of the public or consumer protection goes too far because there is no doubt that sometimes protective measures, whether imposed by the State of by self-regulatory bodies, do restrict competition and innovation unduly and are maintained more for the benefit of existing traders and practitioners than of the general public. The Office of Fair Trading has benefited considerably from the wisdom of Ministers and Parliament in 1973 in placing responsibility for administering certain areas of competition and consumer legislation in one body. Pulling them together with a tightly-knit and tightly-run office was sensible because we were founded on the philosophy that, as a general rule, a competitive environment is the best designed to ensure maximum efficiency and customer satisfaction. On the other hand, competition is often not enough to maximise the chances of customer satisfaction, because adequate information necessary for genuine consumer choice is defective. The Consumer Credit Act, requiring interest charges to be disclosed according to a standardised formula, is a classic example of legislation intended to supplement and amplify competition by making consumer choice more real. But consumer protection or ostensible consumer protection can go too far. The need is for the right balance – a 'trade off' – to be achieved in the particular case. We seek to do this in day-to-day discussions between our Competition Policy and Consumer Affairs Divisions. The Government sought to do the same thing in its 1983 announcement about opticians folowing on our Review of Competition and Opticians. Acting on a reference from this Office, the Restrictive Practices Court likewise sought to weigh up in relation to the travel trade the advantages of greater competition against tht needs of consumer protection in decisions made in 1982 and 1983.

The issue of balance or trade-off between the interests of competition and those of monitoring consumer standards is given added point by the reorganization of work among the professions, the increased competition for it, and the rise of new organizations incorporating a variety of professionals, where before they have worked in specialist isolation. The issue, quite visible on the horizon, is conflict of interest. If an accounting practice audits a company, it is well placed to bid for management consultancy work in the same company, but ought it to be able to? If solicitors go into partnership with estate agents and surveyors, similar conflicts may arise, as they will do on a greater scale when building societies and maybe some banks diversify to take on conveyancing, insurance and estate agency work. But this is not the only issue arising out of the reshuffle of professional work. It is associated with increased competition for work, expectations of falling fees and commissions and increased efficiency. Yet the new patterns are untried and their organizational form undeveloped. It is not only a question of clients being railroaded from one service offered by a giant organization to another, regardless of whether or not it offers the cheapest rate or the requisite package or level of skills necessary to manage it, but of competition and the unfamiliarity of new arrangements leading to systematic errors and to rates being cut too low. Just as in the heart of the City, with the Stock Exchange shake-up, where there are expectations of widespread casualties after minimum commissions go and open competition ensues with the 'big bang', the same may happen more widely in other professional and financial services. And while the pushy partnership of solicitors and estate agents doing cut price house purchase going broke may cause no more than local ripples, the consequences of a major bank or building society having its depositors in its traditional sector jeopardized by expensive failures in diversification would constitute a major scandal.

We come at this point to a discussion of the new financial institutions and their problems which will be dealt with more fully in the next chapter, and to a discussion of the institutions – pension funds etc. – which is the topic of the next section. The point to be made here about the role of the OFT is that it is increasingly evident as a guardian of the public interest, as a researcher – 17 projects completed or in progress in 1983 – trouble shooter and thinktank in relation to the reorganization of financial and professional services. In the flux of the latter 1980s the capacity of the OFT to see ahead and warn bodies engaged in direct supervison of likely future trouble will be of greater importance than its established role of scrutinizing and criticizing the habits of entrenched trades and professions. One suspects that Sir Gordon might go yet further against the trend for quangos and acquire still more staff.

## The Institutions

The place of the financial institutions – pension funds, life assurance companies and unit and other trusts – has been left until last in this consideration of additional factors bearing upon the reform of the City, because the position of the institutions is so ambiguous. About their current size and the rapidity of their expansion there is no room for doubt, however. Some figures on this have already been cited in Chapter 1 and it is difficult to add meaningfully to them. The curious reader will find instructive Plender's review of the rise of the pension funds, which he illustrates with a variety of measures.[25] He estimates the cash flow of the insurance companies of Britain at £10 billion p.a. handling savings which have grown from £7 billion in 1957 to £85 billion in 1981, with the institutions as a whole responsible for over £100 billion. The source of the majority of this massive income, contract savings schemes mostly subsidized by the state through tax relief, doubled between the 1960s and the 1980s to rise to 5% of Gross Domestic Product (GDP). The concentration of these vast flows of millions of small savers' money into great pools of liquid cash creates a number of problems. Where is it all to be invested? Will the normal criteria for investment produce an adequate rate of return? How is the probity and competence of investment managers to be secured? What are the implications for wider economic policy of these enormous investment decisions and in whose interest should they be made?

The answers to the earlier of these questions are a good deal easier than for the latter, but a general point about the institutions which has been made earlier in this book is worth repeating as a basis for the discussion which follows. The size of the sums managed is too large not to be a significant factor in the financial sector, and indeed in economic policy as a whole. Hence the interests which are reflected in the way the investment decisions are made are of considerable importance. Furthermore, the position of investment managers in the financial institutions is significant because of their vicarious responsibility to their numerous small clients with whom they have no direct contact. It is this which produces the ambiguity alluded to above. On the one hand, investment managers are in a relatively independent position. They are relative newcomers to the City, not requiring to protect a long-established position, as is the case in the banking sector, for example.

## Table 1. London's Accepting Houses, Business Indicators, 1979

| Accepting house | Balance sheet totals (£m) | Capital plus disclosed reserves (£m) | Pension funds managed (£m) | 'top 1000' Investment (£m) | No. of corporate clients |
|---|---|---|---|---|---|
| Arbuthnot Latham[a] | 185 | 13.4 | 1.5 | — | 1 |
| Baring Bros. | 475 | 25.0 | 675 | 69 | 27 |
| Brown Shipley | 253 | 19.0 | 17 | — | 5 |
| Charterhouse Japhet | 211 | 15.4 | 207 | 81 | 13 |
| Robert Fleming | 215 | 34.0 | 1,034 | 651 | 16 |
| Guinness Mahon | 304 | 22.7 | 3 | — | 6 |
| Hambros | 1,524 | 81.9 | 274 | 93 | 27 |
| Hill Samuel | 1,411 | 81.9 | 1,450 | 254 | 73 |
| Kleinwort Benson | 2,388 | 110.4 | 405 | 205 | 54 |
| Lazards | 729 | 41.9 | 941 | 83 | 32 |
| Mercury Securities[b] | 1,156 | 79.1 | 1,591 | — | 68 |
| Morgan Grenfell | 1,265 | 45.3 | 1,293 | — | 67 |
| Rea Bros. | 111 | 4.9 | 4 | — | 4 |
| N.M. Rothschild | 528 | 25.0 | 377 | 22 | 47 |
| Samuel Montagu | 1,368 | 57.1 | 96 | 302 | 31 |
| Schroders | 1,817 | 57.9 | 1,384 | 150 | 74 |
| Singer & Friedlander | 317 | n/a | 8 | 15 | 14 |

Sources: Annual reports; *Directory of City Connections 1980–1; Pension Funds Yearbook, 1981; Investment Trust Yearbook, 1981.*
[a]Resigned after takeover, 1982.
[b]S.G. Warburg & Co.
Cited in M. Lisle-Williams, Beyond the market: The survival of family capitalism in the English merchants banks, *British Journal of Sociology,* June 1984.

Further, they do not act for themselves, or for close associates, or even for large investors, as is usually the case in City financial decisions, but for a group of clients, often hundreds of thousands, who must inevitably be seen not just as clients but as an increasingly representative group of the British public. The institutions are, in other words, in a position to exercise a reforming and watchdog role in the City if they are so disposed, and could expect political support from doing so. On the other hand, the clients of the financial institutions are, in practice, in no position to exercise any direct influence over fund managers. Those who are in a position to exercise such an influence are those with whom the fund managers interact, and who in many cases manage the funds themselves for fees and commissions, namely the banks, big stockbrokers and specialist financial advisers, i.e. the most established and entrenched elements of the financial sector. Table 1 indicates, in the case of the accepting houses, i.e. the elite merchant banks, the extent to which organizations with relative limited capital and reserves manage very much larger funds directly.

**Table 2. Ownership of UK Quoted Equities (£m)**

|  | 1957 | | 1963 | | 1970 | |
|---|---|---|---|---|---|---|
| Insurance companies | 1023 | (8.8) | 2750 | (10.0) | 4618 | (12.2) |
| Pension funds | 400 | (3.4) | 1761 | (6.4) | 3423 | (9.0) |
| Investment trust companies | 600 | (5.2) | 2037 | (7.4) | 2875 | (7.6) |
| Unit trusts | 60 | (0.5) | 344 | (1.3) | 1095 | (2.9) |
| Persons, executors and trustees | 7631 | (65.8) | 14848 | (54.0) | 17949 | (47.4) |
| Other shareholders | 1886 | (16.3) | 5758 | (20.9) | 7890 | (20.9) |
|  | 11600 | (100) | 27498 | (100) | 37850 | (100 |
| Combined institutions | 2083 | (17.9) | 6892 | (25.1) | 12011 | (31.7) |

Source: J. Moyle, *The Pattern of Ordinary Share Ownership, 1957–1970*, Cambridge University Press, 1971.

The conclusion of Richard Minns's *Pension Funds and British Capitalism*[26] is that the financial institutions are almost entirely under the influence of the banking sector, and that their inherent capacity for reform and vigilance in the wider public interest is hence stultified. A large part of the reason for this lack of practical independence, and here Minns is emphatically supported by Plender, is the very speed of the growth of the financial institutions and the pressure to invest their huge cash flows. This has meant that existing outlets in equities and government stock have necessarily been extensively used, that existing agencies for their purchase have naturally been keen that their established position should continue to benefit, and that governments have naturally been concerned that organizations buying up to four-fifths of their stock should continue their purchasing on a stable basis rather than start branching out on independent paths of their own. In sum, the existing structure of financial and banking sector institutions was only too glad to accommodate the extra business provided by the new institutions, which have now grown so large that their continued cooperation is seen as vital to the stability of the financial sector as a whole, and to the success of a good deal of government economic policy.

One consequence of this has been the substantial takeover by the new institutions of much of the equity market, especially in leading stocks. Tables 2 and 3 provide an illustration of the way in which this has happened, but must be read in conjunction with Minns's finding that, in the case of pensions funds, although the

**Table 3.   Institutional Holdings of Listed UK Equities**

| | 1978 | | 1979 | | 1980 | | 1981 | |
|---|---|---|---|---|---|---|---|---|
| | £m | Holdings as % of market value | £m | Holdings as % of market value | £m | Holdings as % of market value | £m | Holdings as % of market value |
| Insurance companies | 11376 | 18.0 | 12227 | 18.3 | 16248 | 18.9 | 18744 | 18.9 |
| Pension funds | 15331 | 24.2 | 18305 | 27.3 | 22846 | 26.6 | 27060 | 27.2 |
| Trusts[a] | 6298 | 9.9 | 5761 | 8.6 | 6736 | 7.8 | 7913 | 8.0 |
| Total institutions[a] | 33005 | 52.1 | 36293 | 54.2 | 45830 | 53.3 | 53717 | 54.1 |

[a]Includes unit trusts' holdings of unlisted equities.

Source: *The Stock Exchange Fact Book*, (London; The Stock Exchange[a] J. Coakley and L. Harris, *The City of Capital*, Basil Blackwell, 1984.

Cited in J. Farrar and M. Russell, The impact of institutional investment on company law, *Company Lawyer*, Vol. 5, No. 3, p. 115.

funds owned 16.8% of company shares in 1975 and the banks only 0.7%, the banks controlled 17.6% in respect both of day-to-day and overall policy control. In the case of pension funds' shareholdings, the banks, brokers and others controlled 67% of the holdings.[27] Although the institutions provide the channel for the income, control of investments is hence relatively narrowly circumscribed by the existing structure of City institutions and interests. This conservatism is further reinforced by the conservative restraints imposed upon the institutions both by the law and by internal regulation, requiring them, for example, to place a minimum proportion of their investment income in government stock. This conservatism, coupled with the very large sums it is required to invest, result in an over-concentration in the equity market upon the leading companies, where a major loss on an investment is unlikely, and enough shares are being traded at any time to allow a large block to be bought. The implications of this for economic policy have exercised many, particularly on the left, for two decades.

A minority of the Wilson committee on the functioning of financial institutions recommended a deliberate direction of a limited proportion of financial institutions' funds to smaller companies to encourage genuine expansion in the economy. It has been pointed out that there is something of a paradox in the pattern of investment decisions by institutions whose clients' interests are predominantly long-term – 10–20 years or more – since those investments are predominantly medium-term. This is a criticism often made of the British capital market as a whole, in contrast to that of Japan, most notably. Investments are normally expected to yield steady returns within a year or two, rather than being left to develop for five or ten years before yielding much higher rates of return. Yet it is in their early years that even the most successful companies have their most frequent cash shortages and need every penny to return to the business for expansion, research and development.

This argument takes us into the realm of much wider argument about venture capital in the UK and whether fund managers could ever be realistically expected to acquire the quite different skills necessary to assess such risks. But enough has been said to indicate that the balance of opinion and evidence on the financial institutions suggests that they are very much dependent upon the pre-existing structure rather than an independent force for change.

This does not mean, however, that no initiatives have been taken or that the institutions exist in some kind of straightjacket. Another aspect of their ambiguity is their almost entire lack of legal regulation and the scope which this has offered for activities which have, on occasion, been imprudent and led to serious conflicts of interest. In the words of two legally qualified commentators:

> The interest of the insured under a contract of insurance is very remote from the portfolio company. He has merely a contractual right to a sum of money at a future date . . . There is a similar remoteness in the case of pension schemes . . . There is no legal regulation of pension schemes in the UK at the moment other than under trust and tax laws and the very limited provisions of the Social Security Act 1973 which set up the Occupational Pensions Board. There is no effective power of monitoring investment performance by the insured or member . . . In the case of a unit holder, he has a defined interest in the trust, but this carries no control over the portfolio. A shareholder in an investment trust has the rights of a shareholder in that company but no other control over the portfolio.[28]

The constraints upon investment fund managers of the financial institutions are thus those discussed above rather than of a legal character. There is ample evidence that this lack of a legal structure defining their responsibility has by no means been beneficial to the financial institutions. The evidence is of several sorts: of doubtful practices by fund managers, against which there appears to be little legal recourse; severe and increasingly complex conflicts of interest for fund managers and nominees as their investments have grown larger, on which there is little legal guidance; and of a number of recent attempts by financial institutions, sometimes acting in concert, to improve standards in the City in the interests of their clients and the wider public. In short, the ambiguity of the present unregulated situation and the lack of any substantial collective initiative by the institutions themselves, has resulted in what could have been a significant reform movement failing to crystallize.

Wide ranging evidence of incompetence, arrogance, blatant conflicts of interest and recklessness, entertaining to the cynic and no doubt hair-raising to the member of the funds so put at risk, is deployed by Plender.[29] This is not the place to repeat it, and to attempt to summarize the subtleties of the detailed accounts he provides of asset management by the pension funds of ICI, Unilever, the Post Office and the electricity supply industry would be to risk misrepresentation. What rings clearly through it all, however, is the lack of institutional and legal restraint upon fund managers, even restraints upon such matters as pension funds investing in the shares of the employer's own company, fund managers purchasing shares on their own account in companies in which they are recommending or directing the fund to make purchases, and of funds making money available as loans to members of the fund. If there is one area which stands out in Plender's account as leading to problems, however it is property. As was seen in the discussion of the secondary banking crisis, and as the literature on it documents extensively, the institutions were badly burned by the secondary banking crash and by the accompanying collapse of the property market, in which they were heavily involved. As Plender notes, in 1980 insurance companies and pension funds owned more property than all the 90 or so Stock Exchange listed property companies. It was the one major area in which the institutions branched out from the blue chip shares and gilt edged securities, and even became so adventurous as to take large stakes in property development in the 1970s. Disaster was staved off in a number of cases only by luck and the vast size of the continuing cash flows of the funds. Had these flows been less, a number of funds might well have gone the way of the Crown Agents. Like the Agents, fund managers seem at times to have been naive about the property market, to have had unrealistic expectations about the absolute security of property as an asset, and to have been easily gulled by the variety of sharp operators who flourished in the boom.

The issue of behaviour, upon which Plender concentrates, is not however the most interesting or significant for the institutions or their managers. More important are the conflicts of interest which arise when funds acquire substantial interests in companies, often large plc's, as a result of their substantial investments. As a consequence they may seek or be invited to sit on the board. There are no unambiguous rules as to how such directors should then act. Should they act in the interests of the company, of which they are a director, and if so advise the fund manager to buy more of their shares if this is appropriate? Should they act in the long-term interests of the company and demand divestment of unprofitable sectors and costly reorganization, even if that affects share price and dividends in the short term? Should they advise fund managers of the company's target for a takeover bid, so that the fund can make a smart profit? If the company gets into difficulties, should they resign or soldier on in the hope of resolving the problems, and even seek more fund investments to do so? The problem is manifestly more complex still where a large institution nominates directors to boards of several companies in the same industrial sector, and where the nominees, as employees of the institutions, have had a past career working closely together. As Farrar and Russell remark, 'This is one area where the question must at least be raised, whether English company law should adapt so as to redefine the role of the majority shareholder in general and/or the shareholders in particular'.[30] These are not merely hypothetical issues. The relationship between fund managers and City institutions such as merchant banks and stockbrokers is sufficiently close and substantial, for example, for the terms of a takeover bid to be put over the telephone to institutional fund managers and for their acceptance to determine the outcome before the bid comes on to the open market. The same is true of issues of new shares, where underwriters depend upon the institutions to place the majority of a large issue before trading begins.

What then of the evidence that the institutions can use their muscle in the public interest? There are some indications that what was begun reluctantly is growing in strength, self-confidence and co-ordination, but it has to be said immediately that there is far from a co-ordinated movement yet. One of the earlier examples of institutional pressure was provided by the Thalidomide affair, in which Distillers, the UK licencees, were reluctant to accept responsibility and resisted public pressure for a generous settlement with the victims. Eventually the company's shares began to fall and the offer was increased from £3.25 milion to £21.75 million, after a meeting between the institutional investors, the company's merchant bankers and its senior management. The institutions are reputed to have a predilection for negotiating behind the scenes, and are said to have investigated unprofitable contracts and management incentive and share option schemes and other matters, and to influence senior management appointments. Certainly, the outcome of public litigation by the Prudential in the Newman Industries case in 1980–82, which reportedly cost £750000 at first instance, and was later settled after going to appeal, can only have counselled caution on the institutions taking too aggressive a public stance in individual cases. More recently, there is evidence of a greater move towards a co-ordinated policy by the institutions through their associations, and of a pattern in individual cases of regarding the expression of a firm view of the public interest as normal, even if this cannot always be managed entirely behind closed doors. The area of director's perks and privileges and golden handshakes has provided an issue upon which the institutions have been willing to assert themselves.

*Golden Handshakes*

Ever since Edward Heath denounced the payment of part of the fees of directors of

Lonrho into the tax haven of the Cayman Islands in the early 1970s, as the unpleasant and unacceptable face of capitalism, directors' perks have been a particularly quotable area of criticism. Whereas at that time it was the disproportion between the size of perks and golden handshakes and any conceivable benefit to the company that the director may have provided that caused outrage, by the early 1980s attention was fixed in more detail upon the powers of directors to award themselves such benefits, and of shareholders to control and monitor them. In this latter respect the Companies Act 1980 was helpful, since it requires details of service contracts to directors to be made available, and has given rise to publicity in a number of instances that might otherwise have passed unnoticed. Nor have the 1980s been without their spectacular cases of big pay-ofs. Jack Gill's £750000 golden handshake, when he fell out with Lord Grade (Chairman of Associated Communications Corportation (ACC), the television and films company) after 25 years working together, is the most notorious, but the £400000 compensation paid by Playboy to Admiral Sir John Treacher, when the group decided to sell its Casinos because it had lost its gaming licences, was also important. Treacher had worked only 96 days as a director, though of course the compensation was for the years that he was contracted to work but would not because of the sale of the company. Other less prominent cases abounded, both of substantial golden handshakes and of highly favourable deals on company property – also a feature of the Jack Gill case – and the provision of luxury services for directors, even by sometimes quite modestly sized companies. So much so that a stockbroker and Tory MP, Anthony Beaumont-Dark, went as far as proposing a £75000 maximum for golden handshakes.

This approach rather missed the central point however. For although Henry James, director of the National Association of Pension Funds (NAPF), could come out with such traditional vituperations as 'we are not opposed to generous payments, but we do object to obscene payments',[31] the NAPF's action in seeking an injunction to stop Gill's payment sought to bring the issue of shareholders' power and directors' privilege into open debate. Limited liability companies are supposed to be subject to shareholder democracy – he who holds a majority of shares controls the company; he who has a significant minority can normally press for representation in the board room; and he who has any, can ask questions and vote at the AGM. The ACC case made a nonsense of all this, for the only shares publicly traded were non-voting ones. This suited the IBA, which requires tight control over shares, so that a company cannot be taken over and run in a quite different way than that upon which its licence application was based. In the ACC case, however, the source of private control over the voting shares was the more common one of a successful private company whose directors were used to regarding it as their property, subsequently raising cash from the public. Where directors are also executives, and there are no non-executive directors on the board, and voting shares are controlled by directors, there is little to stop the directors writing anything into their service contracts. From the point of view of the small or non-voting shareholder, this constitutes a conflict of interest which may well reduce the dividend paid. In law, shareholders must approve if the golden handshake exceeds that which a court would award a dismissed director for breach of contract, and many settlements are worked out on this basis. The length of service contracts is, however, pertinent here, and many run over five years where there is an argument for reduction to three, in line with the normal period of election as a director by the shareholders.

That the fight for reform should be led by the NAPF is indicative of the other side of the story. Many institutions refused to invest in ACC because the shares for sale had no voting rights. With a number of limited changes, legal and administrative, the powers of the executive directors to indulge themselves could be rapidly eliminated. One reform is to require at least two non-executive directors on every board; another is to change the law to permit or require directors to be paid at least in part in shares in the company, so that their cash payments reflect, through dividends, the fortunes of the company they administer; another is to modify the tax rules which allow the first £25 000 of the golden handshake tax free, and subject the rest to only 30% tax; and of course the reform of non-voting shares would further serve to give teeth to the requirements of disclosure of the terms of directors' service contracts. Certainly there were those who took the matter seriously: 'The executive director has become the shareholder's worst enemy',[32] said Edgar Palamountain, former director of M & G Trust and now chairman of the Wider Share Ownership Council.

When it came to the crunch, therefore, every hand seemed to be against Jack Gill, and that of his former boss had withered. The NAPF had an injunction to stop the payment, and Robert Holmes à Court, who finally won the battle to acquire ACC, also made his opposition clear. Although the battle over the payment dragged on until late 1983, à Court ensured victory by acquiring 75% of the stock of both classes, so giving him the power to change the company's rules, which he did by enfranchising the non-voting shares. Meanwhile, it was disclosed that the Department of Trade had been conducting a secret inquiry into ACC, and that further investigations would follow. This was paralleled by an inquiry by the Inland Revenue. The source of all of them lies at least in part in the extravagance of directors of a company whose spectacular record of success ended with a profits fall from £11.63 million in 1981 to £2.62 million in 1983, and behind this the perennial problems of the fiduciary duties of companies created by the energy and flair of a successful entrepreneur to the public shareholders to whom they turn in later years to raise capital.[33]

The ACC affair was one in which the institutions could appear as the champions of the public interest and win. The confidence they gained there was no doubt one reason for the reportedly firm line taken by the NAPF and the British Insurance Association in urging their members not to buy the shares of Reuters when they came onto the market in 1984. The shares looked set for a huge success because of the strong position of Reuters, not so much as a mainline news agency, but as the owner of a successful system for the rapid international dissemination of financial information. The institutions' concern, as at ACC, was that the shares on offer to the public carried less favourable voting rights than those retained by the newspapers, which had cooperated to found Reuters news agency in the nineteenth century. The response by the underwriters was an unprecedented propaganda campaign for the launch on both sides of the Atlantic, which succeeded at least in part because institutional funds managed by merchant banks and others outside the institutions themselves were only too ready to snap up the shares. Hambros, for example, almost offered to take on the whole of the UK offering, according to one report.[34] As a result, the underwriting went well and the institutions were defeated by the extent of their embrace by the City establishment.

## Notes

1.   See P. Knightley, The Gilded Tax Dodgers, the *Sunday Times*, October/November 1980, later published as *The Vestey Affair*, McDonald, 1981.
2.   L. Sullivan, The multi-million pound tax dodge, the *Sunday Times*, 18 November 1979.
3.   See the *Daily Telegraph*, 17 August 1979.
4.   *The Times*, law report, 14 December 1979.
5.   See *The Times*, law report, 23 May 1980.
6.   See *The Times*, law report, March 1981.
7.   T.M. Ashe, Tax avoidance: form giving way to substance? *Company Lawyer*, Vol. 2, No. 3, p. 104.
8.   See Ashe, op. cit., p. 105.
9.   Command 8822, HMSO, 1983.
10.   See R. Franey, *Poor Law: Mass Arrest of Homeless Claimants in Oxford*, CHAR, 1983.
11.   See *The Times*, law report, 14 February 1984.
12.   See, e.g. David Tallon, Law Lords hand Revenue the right to read our minds, *The Times*, 18 February 1984.
13.   Quoted in I. Griffiths, Blind man's buff takes over in the Revenue avoidance game, *The Times*, 13 March 1984.
14.   I draw this summary from S. Aris, *Going Bust*, Andre Deutsch, 1985, which is also the source of the examples in the following paragraph. I am grateful to the author and publisher for letting me see pre-publication copy of the book.
15.   See J. Wilson, *Roger Cook's Checkpoint*, Ariel Books, 1983.
16.   J. Wilson, op. cit., pp. 229–30.
17.   *Report of the Committee on Insolvency Law and Practice*, Chairman Sir K. Cork, HMSO, 1982.
18.   Cork, in Wilson, op. cit., p. 232.
19.   Cork, quoted in an interview with S. Aris, the *Sunday Times*, 16 December 1984.
20.   In Wilson, op. cit., p. 234.
21.   *A Revised Framework for Insolvency Law*, Command 9175, HMSO 1984.
22.   This, and the preceding remarks by Cork on the White Paper are taken from Cork's interview with Aris – see note 19.
23.   Alex Fletcher, Junior Minister at the Department of Trade, *Sunday Times*, 11 November 1984.
24.   *Tenth Annual Report of the Director General of Fair Trading 1983*, HMSO, 1984, pp. 10–11.
25.   J. Plender, *That's the Way the Money Goes*, Andre Deutsch, 1982.
26.   Heinemann, 1980, see p. 14.
27.   Op. cit., pp. 145–6.
28.   J. Farrar and M. Russell, The Impact of Institutional Investments as Company Law, *Company Lawyer*, Vol. 5, No. 3, p.108.
29   .Op. cit., see Chapter 6 esp.
30.   Op. cit., p. 111.
31.   Quoted in P. Wheatcroft, Derailing the Director's gravy train, the *Sunday Times*, 11 May 1982.
32.   Quoted by P. Wheatcroft, Derailing the Director's gravy train, the *Sunday Times*, 11 May 1982.
33.   For a further comment on the ACC affair, see L. Sealy, Refloating the Titanic: the battle for ACC, *Company Lawyer*, Vol. 3. No. 3.
34.   See *The Times*, 15 May 1984; the *Sunday Times*, 20 May 1984.

# 6

## Some Problems: Fraud prevention and the new financial conglomerates

### Introduction

In this chapter and the final one which follows I turn from considering the nature of the movement to reform of City institutions and the reasons for it to look at some of the difficulties that are raised. This chapter is concerned with two specific and relatively well-recognized areas of difficulty, whereas the final one will deal with the more general implications of the attempts at reform for the development of British society as a whole.

The first of the two problems considered immediately is one of long-standing intractability in the City – fraud prosecutions. It is notoriously hard to mount successful fraud prosecutions for business and commercial crimes, and dealing with those cases which give rise to most anxiety in City and business circles usually proves even harder. The prosecution of breaches of well-established and legally codified rules is obviously easier, *ceteris paribus,* than framing a charge in preparing a case which will successfully convict an offender and involve appropriate sanctions where what is at issue is precisely the current level of acceptability of certain business practices. As will be seen below, sharpening up the process of criminal prosecutions of commercial fraud has been a substantial preoccupation of Government and others in the context of the reform of the City of London.

The other issue, which has rather wider implications, is the creation of large new financial institutions as a result of increased international competitive pressures. Aspects of this development have been referred to at several points already, but the political economic implications of greatly increased size and diversification, and the introduction of so-called 'financial supermarkets' aimed at attracting a large number of new customers of relatively ordinary means have yet to be considered. The issues of financial stability, competition, co-ordination, conflicts of interest and state responsibility, all of them operating on a hitherto unknown scale, lead naturally into the discussion of general issues raised by the reforms in the final chapter.

## Fraud prosecutions

Criminal prosecution is the sharp end of the system of control of financial institutions, the ultimate sanction for the serious wrongdoer. For that reason there is a variety of arguments, many of them rarely made fully explicit, for fraud prosecution to be a successful and effective weapon when it is used. As will be described below, during the period of reform there was no shortage of critics willing to propose improvements and demand a more vigorous prosecution policy, but the considered view of this writer is that such demands give inadequate weight to the distinctive nature of the difficulties in controlling commercial and financial funds, particularly those of greatest current interest. First though, the arguments for an effective prosecution system for fraud.

A frequently articulated view here is that lack of criminal prosecution with a high chance of success seriously undermines the credibility of the entire system of regulation of commerce and finance: prosecution should act as a kind of longstop and a justification for the proceedings and sanctions of self-regulatory agencies within institutions. Thus criminal prosecution seems to be held (a) to act as a formal seal of approval of tough action by the institutions against their members; (b) as a formal public indication that the behaviour in question commands public attention as seriously beyond pale of current acceptability; and hence (c) that the absence of criminal prosecution as a follow-up to institutional sanction undermines confidence in the institutions and may leave members to wonder why they bother to observe proper standards if others can 'get away with it'. More generally, successful fraud prosecutions may be argued uniquely to fulfil all the requirements of an adequate system of social control, which may severally be managed by various other means, but not all by any other single means. Thus criminal conviction may be maintained to deter other offenders, a successful system of fraud control will involve both detecting and convicting offenders, and the entire process will protect the public. This, however, is to place unreasonably high expectations upon criminal prosecution. Although the critics are never quite as overt as this, their implied position is frequently close to the fetishism of criminal prosecution. To put the point bluntly: if there is a vigorous, well-funded and staffed prosecution system, which is successful in detecting and convicting offenders, it will deter others and protect the public, but this view wholly ignores the fact that criminal prosecution is a formal intervention into social life hedged around with rules to protect the innocent, and that it cannot be generally successful unless the relevant social institutions and their personnel support it by acting both to condemn and denounce unethical behaviour, and to give evidence to the prosecuting authorities formally and informally where it occurs.

It has been one of the principal characteristics of City institutions until recently to keep evidence of wrongdoing under wraps and deal with it informally among gentlemanly equals in the club. Although, as I shall describe in a moment, the principal emphasis of critics has been upon the improvement of criminal prosecution, and although it is essential for this to be efficient, determined and effective, such an attack cannot succeed, as it seems to hope, without also considering what should be the relationship between criminal prosecution and self-regulation, and to this little attention has been given. Rather, the critics' line has been: self-regulation is beside the point if criminal prosecution is ineffective.

Nor is this an approach confined to journalists. It has been adopted by some of the institutions and is a large element in the Government's reaction. Thus one finds not only the accomplished financial journalist Charles Raw remarking that "I suspect that one or two convictions (for fraud) coupled with stiff sentences would do far more for investor protection than any number of state-backed self-regulatory codes of conduct[1], but also the CSI responding to Gower as follows:

> unquestionably the greatest weakness of the present scheme of regulation lies in what is a Government responsibility, but one that goes wider than the Department of Trade, the failure to deal effectively with commercial and financial fraud. Anyone who commits an elaborate fraud knows that he probably will not be prosecuted, and that if he is prosecuted it will take years to formulate charges, and he will probably escape the main charges. There is little point in improving the finer points of conduct if gross fraud goes unpunished.[2]

No doubt the CSI had in mind such cases as that of commodity brokers Miller Carnegie where the trial lasted three months and cost £500 000 before collapsing.

The political implications of being seen to be 'soft' on fraud were painfully apparent to Ferdinand Mount, a commentator with the reputation of being close to the Prime Minister:

> There is . . . nothing to unsettle a Conservative Government two or three years after an election like a fruity financial scandal. It crystallises discontent, offers an outlet for moral outrage and fills the air with the smell of decay. In previous cases this has been intensified by a general uneasy feeling that the British authorities are slow and listless in the prosecution of fraud. We do not, most people think, handle these matters as well as they do in the United States, where crooked tycoons are caught and sent to gaol. And most people are right.[3]

Mount linked his complaint to a characterization of the big fraudster as foreign, but he is not alone in complaining that foreign complications make criminal sanctions even less likely. The Society of Conservative Lawyers complained recently[4] that London was becoming a haven for international criminals because, in part, of a policy by the DPP 'not to bring actions against criminals in this country where the person engaged in fraud is a foreign national and his victims are also foreign nationals'.

They also complained that 'it is ridiculous for our prosecuting authorities to be hampered by lack of funds when London is the leading international legal and financial centre', and recommended that Britain should sign the European convention on extradition, which would make prosecution of foreigners, and the recovery of British nationals for prosecution here easier. The group also recommended the closing of the legal loophole whereby conspiracy to commit crimes abroad is presently not an offence in Britain.

While criminal conspiracies hatched by foreigners for perpetration abroad are no doubt an extreme, if important, instance, more immediate concern about extradition was provided by a number of cases where the principal in a crashed and possibly fraudulently operated company has debunked abroad. A review in early 1984 of losses to the public through licensed dealers in securities alone put losses since 1981 at over £36 million, excluding one case in which the amount of losses was never made public.[5] One prominent in this number was Norton Warburg, whose principal, Andrew Warburg, remained in Spain, safe from a warrant held by the City of London police. Another was Exchange Securities which left 2000 investors looking for £11 million after the desertion of the principal, Keith Hunt, in 1983. Certainly extradition is a major problem, involving time and expense, and it also carries the penalty that, by the terms of the extradition treaties, only the offences named at extradition can subsequently be prosecuted, even if others come to light in the course of subsequent proceedings.

Such special problems were by no means the only basis for concern of Mount and others at the 'listless' attitudes of the authorities. The DPP in particular, being the key authority making the decision as to whether to press a prosecution, has come in for a great deal of criticism, both for the slowness of his decisions and for the restrictive conventions by which he makes them. Prosecutions are mounted by the DPP in fraud and some other cases where it would be cost-effective, that is where the amount of money involved is greater than the cost of investigating the case and bringing it to trial; where there is a better than even chance of success, the so-called 51% rule; and where the public interest, which is never defined, would be served by a prosecution. Given that fraud cases are complicated, that key individuals may die, retire or go abroad and that offences may not come to light until some time after they were committed, delay is a common problem, and the greater the delay the greater the difficulty of mounting a successful prosecution, and hence the greater the chances of the DPP deciding not to do so.

Since the processes which take place in the DPP's office are never made public, although the reports of leading counsel commissioned for opinion sometimes are, the expectant public is only aware of the delay, which, if lengthy, naturally gives rise to suspicions that the issue is being ducked. Thus in the case of the British Telecom launch where the prospectus stipulated one application per person, the Department of Trade and Industry (DTI) called in the police in a few cases of multiple applications uncovered by the issuing bank and their accountants. About ten major operations involving hundreds of applications were centred upon, with smaller offenders simply being refused an allocation of shares. Prosecution for fraud was still pending during the Spring of 1985 and there would seem to be little justification for delay since the evidence had been collected long before.[6] On the other hand, cheques worth £850 000 were sent in with the applications, and they were cashed and deposited with the Bank of England. The stags, assuming they had been allocated shares, quickly sold the allocation supplied for in the expectation of a profit, only to find that they had no allocation and were forced to buy shares on the open market in order to fulfil their commitments to sell. They were punished by administrative action rather than legal prosecution, and of course remain anonymous to the public. Could it be, many ask, that the powers that be favour the continued anonymity of those who might turn out to be respected City figures?

Another group of cases giving rise to complaints about the DPP in particular were those arising out of the Lloyds insurance and stock market cases discussed in earlier chapters. Although, as discussed at the appropriate point, a number of principals were heavily sanctioned by the self-regulatory agencies, and cases against others are proceeding, the DPP failed to commit itself to action in a number of cases and significantly declined to do so in others. This gave rise from 1981 onwards to repeated comment and speculation as to the reason for and justification of this increasingly inordinate delay. Michael Gillard in the following characteristically vituperative account chronicles the tale of inaction.[7]

Recent decisions and inferences emerging from the DPP have only served to increase scepticism about the will to combat the big time or well-connected fraudster.

Take for example the decision not to proceed against the senior partners of Halliday, Simpson, the Manchester stockbrokers already found 'bang to rights' and banned for life by the Stock Exchange.

Those with knowledge of the case fail to see any justice in that decision, based largely on the advice tendered by Treasury counsel Michael Corkery. Especially as among the grounds advanced for it were the highly convenient suicide last year of the Galloping Major, Trevor Dawson of merchant bankers Arbuthnot Latham, the supposed "vegetable" mental state of Halliday's senior partner David Garner (a condition no doubt likely to be exacerbated by the close proximity of men with large feet and pointed heads) and, most extraordinary of all, the length of time since the alleged offences of defrauding clients by booking share deals at phoney prices via the infamous 'put-through' method.

Corkery had already made a similar negative pronouncement regarding the case against those involved in the similar Piccadilly and Chieftain unit trust scandals. But whose fault, it might be asked, is it that these offences have developed whiskers?

The Halliday scandal broke, post-Piccadilly and post-Chieftain, in the summer of 1981. The Stock Exchange report was completed in late 1982. It found the case proven against certain Halliday partners and implicated certain of their clients, like the Galloping Major and Kuwait Investment Office investment manager Bruce Dawson.

It then took until May 1982 for the Stock Exchange to do their thing and boot out Garner and his accomplices. The report – highly detailed – was then passed to then City Police and Michael Corkery. 1982 runs into 1983. Michael Corkery continues to advise. 1983 becomes Summer 1984 when it is decided that the matter, involving deals done in 1979 and before, is far too old to go ahead. Hardly surprising.

So Garner and his three partners Russell Torr, John Norris and Graham Jackson – all banned for life by the Stock Exchange – could no doubt claim today that they were harshly judged as no further action was taken. Similar protestations could be made by Alan Judd and his Piccadilly cohorts along with Ian Hazeel of Chieftain. No wonder therefore that few DPP decisions have caused such unhappiness as that in the Halliday case.

A similar pattern appears to be emerging with the Lloyd's scandals. As disclosed here last month, the DPP has ruled that there should be no further action taken over the £6 million misapplied from the syndicates managed by Brooks & Dooley on grounds of the vintage of the alleged offences and the difficulty of obtaining information from Bermuda through which much of the money was routed. Now there are ominous signs that the results of the Alexander Howden and PCW enquiries will not disturb the lifestyles of those who presided while over $60 million was misapplied. Let Lloyd's kick them out and the Department of Trade reports rubbish them seems to be the DPP policy. That way there need be no need to incur the responsibility for the heavy cost and unforeseeable result of a prosecution.

The DPP can hide behind the advice of senior counsel, like Michael Hill, to the effect of the complexity of the alleged offences and the difficulty of getting a jury to understand them, not to mention those reliable old stand-bys, ancient offences and information only available in uncooperative hideaways such as Bermuda, Switzerland and Liechtenstein.

Should all that fail, the DPP has another good old stand-by in that the chief PCW pillagers – Peter Cameron-Webb and Peter Dixon – are abroad and would need to be extradited, which, as everyone in the DPP's office knows, is prima facie grounds for doing nothing.

A study of the won-lost-drawn record in the war against fraud in recent years quickly reveals that few major scandals have resulted in a prosecution. Where are the prosecutions of not just those at the Stock Exchange and Lloyd's but Norton Warburg, Signal Life, M.L. Doxford? Answer: either still being investigated or already marked N.F.A.

It is unreasonable to place the entire blame on the DPP, though the complaint about unwarranted delay seems just. The DPP decides to press a case in the light of the chances of success, and the chances of success depend crucially upon the effectiveness of the investigative and prosecuting machinery. Mount was in no doubt that it was in the improvement of this machinery that at least a partial remedy lay.

> The first and simplest thing to do would be for (the Secretary of State) to set up at the Department of Trade and Industry a super-fraud unit staffed with highly qualified lawyers and policemen. The idea runs into the usual Whitehall territorial squabble: the Attorney General jealously safeguards his responsibility for the lawyers, the Home Secretary ditto for the policemen. But sooner or later, one fancies, we shall have to have a squad of DTI tough eggs showing, one hopes, the best characteristics of their master (Norman Tebbit): a quick brain, a suspicious mind and a modicum of low cunning.[8]

At about the same time as Mount was writing, the Government was in the process of making a two-pronged response to this very complaint. The first was the establishment on a permanent basis in early 1985 of the Fraud Investigations Group (FIG), with a staff of 30 civil servants, including specialist accountants from the DTI and lawyers from the DPP's office. The Group had been running on an informal basis for 18 months, and is based in the DPP's office. Its function is to co-ordinate enquiries in major fraud cases at an early stage, with a view both to increasing levels of cooperation between the police, DTI and DPP, and to ensuring that the police do not pursue enquiries at length when successful prosecution is unlikely, and do not fail to secure necessary evidence when it is available in their enquiries. The history of police relations with the DPP's office over fraud has not always been happy in this respect, with the police sometimes feeling that substantial cases developed after extensive investigation were unreasonably refused sanction to proceed. The point about bringing in the DPP early is to ensure that his requirements are clearly identified, and hence police time is not wasted.

The initiative is a very limited one, and it remains to be seen how effective the FIG will be. The staff and resources are small, and the formalization of the Group's existence does not affect the division of responsibility and powers between the three bodies involved – more if the numbers of different police forces is counted, though London naturally predominates. Further, other relevant bodies, such as the Inland Revenue and Customs and Excise have not been brought in, even though they often have a major role in frauds, especially where the collapse of a business brings it to light. New institutions with an increasing role in the supervision of financial institutions, such as the OFT and the SIB remain so far uninvolved, as of course do the self-regulatory agencies themselves, despite their increased responsibilities and the great emphasis placed upon them. In short, the limited initiative of the FIG can scarcely be said to constitute either effective funding or effective co-ordination on the issue of fraud investigation and prosecution; at best it is a modest start.

The Government's other initiative was a bolder one in respect of fraud trials. A committee under Lord Justice Roskill was set up by the Government in 1984 to improve legal procedure in the prosecution of fraud, and from the start it was reported as being willing to discuss the abolition of jury trial in fraud cases, or the establishment of special juries drawn from qualified people. The argument here, reminiscent of those deployed a decade earlier by Sir Robert Mark and others over the capacity of professional criminals to exploit the legal system to avoid conviction, was that fraud cases are exceedingly long and complex, and juries drawn these days, especially at the Central Criminal Court with its East End catchment area, largely from working-class panels, are not competent to try cases. One possibly apocryphal version of a comment of this nature by an expert witness at a fraud trial, was that only three people understood the case and they included neither the Judge nor Counsel for the Prosecution.

This is not the place to go into great detail into whether juries are incapable of understanding fraud cases or whether proceedings have to be so lengthy and complex. At the time of writing, Roskill still had to report, but the evidence was mostly in and its balance was substantially in the favour of juries.[9] Not only were such predictable protagonists as the Law Society, the Criminal Bar Association and Justice ready to defend the jury at fraud trials, but also the majority of chief constables. In addition, evidence of the incompetence of juries proved as hard to locate as it did in the case of trials involving professional criminals. Justice lawyers claimed that judges were impressed by the performance of juries, and that there was no evidence of perverse verdicts or verdicts which reflected a failure to understand the case. Witnesses were hard put to cite a single case in which the trial could not be mounted because a jury would not understand it. Length and complexity notwithstanding, therefore, the jury emerged in the experience of court practitioners as neither arbitrary, nor stupid, nor lazy. Further, the argument was made in defence of a uniform system that there are substantial political grounds for retaining the jury as a key element in criminal trials, which are believed to be important in sustaining public support for criminal justice. Any suspension of this right to a jury would be bound to seem arbitrary, since it would have to be based on some judgement as to the complexity of the case or a decision on the nature of the charges preferred. And even if the arguments for trial by expert assessors in some form is made out for a minority of cases, are these numerous enough to justify compromising one of the foundations of British criminal justice?

By contrast the committee began to hear some damning criticism of other parties to fraud trials. Thus it was argued that the time and expense of full commital proceedings under which all the evidence is heard in order to establish a *prima facie* case for full trial is unjustified. More relevant, it was argued, would be the establishment of pre-trial review with wide powers for the judge, who should be a specialist in the field, to examine evidence and try preliminary issues. Further, such hearings should be attended by senior Counsel for both sides, not as now by juniors. The general point of co-ordinating court procedure by bringing together judge and counsel for both sides at an early stage and insisting that all remain on the case and pursue an early trial is clearly relevant to coherent and speedy justice being done, regardless of the personal and administrative convenience of the various learned parties. Another proposal was for the prosecution to prune back charges as far as possible, and for the defence to make the main lines of its position available to the prosecution, to avoid delay in overpreparing for the trial and the needless length and complexity of it. The objective should be for the pre-trial procedure to agree on the facts and the main outline of the disputed items, so that the trial proper could concentrate clearly on them. In addition, the presentation of evidence in fraud cases could be made easier if modern techniques of graphic display were permitted in the courtroom. All in all this amounts to a substantial improvement and streamlining of fraud trials in order to cut time and costs and make them easier for juries to appraise, at the cost of a limited loss of defendants rights, for example, over the disclosure of his defence before the trial.

Thus, the government showed itself to be concerned about at least two aspects of fraud prosecution, investigation and trial, with at least a chance of real improvement in the latter case if the evidence to Roskill is acted upon. In a third area, that of formulation of the law itself on fraud, and hence the offences charged, it has shown itself to be less concerned – although it has engaged, as have all Governments – in attempting to plug loopholes where they have become embarrassing, e.g. insider trading, dealt with by the 1974–9 administration and concert parties, on which action was taken by the Thatcher Government.[10] This is not the place to comment on the general issue of the nature of Company Law in Britain, which forms the wider context for the fraud issue, but it is relevant to note the concern of one legal commentator as to the inadequacy of the law in allowing appropriate charges to be brought in fraud cases:[11]

In some cases, where there is a specific serious offence which fits the circumstances, as in those involving fraudulent and misleading prospectuses and other similar frauds, there will be a reasonable chance of success. But there are no such serious specific offences in respect of many other forms of City fraud, notably those which involve the improper abstraction of funds from a company or the manipulation of market. In such cases the prosecution is faced with a choice between attempting to establish less appropriate ''real'' crimes or falling back on less serious preventive or regulatory offences. If the defendants are charged with ''real'' crimes, like theft or obtaining by deception, there may be considerable difficulty in persuading a jury that what has been done matches the plain man's conception of such offences. If less precise charges of conspiracy to defraud or deceive are laid, the defence will be able to take full advantage of the current legal distaste for vague and general charges.

Some elements of the DPP's difficulties over the chances of a prosecution's success and the public interest involved in bringing it are evident here, although it is fair to say that he has not gone public in calling for new legal weapons for his armoury. Nor is this Hadden's only, or indeed principal, conclusion, which is that

> the traditional criminal prosecution is not an appropriate mechanism for the day-to-day regulation of companies in the securities market. . . . Much of the preventive role of the criminal law may also be carried out more effectively by administrative than by legal procedures. There is a choice in this context between Governmental and self-regulatory systems. In either case, the objective should be to achieve as much as possible through licensing and prior vetting, rather than by prosecution and punishment after the event. This is particularly appropriate in respect of such relatively infrequent transactions as the issue of prospectuses and takeovers and mergers, where the costs can readily be incorporated into the relevant fees or by some form of general levy. Failure to conform with this form of regulation may be dealt with by specific injunctions or directives backed by the ultimate sanction of withdrawal of a licence to trade or of exclusion from the market. There is also the possibility of civil actions for damages based upon a breach of statutory or perhaps even unofficial regulations. This form of action is highly developed in the United States.[12]

What Hadden might have added is that it is only the success of the regulatory machinery as a whole, of which criminal prosecution only forms a small element in the case of fraud, that keeps offences down to a level that can be processed with an degree of efficiency. If wrongdoings, whichever side of the criminal law they are technically on, mount beyond a certain level, many within the fields affected will become cynical, encouraged to sharp practice themselves to compete, and unwilling to give evidence against wrongdoers, still less blow the whistle. Only in an environment where high standards prevail will practititoners feel the sense of indignation and personal security essential to denounce the wrongdoer promptly and accurately. In turn, high ethical standards cannot be encouraged except by measures to ensure competence, disclosure of dealings, and inspections to enforce compliance with public standards and procedures. It is significant that NASDIM should be so concerned with these matters, since licensed dealers have in the past been among the most intractable offenders. The importance of licensing and vetting machinery administered variously by state agencies, self-regulatory industry bodies or quangos like the MIB and SIB and the OFT, is that they enforce standards sufficiently effectively to make it difficult for fraudsters to operate except by brazen lies and deceptions, which will only aid them in the short term. This will not only deter would-be offenders and provide a better basis for whistle-blowers to act, but also enable the formal investigative and sanctioning machinery, including criminal prosecution, to concentrate on a reasonable case-load. Where regular reviews of compliance and disclosure requirements monitored by the self-regulatory agencies do uncover significant wrongdoing, it is essential that adequate sanctions by way of disqualification from further work in the relevant market, and the recovery of illegitimate earnings, and a fine be imposed. If this is the case, however, it leaves the criminal law with only a residual role in adding potential incarceration and an additional public denunciation to the range of sanctions available.

We thus return to one of the major concerns of this book: the means by which City institutions regulate themselves. The conclusion must be that the criminal law can only be a support for regulation, whether it is carried out through self-regulation proper or through state inspectors. It can never be a substitute for it. It has to be borne in mind, however, that whether institutions regulate themselves or whether the state imposes a system of vetting and licensing on them, the events reviewed in this book, and the reform of City institutions discussed, emphatically indicate that it is the state which is the ultimate guarantor of the system. It may, as in Britain, and particularly under a Conservative Government, wish to distance itself from its status as guarantor and to emphasize the independence of City institutions even in the revamped regimes, but the enhanced role of the Bank of England, the established place of the DTI, the increasingly wide range of the OFT, and the creation of the SIB and the MIB should leave us in no doubt of the essential role of the state in determining the nature of the order and the extent of the guarantees to investors, clients, depositors and other customers of City institutions.

The implications of this enhanced role for the state will be the concern of the next chapter, but it bears pointing out in the present that, if the above analysis is correct, it involves the recognition by the state, albeit nor a very articulate one as yet, of an administrative obligation to intervene and maintain benign vigilance in the public interest to restrain capitalist institutions, rather than to rely upon a formal framework of law to establish boundaries within which institutions may act. It involves, in other words, a positive intervention by the state in defining objectives and good practices, rather than the traditional negative restraints of the rule of law, which states what is illegal but leaves the citizen free to do anything which is not illegal. Whether such an analysis would appeal to a right-wing Conservative administration is a moot point, but it is one whose essential correctness is also argued for by the developments discussed in the latter part of this chapter in the new financial institutions.[13]

## New Financial Institutions: Conglomerates and Financial Supermarkets

Mention has already been made in the discussion of the Stock Exchange of the considerable upheaval in financial organizations consequent upon the 'big bang', with almost every significant jobber and broker having at least firm plans by the beginning of 1985 to merge with a bank or similar large organization, so as to provide the capital necessary to survive in the large and more competitive market that will operate from late 1986 onwards. Because of the need not to make the account of quite complex changes in the Stock Exchange even more complicated, only certain aspects of this process of agglomeration and diversification were commented on. It is time now to note other aspects, and in particular some of the new risks involved. The two essential moves, which do not affect all the organizations involved, are agglomeration and financial supermarkets. In the former case, existing large organizations, principally banks, are diversifying their activities by buying up stockbrokers and jobbers with a view to dealings in both equities and gilt-edged Government securities under the new regime, and in some cases the discount houses also, with a view to more extensive dealings in the money markets and Government lending and borrowing.

In some cases, mergers and takeovers simply constitute a defensive agglomeration in order to continue operating more or less in the traditional pattern of City institutions in the wholesale share markets and merchant banking. A prime example of this is the merger in 1984 of the stockbroking firms Rowe and Pitman, and Mullens and Co, and the jobbers Ackroyd and Smithers with Mercury Securities, owners of merchant bankers S.G. Warburg, in a deal worth £245 million. The deal was followed by rumours of widespread problems of adjustment, as the new partners settled in with each other and began to accommodate what came to be called the different cultures of bankers (said to be budget-conscious and committee-driven), brokers (said to be sales-oriented), and jobbers (said to be anxious observers of market movements). How much is to be made of the substance of these different professional cultures remains debatable, but it would appear that there is a good deal of jockeying for position within the new organizations.

This personal aspect of the reorganization was given added impetus, because of the so-called marzipan layer of specialists just below the partners, who could not sell their shares on takeover for princely sums, but who could, if their expertise as revenue-earners was well-rated, command substantial increases in salary, by taking advantage of openings created by the realignments, particularly since it began to be realized that top-grade talent would be at a premium because it alone could secure the position of the new conglomerates in world markets. And specialists left not only in singles but in teams, sometimes poached aggressively by rivals. Thus, for example, a few weeks after the merger of Alexanders Discount with Jessell Toynbee, four specialists in gilts, floating rate notes and certificates of deposits, left to join Hill Samuel;[14] three of the four in Scrimgeour Kemp Gee, taken over by Citicorp in 1984, left for various destinations in early 1985;[15] five of the award-winning team of retail analysts were poached from brokers Capel Cure Myers by rivals Wood Mackenzie in early 1985 in a deal estimated at £300 000–£400 000;[16] and in the same period leading jobbers Webb Durlacher Mordaunt lost seven of its eight European equity trading team who were expected to join brokers Savory & Milne, itself recently linked to the Scandinavian financial group Dow Scandia, at a potential cost of £750 000.[17] The implications of these extensive moves of personnel and the cash sums involved is, first, that they accentuate a widely agreed prediction that job security will decrease in the City, and secondly that this and the greater emphasis on performance will put a strain on the loyalty of an individual to his colleagues and his organization, and increase the temptation for him to contrive to shine, even at the price of cutting a few corners. This in turn will put pressure on the new regulatory arrangements.

Nor is this the only aspect of the problem. Conflicts of interest in the new conglomerates are endemic. As the Prudential's Michael Newmarch pointed out at a seminar in 1985,[18] where erstwhile brokers and jobbers work side-by-side in a new organization they 'might use their research to establish positions in stocks before releasing the good news story to an unsuspecting world'. The more effective the separation of research, sales and the market-making mechanism within the same firm by administrative means (the so-called 'Chinese wall') 'the less was the scope for realising benefits from joining disparate functions together'. Or in the words of a broker, 'there isn't much sense in sending out a circular on a stock unless the firm has already taken a line of shares on board'. And Lord Camoys at Barclays de Zoete Wedd, the equity dealing subsidiary resulting from Barclays' takeover of brokers de Zoete and Bevan, and jobbers Wedd Durlacher Mordaunt, echoed this sentiment, saying that the various functions would have to be 'tolerably linked, but not intolerably linked', and that an internal police force was needed to achieve this fine balance, while recognizing that 'you have to be careful that you don't shake the business up so much that you lose whatever you bought'.[19]

This is not the only area of conflict of interest. In early 1985, Barclays began to offer their share-dealing service to customers at five selected branches with the object of encouraging its existing retail customers to diversify their financial dealings. However, what guarantee was there in these circumstances that shares favoured by Barclays would not be stuffed down unsuspecting throats, or even, in the longer term, that the customers' entire financial needs might become enmeshed in the various services offered by the bank, and the customer end up feeling unable to escape because of the pattern of borrowing, savings and investments he had entered into? This so-called 'cradle-to-grave' pattern of financial services is the most developed version of the financial supermarket idea. Here the object is to provide a wide range of financial services – insurance, mortgages, personal loans, savings and current accounts, unit trusts, pensions, equities and so on – within the same organization to new customers. This may be done, as Barclays hope, by diversifying from an existing set of retail outlets with well-established customers and certain services, and encouraging them to consider others. Alternatively, it may be done by a retail outlet with a consumer goods background, using its premises to diversify into financial services. This was initiated by House of Fraser in Spring 1985 when it opened its first financial services shop in Birmingham, with the prospect of extending it to another 250 outlets. It offers credit cards, insurance, personal loans and the services of a building society.[20] Given the enthusiasm of the relevant representative of the Government, Alex Fletcher, Junior Minister of the DTI for financial supermarkets, it is worth considering the difficulties and their implications.[21]

In mid-1984 Marks and Spencer was reported as being poised to introduce money centres in some of its 266 stores, inspired by the example of Sears Roebuck in the USA. Although M & S duly launched its own credit card, it held back from rushing ahead with full-blown money centres. Dean Witter, the securities firm involved in the Sears Roebuck scheme, lost $33 million in 1984 and Hambro Life's more upmarket financial management programme cheque account with investment services attached attracted only 1000 accounts in its first year and had to be relaunched.

Perhaps the greatest shock to the rapid development of diversification by financial institutions, however, came with the collapse of the merger between Mark Weinberg's Hambro Life insurance group and Jacob Rothschild's Charterhouse J. Rothschild (CJR) in mid-1984. It was the more surprising because of Rothschild's strong track record in favour of growth and diversification. He broke with the family banker, N.M. Rothschild in 1980, because he regarded it as unadventurous, and proceeded to build up the largest merchant banking group in Britain in a very short time, merging with a larger investment trust, buying half a leading Wall Street firm and then a stake in brokers Kitkat and Aitken, and finally merging with the Charterhouse group. He went on record as saying fairly forcefully that better capitalized, more competitive organizations were required in the City, and regarded financial services in the 1970s as too fragmented. The deal with Hambro Life, proposed only five months after the merger with Charterhouse, would have created a group larger than the Midland Bank, and brought together insurance salesmen, international investment bankers and stockbrokers. The deal fell apart as investors took umbrage at the combination of consumer and entrepreneurial business, the difference in the styles of management of the two sides, and the fact that CJR had not time to integrate its own portfolio of investments. Despite this debacle, Rothschild remained committed to diversification:

> I think it is perfectly possible to mix retail and wholesale financial services businesses. In this country we have no retail stockbrokers, but in the US Merrill Lynch, E.F. Hutton and others have large sales forces. Due to the fiscal and regulatory system that has grown up here, it has been impossible de facto to sell shares through a sales force, yet by a quirk you could sell unit-linked life assurance that way. Now you have a Government that, as we have seen, with the British Telecom issue, is keen to encourage distribution to the small investor. If a life insurance company bought a stockbroker and chose to make a proportion of its sales force stockbrokers, it could change. In the US, firms like American Express have developed just that kind of retail/wholesale mix . . . [but] . . . there will be mishaps. We have just had a well-advertised difference of culture between the Trade Development Bank and American Express, for instance.'[22]

Notwithstanding Rothschild's optimism about diversification and bringing extra customers in over the longer term, the immediate future of financial supermarkets of a fairly distinctive kind seems more likely to lie with the building societies, whose growth in the post-war years has been enormous, being the Government's tax subsidized and preferred means of moving from 30% to 60% owner-occupation. Growth in total size of assets has been accompanied by a continuing fall in the total number of societies, the large taking over the smaller ones, but by the mid-1980s the societies, now with a wide network of high street branches and an established position in the minds of public, rivalling and in some respects exceeding that of the banks, were itching for permission to change their legal rules and diversify. The Government was only too ready to comply, and a Green Paper in 1984 envisaged legislation in 1985–6 to allow this. The Green Paper effectively proposed to allow societies, or at least the top 10 or 20 of them, to act as banks, offering cheque books, overdrafts, cheque cards, cash machines and unsecured personal loans to an extent of around £4 billion, so creating direct competition with the banks in almost all fields, the banks' non-mortgage personal lending being around £9 billion. In addition, the societies have asked to be allowed to offer estate agency services which, they point out, Lloyds Bank already does, insurance broking, conveyancing and valuations. If all these are permitted, pressure towards the further amalgamation of smaller societies not eligible for diversification will increase and the larger ones will achieve a very powerful position in respect of many of their clients, which means large numbers of householders. The risks of conflict of interst here are obvious. Given that a mortgage at the right time, of the right amount and at the best rate, is something avidly sought by house buyers, they would be highly vulnerable to being penalized by terms far less than the best on offer in the market in respect of the other services necessary to house purchase. On the other hand, there are arguments that in-house services allow for economies and a cheaper overall service.

Further examples of developments along these lines could be given, but enough has been said to identify the range of risks involved and to draw the major conclusion. The risks may be itemized as follows:

1. Increased size of organization through mergers means that any failure will have a much more disruptive effect on markets as a whole and is likely to involve a much larger section of the public.
2. Personnel problems during the period of reorganization have been identified above, together with the dangers of undue pressures upon individuals for high performance at all costs, and its effects upon probity.
3. Conflicts of interests in diversified organizations are endemic and only time can tell to what extent they can be prevented from having an adverse effect on clients.
4. It is agreed that increased competition is inevitable in the future and that casualties are likely. This further increases the pressures to cut corners and reinforces the dangers of crashes where organizations are large (see 1).
5. Diversification raises increased chances of knock-on effects from one organization to another, with misjudgements or improprieties in a limited area bringing the whole edifice crashing down, unless the organization of finance is both prudent and strict. Rules for the management of this issue have, of necessity, yet to emerge.
6. The greatly increased numbers of clients implied by diversification, and especially by the financial supermarket idea, mean that the political impact of failures or serious difficulties is greatly magnified. It is bad enough, as was seen in the cases of the Lloyds scandals, when a few well-heeled participants are exploited by fast and loose operators, but where the clients are citizens of ordinary means and run into thousands or even tens of thousands, local organizational problems spread to scandals affecting not only that sector of the City, but the Government as well.

The overall dangers and their implications can be illustrated by the development of an organization which has been referred before. Citicorp of New York is the world's largest group with worldwide assets of $151 billion and reported pre-tax profits of $1.54 billion dollars in 1984, of which rather less that 10% came from the UK, where it has a major presence. Its British head states that he would be 'very happy to become the fifth force in banking in the UK'.[23] This cannot be achieved by challenging the big four clearing banks in the retail market, but Citicorp is going all out to do so in other areas. To that end, it became the first bank to buy a discount house in February 1985. It was also the first foreign bank to become accepted into the British cheque clearing system, and the first foreigner, in 1984, to arrange a new share issue. It also owns Scrimgeour and Vickers, two major stockbroking firms, and is intent on making a major impact in bond trading and equities, concentrating on a limited range of stocks, where it will become a market-maker, and becoming a leader in corporate finance, such as takeovers and new issues. It will also become a primary gilts dealer. In these latter fields it admits to lacking internal skills at present. In the words of its UK head: 'It's going to be tough and we're going to make mistakes. We're going to have false starts. We're going to lose some money. But we're going to to help a lot of people.' Nor is it only in the corporate finance side that Citicorp is involved. It owns 51% of Diners Club, provides consumer credit of £770 million, including mortgages, life assurance, savings and current accounts and travellers cheques. It already has around £750 million loaned to medium and small companies, and is engaged in foreign exchange dealings.

This is a formidable range of diversification, and despite its huge strength, there is evidence that past errors have hurt it and could yet do so again. It was badly over-exposed to Third World debts that went sour with the strong dollar and high interest rates in the 1980s. It lost millions from retail banking in the US. It took the wrong view of UK interest rates in 1980–81 and lost heavily there. One of its techniques for thinking about developments is to ask 'what if?', e.g. what if it had been able to manage the British Telecom issue through Scrimgeour Vickers, with retail distribution through Diners Club and Citibank savings? Equally one might ask: what if several things started to go seriously wrong in different areas at the same time? Citicorp has large reserves, and perhaps the parent company would help out. But US banks are by no means immune to failure, as the string of failures in Ohio in 1985, and the collapse of the mighty Continental Illinois and its rescue at a cost of $4 billion dollars in 1984, indicates.

If Citicorp, with its bounding self-confidence and vast resources is going to develop fast and take risks in doing so, where does that leave the competition? A number have gone on record as seeing Citicorp as their major rival in establishing themselves in the new markets after 1986, and the pressure to be bold will be enormous. It is all very well to say there will be casualties, but the question is not the same if they are small stockbroking firms being hammered as if they are major conglomerates avidly pulling in customers on a big scale. The risks of the new markets, diversification into new areas, greatly increased size and, most of all, the active search for new customers of modest means, will put tremendous pressures on the regulatory systems. No such system exists to prevent failures, only to try and ensure prudence and probity, and the political consequences of any major crash will necessarily be borne by the Government. It is the state who stands as guarantor behind the regulatory system, and who supervises it, and the Government which determines the extent and mode of that supervision, the detailed development of which has been described in its various respects in earlier chapters. The major conclusion here, then, is that for all the Thatcher Government's commitment to free market competition, events have acted to increase state intervention. So far, it has been held at arms length, and institutions encouraged to police themselves, albeit with an enhanced measure of state surveillance, including the appointment of nominees to supervisory bodies. The implications of this paradox have yet to be grasped and will be taken up more fully in the next chapter.

# Notes

1.   City cops out of policing plan, the *Sunday Times*, 20 June 1982.
2.   See P. Robinson, Time to tighten up policing of the fraud law, *The Times*, 10 November 1983, which also makes a number of other interesting points.
3.   Keeping the City off the limits to fraud, *The Times* 11 June 1984.
4.   See C. Clifford, London haven for fraudsters, the *Sunday Times*, 27 January 1985.
5.   P. Robinson, Financial markets prepare a few antidotes to rogues and fools, *The Times*, 17 January 1984.
6.   Police investigations were only sanctioned by the DPP in May 1985.
7.   In the City, *Private Eye*, 10 August 1984, No. 591, p. 25.
8.   Op. cit.
9.   See the review by T. Gibb, Jury still out on fraud trial review, *The Times*, 21 March 1985.
10.   See, e.g. Can the law silence concert parties? *The Times*, 6 July 1981, and compare *The Times* Business News Editorial, 19 April 1985 which, commenting on the Takeover Panels latest revision of its rules said:

> Struggle as they might, the architects of the updated code have not been able to come up with a water-right definition of a concert party. This quaint term covers all attempts by groups of investors to gain control of a company without being forced to make an outright bid. If they can be deemed a concert party, then they are treated as a single entity and must obey the rules as such. Many and varied have been the strategems to depict a cohort as a rabble of infantry clustering round a beloved general. This, it can be confidently predicted, will continue to be a source of friction and resentment on both sides.

See also L.H. Leigh, *The Control of Commercial Fraud*, Heinemann, 1982, which gives a comprehensive account of the British machinery for the control and prosecution of commercial fraud, and a lawyer's review of leading recent cases. His conclusion, suggesting some reforms, acknowledges the difficulties of achieving success. For a review of company law by a lawyer with social scientific sympathies, see T. Hadden, *Company Law and Capitalism*, Weidenfeld, 1972. The literature on insider trading is now extensive. I have made some comments on the difficulty of legislative control in *Fallen Idols*, op. cit., pp. 199 ff. Other interesting discussions on it are to be found in, e.g. D. Sugarman, The regulation of insider dealing, *in* B.A.K. Rider (ed.), *Regulation of the British Securities Industry*, Oyez, 1979, and B.A.K. Rider, Self-regulation: the British approach to policing conduct in the securities business with particular reference to the role of the City Panel on Takeovers and Mergers in the regulation of insider dealing, *Journal of Comparative Corporate Law and Securities Regulation*, 1978, pp. 319–48.
11.   T. Hadden, Fraud in the City: the role of the Criminal Law, *Criminal Law Review*, 1983, p. 506.
12.   Op. cit., pp. 510–11.
13.   Some of these issues are further debated by me in: Prosecutorial and administrative strategies in the context of Business crime and the role of private and state policing *in* C. Shearing and P. Stenning (eds), *Private Policing*, Sage Publications, 1986.
14.   *The Times*, 9 October 1984.
15.   *The Times*, 14 January 1985.
16.   *The Times*, 2 February 1985.
17.   *The Times*, 14 February 1985.
18.   See the *Sunday Times*, 10 February 1985.
19.   Quoted in ibid.
20.   See *The Times*, 22 February 1985.
21.   See, e.g. his statement reported in *The Times*, 26 October 1983, that he would like to see a network of 'high street investment shops where small savers could buy and sell stocks

and shares in the equivalent of a stockbroking supermarket . . . If the securities industry in this country is to grow similarly (to that in the USA), we must tap the savings of the community where they are to be found.'

22.   See the extensive interview with Rothschild, *The Times,* 11 December 1984. It is perhaps not irrelevant in this connection that the major US brokers and investment bankers E.F. Hutton, to whom Rothschild refers, were ordered in May 1983 to pay $10 million in fines and compensation, including a maximum $2 million fine, for a fraud involving the transfer of paper money between accounts in order to obtain effective overdrafts, at a daily rate of $250 million, interest free. Shortly afterwards the firm was named as liable to the extent of $34 million in the settlement of a suit over the failure of annuities which, it was alleged by clients, brokers should have known were unsafe. See *The Times,* 3 and 7 May 1985.

23.   See *The Times,* 19 March 1985.

# 7

## Conclusion: Everyone a capitalist?

One of the objects of this book has been to show the extent to which reforms have been taking place across a variety of institutions in the City of London. Chapters concentrating on banking, insurance and the stock market have described developments in three major areas, and further comments on other areas have shown that the impetus to reform is more wide-ranging than that. In all cases, a move was discernible away from the traditional regulatory mode of the informal, socially exclusive and private gentlemen's club towards the more formal, bureaucratic and public accountability, characterized by higher levels of disclosure of the activities of members of the institutions, stricter surveillance, more extensive compliance and qualification rules for membership, and a measure of state-nominated participation in the main regulatory bodies. None the less, the emphasis has remained upon the preservation of self-regulation, to which the government remains committed. In addition, the extent of the move away from the old, informal mode is nowhere complete, and varies from institution to institution. Of critical importance here is the enhanced role acquired by the Bank of England as a supervisory body for City institutions. The Bank has retained its role as the mediator between the City and the government and acquired the power to put its nominees on the ruling councils of various institutions, nominating the chief executive of Lloyds, having a powerful say in the nomination of lay members of the Stock Exchange Council, and in the nomination of members of the Securities and Investment Board (SIB) and the Marketing of Investments Board (MIB), besides its continuing direct responsibilities for the banking sector. Yet the Bank remains strongly committed to the traditional gentlemanly mode of supervision, seeing it as more flexible and effective, more conducive to the establishment of trust, and more civilized. It hence continues to run the risks associated with this regulatory mode, as was illustrated by the JMB rescue and its aftermath.

The move to a new style of formal accountability, while substantial, is hence by no means complete. To take up the language so often used by City figures, the City is opening its house to outsiders, and in doing so reducing the number of restrictions and esoteric customs that have characterized and supported it in the past. But although its institutions and markets will become compatible with those of other markets abroad, it is still a distinctive place, and newcomers will be required to respect this if they are to become fully established and successful. The difficulty with this sort of rhetoric is that it confuses the old with the new. Outsiders, certainly those from America, will have been used to checking carefully on the rules and keeping a wary eye open for the state regulatory body, the SEC. Within those clear and visible constraints, the rhetoric of tough games playing, whose only object is to win, is the counterpart of the City of London's now slightly fey-sounding concern with the conventions and manners of the house. In crude terms, the danger of allowing the old informalities and niceties to hang on is that they will be ignored by newcomers. This tendency can only be enhanced by the greater competitive pressures which will prevail in the more open markets. If rules are not clear and emphasized unequivocally by regulators, the tendency to ignore them will be significant and dangerous. Considerable progress has thus been made by way of regulatory reform, but serious doubts must remain that it has gone far enough to meet the requirements of changes.

As has been evident throughout this book, and as I made plain at the outset, the pressures necessary to achieve real change came from the interaction of several sources. Scandals, as have been illustrated, played a significant part in focusing public attention on regulatory failures, and their repetitive nature in many areas has served to keep those involved in developing the reformed regulatory machinery on their mettle. The rise of the institutions – pension funds, life assurance and others – has played a background role, bringing a new mass clientele to the City by proxy, and now constituting rather somnolent and largely easy-going giants in the City markets. So great is their financial clout, however, that even if they are over-compliant to the existing pattern of practices and institutions in the City, and have failed to assert themselves as much of an independent force, the City must remain anxious that nothing should go seriously wrong with them, for if it did do so while they were following the investment advice and practices of the other institutions, all parties would be bound to be caught up in the scandal. More important has been rising international competition in all sectors, which has forced the City into making a clear choice as to whether to become a protected backwater, serving a domestic market only, or whether to vie for a leading place in international markets. In most cases there seems little doubt about the preference of institutions for the latter course, but if there were any doubters they were certainly harried out of sight by the determination of the Thatcher government that being big in world terms was the only objective worth striving for. This was coupled with a strong commitment to end restrictive practices and closed shops and improve access to the City both for foreigners and for the majority of the British population.

In retrospect, the decision to abolish exchange controls in 1979 was a vital one for City reform, since it immediately allowed much easier access to the City by foreigners and allowed British investors the option of diverting funds onto foreign markets, so increasing the competitive pressures upon the City to provide the best buys and the best facilities. It could be said that the multiplication of institutions and the influx of foreigners significantly preceded 1979, a point put by Moran,[1] and for the banking field at any rate this is the case. Certainly one should not discount the proliferation of trading entities, the fragmentation of markets and the increase in size of organizations in the 1960s and especially the 1970s – the influx of foreign banks, the great increase in Lloyds membership, the proliferation of specialist markets for shares, commodities and currencies and their futures – also bringing pressure to bear upon the sustainability of old patterns. Closeness, privacy and informality become impossible when there are too many strangers involved in too great a variety of novel organizations. Determination to achieve real reform in a sector as entrenched as the City requires, however, a combination of a sudden increase in pressure, coupled with a strong call for public debate. This arguably was provided by the consequences of exchange control abolition and the government's moves in a combination of fields: the Office of Fair Trading (OFT) case against the Stock Exchange and the Parkinson-Goodison deal, the Gower reports and the Investor Protection Bill, the Lloyds Act, and the government's less enthusiastic response to Cork with its Insolvency Bill, and the Chancellor's committee on Banking Regulation in the wake of the JMB affair, besides initiatives on fraud prosecution discussed in the last chapter.

This brings us to confront the principal topic of this chapter. The effect of the processes of reform has been to bring government, and the state more widely, into much greater involvement with the City. What are the implications of this? There are always difficulties in the state becoming more heavily involved in any section of the economy since public expectations inevitably rise that the state will act as guarantor when anything goes wrong. Conversely, the state will acquire some of the odium if organizations of which it expressed approval, or their members, engage in incompetence or gross exploitation to the detriment of public clients. The City has in the past been a peculiarly segregated sector of the British economy, able to exercise its influence to protect its interests through the Bank of England, and largely immune to government intervention, socially closed to most of the population and occupationally esoteric: in both the modern and the archaic meaning of the word, a mystery. In this it has contrasted sharply with the industrial and agricultural sectors which have long been fully integrated into the life of the mass of the population as employees, who have over time developed tenuously held patterns of rights and privileges exercising a degree of restraint upon management, and expressed most evidently in trades union organizations. The relationship of the mass of the population to the City, however, has been of a quite different character.

Until the last generation or two it was almost totally obscure, being constituted by the unseen abstraction of surplus value in the form of shares and dividends. More recently, large numbers of the more securely employed population have come to entrench their security by organized savings through pension schemes, life assurance, and to a lesser and more recent extent, unit trusts, which have channelled their individual drops into a stream which has now become a flood. Still, however, the relationship between these small savers and the City is largely obscure: the amounts are abstracted automatically from salaries and bank accounts,

and what is done with the aggregates is not contemplated very actively b
for the most part, though unit trusts do of course encourage a more activ

Widespread home ownership and the impact of the cost of money upon m
rates has acted to improve the awareness of the major workings of the City, b
involvement of small savers in what becomes of their money has remained sli
True, there have been straws in the wind: particular campaigns to obta
disinvestment in South Africa for political reasons, most notably in the churches
charities and universities; limited but sustained attempts by ordinary members to
obtain boardroom places in building societies; much further upmarket, we might
note the revolt of Lloyds external names over the scandals there, which was much
more organized and effective. We are, however, a very long way yet from organized
bodies of employees demanding that their pension funds be directed to particular
investments; even though most funds have trade union representatives on the board,
they are largely quiescent, and willing to defer to the expertise of others in
protecting the long-term security of their members by established investment
patterns.

Recent reforms have, however, gone some way to create the conditions for mass
interest in the City. If more goes on in public, if rules, objects, practices and
procedures are available for inspection, and if senior figures are more publicity-
conscious, the cultural seclusion of the City, at any rate, is under considerable
threat. Whether the general population or significant sectors of it become actively
concerned with particular institutions and events is another matter. Certainly, at a
party political level, neither the Labour Party, nor the mould-breaking Alliance,
have shown an increased inclination to seek to involve their members in active
concern over the functioning of the City. The initiative for the integration of the
public into the financial sector has, on the contrary, come from the Tory
government, with its encouragement of individuals to set up in business, of
management buy-outs of failing companies, of wider share ownership, and its
enthusiasm for financial conglomerates, diversification and financial supermarkets.
The objective is clear: get the mass public to participate in the institutions of
capitalism more fully and they will become more appreciative of them; get them to
take wider responsibility for their lives, and they will be able to struggle more
effectively and gain the rewards of doing so; and all of this will increase investment,
create wealth and jobs, and benefit the economy as a whole, and so shift irreversibly
the balance of the dominant political consensus in the direction of free enterprise.

The trouble is, that despite the evident sustained resolution of the government to
this end, and its seeming effectiveness in persuading at any rate significant numbers
of the population of the merits of such a move in the early 1980s, it is subject to a
variety of paradoxes, or as Marxists would have it, contradictions, some of them
evident in the government's very behaviour. They all derive at root from the
paradox of a government committed to free and private enterprise being actively
engaged in intervening in a sector of the economy, and using the apparatus of the
state to do so, with the object of securing and promoting private enterprise. Surely a
government genuinely committed to private enterprise would disentangle itself
from all sectors of the economy and leave business free to do business. It has indeed
been a large part of the rhetoric of the right-wing government to argue just this, and
to talk of the importance of easing the burden of taxes and regulations upon

...nic revival has centred upon creating the conditions ... to invest, to prosper and to create wealth and jobs, not ... prod them into doing so. There are several answers to ... more convincing than others. One is the point already ... been a segregated sector of the economy, and that it ... ctive to open it up as a possible area of activity to all ... ugh, and a feature of the requirement of pro-capitalist ... that sectors of capital modernize and do not monopolize, ... gnate.

... argument might, less plausibly, be that state intervention to promote ... unshackle private enterprise is necessary because of 30 years of state intervention to take it over and tie it down. While this argument may be relevant in respect of coal, steel, engineering or shipbuilding, it is much less pertinent to finance. The aspect that the government is naturally much less reticent about trumpeting, though it is quite willing to practice, is that of investor/consumer/depositor protection. If the activities of City institutions are to be accessible to public scrutiny, let alone wide public participation, they must be seen to be efficient and above board. As Walter Wriston of Citicorp is fond of saying, what are required are clear rules and a level playing field. One essential necessity to encourage wider participation in the principal markets of the City is thus the bringing of the regulatory system clearly into the open and ensuring that it works effectively.

There is another aspect to investor protection, however, that brings out another paradox. The government has felt constrained, under the accumulated weight of established consumer sentiment and institutions, to go further than trying to ensure mere clarity of rules, probity of action, and equality of access, to include controlling and limiting risks for new participants of limited means. The BT share issue was perhaps the grossest example of this, where a massive campaign was mounted to secure wide public participation, and the launch was contrived to ensure that the mass of the new shareholders would make an instant profit. But can it always be done? The institutions devised for the mass public – pension funds, life assurance, and units trusts – have been devised to minimize risks to the individual by spreading them very widely, and have been on the whole highly successful in avoiding major losses to individual small savers. If these same small savers are encouraged to move upmarket, they also increase risk. Nothing that governments or self-regulation can do to ensure competence, prudence and probity can escape the fact that increased risks mean increased chances of major losses as well as major gains. The danger is, then, either that higher rates of participation will not spread very far upmarket or that, if they do, major losses will cause a powerful adverse reaction for which the government, having encouraged their participation, will be held responsible and state guarantees demanded.

The danger, in short, is of the very same thing happening in the financial sector as was derided and denounced by Thatcherites in the industrial sector. There, well organized employees of major companies successfully demanded state aid when the company went bankrupt. The antidote against this proffered in the financial sector is careful checks on organizations to detect trouble early and various risk-limitation and compensation fund devices organized and financed by the institutions themselves. These may help, but they are not a complete solution. Capitalism is about taking risks, and riks must mean losses as well as gains.

What is likely to be even worse in practice, in the financial sector, is that the astute operator who is full-time and has his ear to the ground, i.e. has good contacts with the relevant grapevines, is able to get in and out of situations fast enough to be able to show a good profit on the year. The small-scale outside participant is liable to find himself insufficiently well-informed, and indeed on occasion to be the dupe of the slick operator. All markets in the financial sector are prone to sudden changes, and unless the investor is able to switch promptly or to employ a good agent to do it for him, he stands to get caught. In general, then, not only is it difficult in principle for investor protection to contain risks, except at the price of limited returns (i.e. by spreading it), but the small new player may find himself at a distinct disadvantage and loss in comparison with the larger, established one.

To push the paradoxes further, the greater the investor demand for protection from risk and wrongdoing, the greater the temptation towards greater state intervention to achieve this. The tighter and tougher, more public, and better funded and staffed and integrated between sectors regulation is, the better the investor is protected, but the greater the perceived involvement of the state, the greater the reliance placed by the public upon such involvement as a guarantee, and hence the bigger the backlash if things go wrong. The danger of creeping consumerism for the state is that the state is in fact induced to take on risks that, if private enterprise is private, should be taken by the investor or depositor.

The government has responded to these sorts of difficulty with due caution, but without entire success. Its strong support for diversification, agglomeration, international competition and wider public participation in the City clearly has exposed it to a higher degree of risk if these experiments do not work well. Further, the risk of a backlash is arguably the greater because of the very success so far of mass savings institutions which spread risks, and the high expectations of security in financial institutions that have grown up in the public eye – in contrast to industrial ones where whole industries have gone into liquidation. The government's strategy has been to attempt to get the City itself to absorb as much of the burden as possible, by emphasizing continuing self-regulation and independent responsibility to investors, with state oversight. An important weakness here, as was evident in the ideologically if not practically important field of fraud prosecution, is the fragmentation of authorities involved in supervising markets and defining and enforcing the rules. Not only is there a considerable diversity of bodies with complementary and overlapping jurisdictions, but their status varies enormously, from state bodies like the DPP's office and DTI, to independent self-regulatory bodies. The Crown Agents were no doubt an exceptional case, but their catastrophic and unrestrained career in the 1970s clearly shows how badly things can go wrong when the responsibilities of supervisory bodies are not clearly demarcated. The safeguard proposed here is the SIB, but in 1985 that is all potential rather than reality. The SIB's potential is that it has a wide scope for intervention, and is clearly to be encouraged to use its discretionary powers; in addition the Secretary of State will have powers to modify its powers at short notice to make it the equivalent of British SEC if that turns out to be necessary. This sounds a bit like saying to the City: 'You had better be careful, we have a secret weapon which can do anything.' Star Wars notwithstanding, arms negotiators would have greater sense than to deploy that kind of hollow threat.

There seems to be no escaping the government's dilemma. It seeks to enhance the legitimacy of capitalist institutions by making them more widely participated in, but in doing so it is driven to undermine their function in a way and to a degree that is fundamentally at variance with the fluctuations, cycles and risks intrinsic to capitalist markets. The only way to cut those risks is to intervene to control the markets themselves, which as far as the Thatcher government is concerned is the opposite of what it was elected to do. It would be a mistake, however, to confine remarks on the problems raised by City regulation to strong pro-capitalist governments. The paradoxes involved for such a government are clearly fiercer and more numerous than one which regards capitalism as a bit rough and ready, and in need of some general reining-in to control its natural instabilities and tendencies to excess, that is, a social democratic government. A socialist government committed to abolishing capitalist institutions would, of course, solve the dilemma, but since such a government has never been elected in the Western world, and shows no prospect of being so, I will not pursue that possibility.

Social democracy is the compromise, or to put it less politely, the bastard offspring of the conflict between capitalism and its utopian rival, socialism. The essence of social democracy is that the beast of capitalism need not be slain, but may either be tamed or tethered (depending on particular predilection), and its undoubted strength in increasing total wealth and income used to secure the prosperity of the majority. Such a solution accepts some continuing failings of capitalism: substantial inequalities, a measure of poverty and unemployment, but compensated for by increased prosperity for all or nearly all, and the security of all, either through employment and/or welfare measures financed by taxes. Prophecies of doom in the late 1970s notwithstanding, this compromise has continued to work, albeit with less evident ease. The security of the majority continues, even though an increasing minority suffer from unemployment and welfare cuts. It is not that social democracy is not working, but that it is not working as well as it has in the past. The election of radical conservative governments in both Britain and the USA is evidence enough of the continued popular faith in the legitimacy of the major institutions of capitalism, and an acceptance that it is more important to preserve the wealth-creating strength of the beast than to beat and chain it to the point of collapse. This becomes a more intelligible claim when it is recalled that the sectors of the population which have most benefited from social democracy in the post-war years have been those who have moved, usually with the help of education, from parental backgrounds characterized by the insecurity and frequently manual work of the 1930s into the expanding white-collar jobs whose upper reaches in particular have grown dramatically.[2]

It is this sector, the salaried sector of the population – often these days the double-salaried sector, with most wives earning and many with qualifications – that is being encouraged to commit itself further to capitalist institutions and dabble in the markets, the very sector with the highest level of reward from social democracy in terms of security – reasonable security even in the mid-1980s of job, and reasonable financial security through pensions, life assurance and home ownership. However much the more upmarket institutions of capital are bullied into displaying their acceptable face, they can never offer security to the small-time operator. To the extent that the government induces participation in them and it results in loss of security, the outcome will not be an increase in belief in the legitimacy of capitalist institutions, but a decrease. For every smart or lucky investor who wins out, there will be more who lose.

Welfare or security as a universal objective and as a sustained political achievement for the great majority is absolutely essential to the social democratic compromise. The growth in interventionism of the state to guarantee this, characterized in somewhat different ways under the general term 'corporatism' by a number of writers, is a millstone round the neck of any government with a strongly pro-capitalist ideology. It may lumber about in various directions, but it will not be able to throw it off. Writing on corporatism, while being centred upon the issue of the size and place of the state in the industrialized West, tends to concentrate on the consequences for party politics, and more frequently upon the industrial and welfare sectors, where corporate institutions in the charge of industrial and trade union representatives and negotiating bodies have been established, and overtly corporatist policies developed by parties.[3] The evidence of this book is an indication that the fundamentals of corporatism pervade the financial sector also. What has been taking place in the past few years in Britain has not just been the demystification of the financial sector and the dragging of its institutions into the public realm, but also arguably the laying of the foundations for their accountability in policy terms.

The City has long been criticized for ignoring the rest of the economy and insisting on running its own affairs in its own interests, and arguing that where these conflicted with the interests of others, most notably those of industry, those of the City constituted the national interest. The autonomy of the Bank of England in particular was directed to this end. There, repeated criticisms gave rise to the Wilson Committee on the functioning of financial institutions in the 1970s to consider whether they did in fact act against the national interest. The Committee's conclusions were blandly reassuring in the main, but then, given its composition and the weight of evidence from City practitioners to it, this was scarcely surprising. There were those, mainly trades union representatives, who favoured a radical change of policy with investments by, for example, banks and pension funds being directed to industrial projects over the longer term rather than to whatever offered maximum short-term gain, and some of this became at least nominally Labour Party policy. Arguably, however, the necessity for such a change, and the reasoned evaluation of the undesirability of traditional techniques in investment policies by significant sections of the general public is not possible without a much higher level of awareness of how City markets work than is presently the case. If the bringing of City institutions into public accoutability and access, even it it is not accompanied by a rush to participate in direct investment, results in a greater awareness of what the City does, and even more of how and why and who benefits, it will be progress of a sort.

My arguments can be summarized as follows:

1.  One important aspect of substantial involvement by a right-wing government in promoting serious reform of the City is the modernization of finance capital to make it internationally competitive and efficient, and hence a major

revenue earner, which can to some extent substitute for the decline of the industrial sector, whose recovery is taking rather longer than expected.

2.  Another and possibly the other primary objective of the reform of the City is to break the social democratic mould of politics and to bring City institutions into the mainstream of political life, rather than leaving them as powerful and privileged players on the margin. This involves encouraging a significant section of the population to participate in the reformed institutions in the expectation that this will create a major shift in loyalty to them: to practice capitalism is to believe in it. Demystification of the traditional secluded and privileged character of the City is an important aspect of this because it involves eliminating an alienating elitism.

3.  The price of doing this for the government is greater involvement by the state in sustaining the security, probity and efficiency of City institutions, and hence acquiring an unwanted role as guarantor.

4.  Hence the attempt to solve problems of the efficiency and legitimacy of capitalism is bought only at the cost of a lesser ability of the government to distance itself from the vagaries of capitalism, the reverse of the successful strategy adopted in respect of employment in the industrial sector. The arguments that the unemployed should get on their bikes and look for work, that the employed were pricing themselves out of jobs, were strike-prone and hamstrung by restrictive practices, all shifted responsibility away from government. It is hard to see how the same arguments could be applied to participants in savings and investment through financial institutions, if things go wrong.

5.  Finally, there is a contradiction between the expectations developed among a large sector of the population of the institutions of the City which have been the instruments of their long-term financial security, and the actual operations of City markets, with their booms and slumps and relatively high risks, particularly for small-time novice players.[4] This can only reinforce pressure upon the state to act as guarantor, and increase general expectations that financial institutions will deliver even if industrial ones must be recognized as failing to do so. In short, the incorporation of the financial sector into the lives of a large sector of the population cannot be used as a substitute for the failure of the industrial sector to continue to deliver security as part of the social democratic compromise.

## Notes

1.  M. Moran, *The Politics of Banking*, op. cit.
2.  See J.H. Goldthorpe, *Social Mobility and Class Structure in Modern Britain*, Open University Press, 1980 and A. Heath, *Social Mobility*, Fontana, 1981.
3.  The literature on corporatism is now extensive, but it remains unclear whether it is in the end more than descriptive of the trends to the increased size of the state and its relations with consolidating big business and labour. See, e.g. P.C. Schmitter and G. Lehmbruch (eds), *Trends Towards Corporatist Intermediation*, Sage Publications, 1979; G. Lehmbruch and

P.C. Schmitter (eds), *Patterns of Corporatist Policy Making,* Sage Publications, 1982; A. Cawson, *Corporatism and Welfare,* Heinemann, 1982; M.C. Harrison (ed.), *Corporatism and the Welfare State,* Gower Press, 1984; and the references cited in all these works.
4. G.C. Offe, *Contradictions of the Welfare State,* Hutchinson, 1984, Ch. 4 and pp. 23–4. I have found Offe's work the most stimulating of those writers I have read in attempting to draw conclusions.

# Index